Older
Volunteers

Older Volunteers

A Guide to Research and Practice

Lucy Rose Fischer and
Kay Banister Schaffer

SAGE Publications
International Educational and Professional Publisher
Newbury Park   London   New Delhi

For information address:

 SAGE Publications, Inc.
2455 Teller Road
Newbury Park, California 91320
E-mail: order@sagepub.com

SAGE Publications Ltd.
6 Bonhill Street
London EC2A 4PU
United Kingdom

SAGE Publications India Pvt. Ltd.
M-32 Market
Greater Kailash I
New Delhi 110 048 India

Printed in the United States of America

Library of Congress Cataloging-in-Publication Data

Fischer, Lucy Rose.
   Older volunteers: a guide to research and practice / Lucy Rose
Fischer, Kay Banister Schaffer
          p. cm.
   Includes bibliographical references (pp. 231-243) and index.
   ISBN 0-8039-5008-X (cloth). —ISBN 0-8039-5009-8 (pbk.)
   1. Aged volunteers—United States.   2. Aged volunteers—United
States—Case studies.   3. Volunteerism—United States.   I. Schaffer,
Kay Banister.   II. Title.
HN90.V64F53   1993
302'.14—dc20   92-40085

        97 98 99 00 01   10 9 8 7 6 5 4 3

Sage Production Editor: Diane S. Foster

Contents

Acknowledgments

The Older Volunteers Project began as part of a new initiative at the Wilder Research Center to create "guides to research in the human services." Each "guide" is a synthesis of research on a particular topic in the human services. The purpose of these guides is to improve the effectiveness of human services by making research findings available to practitioners.

The Older Volunteers Project was funded by the Amherst H. Wilder Foundation and by six foundations affiliated with Grantmakers in Aging: Florence V. Burden Foundation, H. W. Durham Foundation, Ittleson Foundation, Medtronic Foundation, Meyer Memorial Trust, and C. S. Mott Foundation.

Many people made important contributions to this project. As the lists below reveal, we had access to a rich resource of expertise. Researchers, policy planners, practitioners, and national leaders in volunteerism consulted on this project; many generously donated large amounts of their time.

We cannot name the 57 volunteer professionals who participated in our case study interviews because we promised them anonymity. We want to express our gratitude to all of them for their time and for sharing insights about their remarkable programs.

Fifteen nationally recognized authorities on volunteerism and aging served on the Older Volunteers Advisory Board, including researchers, representatives from national organizations, and funders. The Advisory Board met at Wilder Research Center in

St. Paul twice: near the beginning of the project in June 1991 and toward the end of the project in March 1992. Between meetings, individual members consulted over the telephone, provided referrals and references, and reviewed manuscript drafts. We want to thank the following people for serving on the Advisory Board:

Donna Anderson, National Retiree Volunteer Center
Fran Butler, Washington Representative, National Association of RSVP Directors
Susan Chambre, Baruch College, City University of New York
Trudy Cross, C. S. Mott Foundation
Laura Lee Geraghty, Minnesota Office on Volunteer Services
Eunice Green, Martin Luther King Center, St. Paul, Minnesota
Barbara Greenberg, Florence V. Burden Foundation
Judy Helein, Office of Volunteer Coordination, AARP
A. Regula Herzog, Institute for Social Research, University of Michigan
David Kachel, Division of Elderly Services, Amherst H. Wilder Foundation
Marty Lemke, Meyer Memorial Trust
Jenks McCrory, H. W. Durham Foundation
David Nee, Ittleson Foundation
Jan Schwarz, Medtronic Foundation
Robert Worchester, Minnesota Senior Federation

In addition, the manuscript was reviewed by a focus group of volunteer managers in Minnesota and by a number of other reviewers. We are grateful to the following experts in volunteerism for their general feedback, specific comments, editorial suggestions, and corrections:

Jennifer Crotteau, Buffalo Senior Center, Buffalo, Minnesota
Melissa Eystad, Minnesota Department of Human Services
Linda Jackson, National Caucus on Black Aged
Elizabeth M. Kiernat, United Way of St. Paul, Minnesota
Sandra Marriquin, La Vos Del Ancinano, Dallas, Texas
Vicki McKay, RSVP, Rushford, Minnesota
John Paiz, Indian Social Services, Minneapolis, Minnesota

Bob Papke, Honeywell Retiree Volunteer Program

Cid Perez-Randal, Center for Intergenerational Learning, Temple University, Philadelphia, Pennsylvania

John Pribyl, National Association of Senior Companion Programs Directors

Bev Robinson, Minnesota Association of Volunteer Directors

Lisa Taylor, Courage Center, Golden Valley, Minnesota

Helen Waddick, Riverside Medical Center, Minneapolis, Minnesota

Other experts, including researchers, volunteer managers, and policy planners, consulted on the project. Their input was invaluable at various stages of the project. We want to express our appreciation to the following people:

Neil Bull, Center on Aging Studies, University of Missouri, Kansas City

Frank Caro, Gerontology Institute, University of Massachusetts

Arlene Cepull, RSVP, St. Paul, Minnesota

Gil Clary, Department of Psychology, College of St. Catherine, St. Paul, Minnesota

Miriam Charnow, National Council on Aging

Freddie Dowling, National Association of RSVP Directors

Barb Gustafson, National Retiree Volunteer Center

Dorothy Height, National Council of Negro Women

Robert Jackson, ACTION, Minneapolis, Minnesota

Claire Martin, Points of Light Foundation, Washington, DC

Vicki McGown, Amherst H. Wilder Foundation

Maureen Mulligan, National Association for RSVP Directors

Judi Parks, Carlson School of Management, University of Minnesota, Minneapolis

Janet Preston, St. Paul Voluntary Action Center

Dwight Rasmussen, National Association, Senior Companion Programs Directors .

Miriam Reibald, Metropolitan Senior Federation, St. Paul, Minnesota

Mary Jo Richardson, Minnesota Department of Education

Joseph Ripple, Gay Men's Health Crisis Center, New York

David Rymph, ACTION, Washington, DC

Joan Sirek, Wilder Health Care Center, Amherst H. Wilder Foundation

Mark Snyder, Department of Psychology, University of Minnesota, Minneapolis

This project benefited from the work of volunteers, including four student interns: Karen Brand, Denise Davis, Tammy Lund, and Frank Romero. In addition to the authors, other staff at Wilder Research Center made major contributions to the Older Volunteers Project, including Cheryl Arechigo, Marilyn Conrad, Jeff Frye, Louann Graham, Jim Hulbert, Paul Mattessich, and Daniel Mueller.

Although the authors take responsibility for whatever errors might be in this book, we are aware that the Older Volunteers Project, like virtually all large projects, was a team effort. Many excellent ideas came from other people who contributed to the project in various ways. We are deeply grateful.

Lucy Rose Fischer
Kay Banister Schaffer
Wilder Research Center

About This Book

Older Volunteers: A Guide to Research and Practice is designed to make research on older volunteers accessible to practitioners who work with and develop policies concerning older volunteers. Based on a comprehensive synthesis of research on volunteering and case studies of exemplary volunteer programs, this book is a central source of information on the effectiveness of various practices for recruiting, retaining, and working with older volunteers. A major purpose is to bridge the gap between research and practice so that volunteer programs can enlist more effectively the time and talents of older persons.

Older Volunteers is not a usual how-to manual. Although numerous handbooks and manuals on volunteering are available, these are almost never based on research. Conversely, practitioners who work with volunteers rarely read research reports that are published by social scientists in technical journals.

We have brought together two types of information: research literature on volunteering and case studies of exemplary programs that recruit and work with older volunteers.[1] We have reviewed about 350 articles and monographs, including research literature on volunteering—not just older volunteers. We were especially interested in research literature that is relevant to practical issues of interest to those working with volunteers, such as, What motivates people to do differing kinds of volunteer work? What are the most effective ways of maintaining the commitment of volunteers? What problems are confronted in working with volunteers, especially older volunteers, and what are the solutions to these problems? What are the special issues in recruiting and working with older minority volunteers? How can organizations avoid exploiting older volunteers?

Because volunteerism as a field of research is relatively new and the research is quite limited, we supplemented the literature review with 57 case studies of exemplary and innovative volunteer programs. The sample of volunteer programs was identified by national experts and volunteer leaders around the United States. Although it was not feasible to cover all types of volunteer programs, the sampling method helped identify a diverse set of volunteer programs, including cultural, health, social welfare, civic, counseling, educational, community action, religious, intergenerational, services for the elderly, fund-raising, and corporate retiree programs. Ten volunteer organizations recruit and work with minority elderly as volunteers.

With these case studies, we have addressed questions such as, What are the differences among types of volunteer programs? Under what circumstances do volunteer organizations have problems recruiting and/or retaining older volunteers? What evidence is there for ageism or antivolunteerism, and how do programs confront such biases?

The chapters that follow are organized into four parts. Part I offers background information—the numbers of volunteers, demographic and other social factors that predict who volunteers, types of volunteer work, and motivations for volunteering. Part II is the central part of the book, with chapters on recruitment, retention, and managerial issues in working with older volunteers. Part III examines special topics of interest to volunteer managers: ethical concerns, minority elders as volunteers, and how older people benefit from doing volunteer work. Part IV, the conclusion, both summarizes key themes from the book and offers guidelines for assessing and improving programs for older volunteers.

OUTLINE OF CHAPTERS

Part I: Background

Chapter 1 Making Miracles. In this century we have witnessed a miracle of survival. But our society currently underuses the productive potential of the elderly population.

Chapter 2 Who Volunteers? There are conflicting definitions of volunteering and wide variations in estimates of the numbers of people who volunteer. Several demographic and social factors seem to influence who volunteers.

Chapter 3 Politics to Bake Sales: Types of Volunteering. Volunteer programs differ from each other in many ways: size, structure, sponsorship, age, type of membership, and the types of activities and services they offer.

Chapter 4 Why Volunteer? People tend to have multiple motivations for volunteering. Whether people volunteer is affected both by personality factors and by social conditions. Religion and religious involvement have a significant impact on volunteering, especially for older volunteers.

Part II: Working With Older Volunteers

Chapter 5 Recruiting Older Volunteers. The most efficient way to recruit volunteers is through word-of-mouth or personal contacts. Relying only on word-of-mouth recruitment, however, limits both the growth of volunteer programs and the types of people who are recruited. Several distinct factors affect the recruitment of older volunteers: aging, access, scheduling, and experience.

Chapter 6 Keeping Volunteers. There appears to be less turnover for older volunteers than for younger volunteers. Volunteers who believe that they are competent and successful are more likely to become committed and to continue volunteering than those who feel frustrated and rejected in their efforts.

Chapter 7 Older Volunteers as Workers. A potential tension exists between quality control and compassion. Volunteers are motivated to do good work by intrinsic rewards—especially by having jobs that are challenging, interesting, and important. It appears that the most successful volunteer programs are those that ask the most of their volunteers and invest the most in their volunteers

Part III: Special Topics

Chapter 8 Ethics and Other Thorny Issues. Volunteer programs confront diverse ethical dilemmas: problems of discrimination, the potential for exploitation of volunteers, and the issue of replacing paid workers with volunteers. Ethical dilemmas, by definition, do not have clear or easy answers.

Chapter 9 Minority Elders as Volunteers. Volunteering has different meanings for older persons in differing ethnic groups. In recruiting and working with older minority volunteers, the following factors must be considered: history and life experiences, language and culture, and access to resources.

Chapter 10 The Benefits to Older Volunteers. Although some research indicates associations between volunteering and good health, greater life satisfaction, more friendships, and so forth, it is difficult to prove that volunteering actually causes these benefits.

Part IV: Conclusions and Implications

Chapter 11 Thinking Strategically About Older Volunteers. There is an untapped potential for developing an older volunteers' movement. But to realize this potential will require creative strategies for recruiting and working with older volunteers.

Part I

Background

ONE

Making Miracles

A retired musician was working as a volunteer in a medical center in a large Eastern city. He found a room in the medical center, a solarium, where very old patients were sitting, staring off into space. So he put together a band of retired musicians, including a 93-year-old woman who used to play the piano in silent movie theaters, and now they give concerts twice a week for these patients. The band plays the songs they knew when they were growing up. As the patients listen and clap and tap their feet, they come alive again.

▼

Retired engineers from a large Midwestern corporation work as a team of skilled volunteers at a residential facility for disabled persons. They have a program to design and manufacture mechanical devices for people with handicaps. Most of the people they have helped never could have afforded such devices without the donation of their talent and time.

▼

A 100-year-old woman living in a residential facility in a small town in New York started doing volunteer work about 6 years ago. Although she needs help herself, she offers telephone outreach to other elderly people who are homebound and isolated.

▼

In a large Midwestern community a volunteer mentor, a retired executive, was assigned to work with a high school student who is very talented in art. Her parents had told her that there was no way of making a living through art. But her mentor took some of her

artwork to a local art institute, and the director said that this was
the best artwork for that age he had ever seen! So he managed to
get her a scholarship with [a well-known arts academy].

Older volunteers make "miracles." They provide loving care to
children who are starved for attention; they provide transportation, homemaking, caregiving, and a whole range of other kinds
of help to frail elderly; they run cultural programs at museums,
theaters, and music centers; they are mentors for university students; they repair leaky faucets for poor people; and the list goes
on. Older citizens working as volunteers make enormous contributions to their communities, to charitable and cultural organizations, and to individuals who depend on their help.

We hear more frequently, however, about how much older people
cost to society rather than how much they contribute. The elderly
are described sometimes as enjoying special privileges whether
or not they are needy and as using up a lion's share of health and
social services. In the last 20 years or so, there has been a tremendous growth in benefits, programs, and services for the elderly—
many of which are paid for by public funds. Health care costs have
soared. Social services are strained. The budget deficit seems un-
containable. More and more children are living in poverty. And
older people are blamed. Moreover, as the numbers of elderly increase, there will be burgeoning demands for public funds to support the elderly population—with economic assistance, health
and long-term care, social services, transportation and nutrition
programs, and special housing for seniors. The projections seem
bleak.

And yet this portrait of an aging society has another side. Older
citizens can and often do contribute their time and talents to the
benefit of others, as the above examples show. Millions of older
persons in this country serve as volunteers; even many people
who are very old—in their 80s and 90s—continue to volunteer. According to a national estimate, older volunteers contribute about
3. 6 billion hours of voluntary service to organizations every year
(Marriott Seniors Volunteerism Study, 1991). If valued at the mini-

mum wage,[2] this amounts to a contribution to American society of about $15,300,000,000. And this does not even count all of the hours that older people spend in "informal" services, helping their neighbors, friends, and relatives.

The Age Revolution

In this century, we have witnessed a miracle of survival. Of all the revolutions in recent times—the rise and fall of communism; the exploration of outer space; the astounding inventions, from mass-produced automobiles to airplanes to computers to miracle drugs to satellites to fax machines—the age revolution is in some ways the most miraculous, the most dramatic, and possibly the most significant in its impact on our everyday lives.

The number of people who are age 65 and older in the United States has increased tenfold over the century, from about 3 million at the turn of the century to 30 million now. By the year 2030, there will be a projected 65 million older persons in this country. In the last 50 years or so, life expectancy has increased by as much as 50%, and the number of people who survive into very old age has risen sharply. Demographers in the past projected that life expectancy would increase somewhat, but few anticipated the dramatic improvement in longevity that actually occurred (see Myers, Manton, & Bacellar, 1986). One consequence is that larger and larger numbers of individuals are in their 80s, 90s, and even older. "Had the 1940 survival rate prevailed, 540,000 (native-born) persons aged 85 to 94 could have been expected to survive. There were, however, *more than three times as many such persons in 1980: some 1. 7 million* [italics added]" (Rosenwaike & Dolinsky, 1987, p. 277).

Paradoxically, people are both living longer and retiring at earlier ages, so we spend an ever larger portion of our lives in our post-retirement years. Most people retire early—by age 62 or 63—although we are not eligible for full Social Security benefits until age 65. Retirement, however, is not necessarily the end of productive activity. Some retirees return to the work force and begin new postretirement careers. Retirees also do various unpaid work, including volunteer work. One of the most important benefits of early retirement is that it gives workers a choice about how they spend their time and energy. "Today's early retirement pattern does not preclude productive roles later in life. On the contrary, the opportunity to 'retire' relatively early from a long-term job creates a choice for mature persons about whether and how to continue productive social participation" (Morrison, 1986, p. 354).

Today's older population spans a large age spectrum, from the "young-old," who are just entering their retirement years and often resent being labeled as "senior citizens," to the "old-old" (75+) and the "oldest-old" (85+), whose children are likely to be retired and whose grandchildren may themselves be grandparents. A generation gap exists among the elderly, especially because the very old tend to be less educated than younger cohorts of elderly (see Bould, Sanborn, & Reif, 1989; Koeck, Gagnier, Shreve, Lackner, & Jensen, 1981). Given the wide disparities among older persons in education and in other ways, it is misleading to make generalizations about *the* elderly. It also may be difficult to base projections about future elderly on the experiences of older generations.

Productive Aging

Gerontologists and other policy analysts argue that our policies are out of step with the age revolution. Matilda White Riley and John Riley (1989) pointed out that although about 28 years have been added to our life span, there is a problem of "structural lag, because the age structure of social opportunities has not kept pace with the rapid changes in the ways people grow old" (p. 15). In *Productive Aging,* Robert Butler and Herbert Gleason (1985) wrote: "At present, no government or private institution within society has addressed effectively and comprehensively the multiple challenges posed by societal aging" (p. 10). Others have noted that our society currently underuses the productive potential of the older population and that there will be increasingly serious problems if we do not create greater opportunities for productive aging.

When a society has vast unmet needs at the same time that there are large numbers of healthy, energetic, productive human beings for whom the society can find no use—even though they would like to be useful—then something is wrong. (Cahn, 1988, p. 232)

Given that many "older" people have few significant personal barriers to continuing their productive contributions to society, both economic and non-economic, it is reasonable to question whether limiting the overall productivity for as much as 20 percent of the U. S. population is a "good" social policy. (Morrison, 1986, p. 344)

Several studies have revealed that, with retirement, *much of the time that was formerly used for work is spent on passive activities* —such as watching television. Although ostensibly retired persons should have more, not less, time for cultural and other leisure activities and for volunteer work, it appears that most older persons do not spend more time on such activities (Bosse & Ekerdt, 1981; Chambre, 1987; Kelly, Steinkamp, & Kelly, 1986; Moss & Lawton, 1982).

Research suggests that older people want to be productive and that they are often not as active and productive as they would like to be. One recent study found that older persons are much more likely than younger persons to agree strongly that retired people should contribute through community service and also that "life is not worth living if you can't contribute to the well-being of others" (Herzog & House, 1991, p. 53). In another survey of retirees, 86% said they believed that "others think more highly of those that work" (Lazarus & Lauer, 1985, p. 49). And in another study, over a third of union retirees said they "feel useless at times" (Charner, Fox, & Trachtman, 1988, p. 115).

In research on time use, Herzog and her co-authors (Herzog, Kahn, Morgan, Jackson, & Antonucci, 1989) noted that older people spend less time than younger people in "productive" activities; but, they added, this situation largely reflects retirement from paid work. Housework, another form of productive activity, does not differ much by age; that is, people of all ages do equivalent amounts of housework. These researchers also reported that volunteering does not decline much until *after* age 75. This finding suggests that postretirement volunteer "careers" may last for many years and that there is ample time for "career development" among retired volunteers.

A wealth of research shows that the great majority of persons in old age are competent and are capable of leading productive lives. Studies of older workers, for example, indicate that, for the most part, competence is not a problem. In fact, older workers have fewer accidents and miss fewer workdays, and retirees who are hired on short-term jobs require less supervision than other temporary workers. A number of studies have found that, except for psycho-motive speed (people tend to process information more slowly in older ages), cognitive abilities are well preserved in healthy elderly, even in very old age (see Lazarus & Lauer, 1985; Sheppard & Rix, 1977; Svanborg, 1985). Research shows that health is a much more serious barrier to having a productive life-style than age per se. Moreover, some studies indicate that keeping active can improve cognitive functioning—the "use it or lose it" factor (see Riley & Riley, 1989).

Opportunities for Older Volunteers

In the last 20 years or so, volunteer programs for seniors, both public and private, have developed and flourished. Both locally and nationally, there are now thousands of senior volunteer programs—through church and interfaith groups, health care institutions, and a broad range of cultural and social service organizations. These programs are mostly of recent vintage. The Retired Senior Volunteer Program (RSVP), the Senior Companion Program, and the Foster Grandparent Program, which are partially funded by the federal government, were initiated between 1965 and 1973. Many other programs are even newer—experimental programs to integrate education and volunteering for retirees, to link nurturing older persons with troubled teenagers, to offer caregiving to isolated and frail elderly, to provide mentors for children in inner-city schools, to serve as companions for homeless children, and so forth.

The development of these programs has meant a substantial increase in opportunities for older persons to volunteer, as well as in services provided by older volunteers. Even so, many successful programs are found in only a few local areas, while elsewhere older persons with comparable interests and skills have no such volunteer opportunities. Moreover, many fine programs have very small budgets, which constrict their services and limit their ability to recruit and work with older volunteers.

It may be surprising to learn that older people seem to be *less* likely to volunteer than other adults, according to a number of surveys. Various researchers also have reported that most older volunteers spend no more than an hour or two a week in voluntary service (Fischer, Mueller, Cooper, & Chase, 1989; Independent Sector, 1990; Worthy & Ventura-Merkel, 1982). Studies have found that a major reason many older people give for not volunteering is that no one asked them (Independent Sector, 1990; Kieffer, 1986; Marriott Seniors Volunteerism Study, 1991; Perry 1983). Many policy analysts, researchers, and other professionals believe there is an untapped potential for recruiting and working with older volunteers.

Why Older People "Should" Volunteer

Several reasons have been offered for encouraging older citizens to volunteer. One rationale is that volunteering is "good for them." This is a fundamental assumption of a number of volunteer programs for older persons. Another reason, which is perhaps more implied than stated explicitly, is that productive aging is important as an antidote to the "greedy geezer" image. A third perspective is that volunteering is an interesting leisure activity, especially because of the opportunities for socialization. Policy planners, researchers, advocates, professional volunteer coordinators, and others have articulated these perspectives, which we have labeled the *inoculation, debit,* and *leisure* perspectives.

The *inoculation perspective* suggests that keeping active (and doing good) is "good" for the elderly; that is, older people who are active are happier and healthier than older people who are withdrawn or "disengaged. " Thus volunteer work can inoculate, or protect, the older person from the hazards of retirement, physical

decline, and inactivity. "Keeping busy" is valued in and of itself
(see Ekerdt, 1986). If we extended this idea to its logical implication, we might infer that the quality of the older volunteer's products or services is irrelevant; what matters is that the older person
feels good by keeping active and, perhaps in some general way,
doing "good. "
    In fact, the research evidence for the inoculation perspective is
slim. As we show later in this book (see Chapter 10), it is difficult
to get convincing evidence that volunteer work *causes* older people
to be healthier and happier, because healthier and more active
persons are more likely to choose to do volunteer work, as well
as other activities.
    The *debit perspective* reflects a contemporary economic concern
—that older people are a drain on society, that the elderly have
received special privileges and benefits from policies and programs
based on age rather than need, and that there are too many of
them. Under this perspective, both the quality and the quantity
of what the elderly produce are significant. One type of service
that is particularly relevant to this perspective is service to the
frail elderly, or "eldercare." Thus, when older persons serve as
"senior companions," when they deliver Meals on Wheels, when
they work as volunteers in hospitals and nursing homes, and so
on, they potentially are reducing the drain on public funds from
other elderly in need.
    However, the idea that older persons have a special debt to society
to compensate for the burdens they are imposing is ethically
troublesome. A possible implication is that the elderly should be
induced—or coerced—to be "productive;" that is, the precept that
older persons "should" volunteer could be used as a rationale for
mandating some form of community service as a condition for
receiving retirement benefits.
    The third perspective, the *leisure perspective,* is different from
the other two. This perspective defines *volunteerism* as a form of
leisure activity. Retired persons, under this rubric, are consum-
ers. Volunteer work is *their choice;* if it is enjoyable and meaningful *to them,* then maybe they will choose to participate in volunteer
activities. Chambre (1984, 1987), among others, has argued that
volunteering is essentially a form of leisure activity, most espe-

cially for older persons. Her research supports this perspective. One of the important tenets of this framework is that older people have control over their volunteer activities.

Volunteer activities compete with other opportunities for use of leisure time, such as sports, reading, playing cards, and passive entertainment, such as watching television. From this perspective, recruitment of volunteers ought to be based on a consumer-rationale—that is, representing volunteer work as filling social needs and as being an enjoyable activity.

The leisure perspective, however, may deemphasize the special nature of volunteer service and suggest that volunteerism is no more (or not much more) important than playing bridge or tennis, in terms of its social impact. This suggestion is in direct contradiction to what volunteers say about their own motivations and experiences in voluntary service. Virtually every survey has found that the predominant motivation expressed by volunteers is a desire to "do something good" for other individuals and for their communities. Even if we assume that what people say and what they do are not always consistent and that there are other reasons for volunteering, it seems inappropriate simply to dismiss altruism as a significant factor in motivating volunteerism. In this sense, volunteering is different, in a fundamental way, from most other forms of leisure activities (see Chapter 4).

* * *

In our review of research literature and our case studies of volunteer programs, we have observed that research, programs, and policies related to older volunteers often are shaped by these three perspectives. Each of these perspectives has some validity, but each in its own way is problematic. On the basis of our review of research, volunteer programs, and other literature, we offer the following caveats.

- *In most ways, older volunteers are no different from other adults who volunteer.* Of course, some obvious distinctions are related to social and physical aspects of aging. For example, retired persons have more time during the day to volunteer (see Chapter 5). But the differences appear to be much less significant than the similarities. Thus we need to view volunteering from a life span perspective. If volunteering is "good" for older people, then it is probably beneficial to people of all ages and should be encouraged for everyone. Moreover, as a number of studies have shown, people who volunteer in old age tend to be those who have volunteered when they were younger. We ought to conclude that if we want to encourage older persons in the future to volunteer, then we need to find ways to recruit them (and socialize them into volunteering) when they are younger.

- *There ought to be no implication that older people have any special obligation to volunteer.* Certainly older people have much to contribute if they choose to volunteer. It is also very likely to be true that there is some level of untapped potential—that more older volunteers can be recruited and that more effective opportunities can be developed for them. But we are leery of any suggestion that older persons have any special obligation to contribute through voluntary service, except to the extent that all citizens are obliged to help one another and to serve their communities.

- *Voluntary service is a special type of activity.* As we discuss in the next chapters, volunteering takes many forms and is even difficult to define. But most voluntary service has a component of altruism, helping, and doing good. This quality makes volunteering different from most other leisure activities. And this special nature of volunteerism needs to be understood in order to effectively motivate, recruit, and work with volunteers, including older volunteers.

TWO

Who Volunteers?

The questions seem simple: How many people in the United States do volunteer work? Do people start volunteering more after they retire? Why does it seem that some people are more willing to volunteer than others? Do rich people volunteer more than poor people? Do men or women volunteer more? How does education affect volunteering?

The questions seem simple, but the answers are complicated. Even the most basic question—What is volunteering?—seems to have no easy answer. The types of activities subsumed under the term *volunteering* are extraordinarily diverse. A volunteer might be the president or chair of a charitable foundation, an usher for a church function, a campaign worker who stuffs envelopes for a political candidate, a driver who delivers Meals on Wheels, or a friendly visitor at a hospital. People who do any of these types of jobs might be called volunteers, and this is just a small sample of types of volunteer jobs or positions.

Unfortunately studies of volunteering have been based on differing definitions, and the wording of questions has varied from one survey to the next. There is enormous variability in estimates of how many Americans volunteer—from 18% to 55%. Even surveys conducted in the same year report different numbers of volunteers. How can we know what to believe?

What Is a Volunteer?

Although definitions of volunteer work vary, there are some common themes: Volunteering is an activity intended to help others, it is not done primarily for monetary compensation or material gain, and it is not based on obligation (see Ellis & Noyes, 1990;

Fischer, Mueller, Cooper, & Chase, 1991; Kieffer, 1986; Manser & Higgins-Cass, 1976; Payne & Bull, 1985; Smith, 1982; Van Til, 1988). Interestingly the defining terms are often negative. The definitions, however, have important differences. Some definitions focus on volunteering as nonpaid employment, while others emphasize social needs. Sometimes volunteering is defined as belonging to the private, nonprofit sector (the "third sector"), although, in fact, some volunteer programs are governmentally sponsored, including programs for the elderly. Some definitions include both formal and informal services (services arranged through organizations versus help given by neighbors, friends, or relatives), while others include only formal volunteering.

In this book, because the focus is on organizations that recruit and work with older volunteers, we discuss primarily formal volunteering. But we cannot completely ignore informal volunteering. Formal volunteer work leaves out a wide set of unpaid services that people do for others. If a "volunteer" for a church, for example, provides transportation services to a neighbor as part of a church-sponsored transportation program, why should the same type of service (giving a ride to a neighbor) not be counted as volunteering if this service is provided on an informal basis? (See Chambre, 1984; Fischer et al., 1989, 1991; Kieffer, 1986; Morgan, 1986.) Moreover, there are systematic biases in only "counting" formal services as volunteering. It seems that certain groups of people, such as women and minorities, are much more likely to be involved in informal helping networks than in formal volunteer organizations. Some major surveys, notably the recent Gallup surveys, include informal helping in their statistics on volunteering (see Independent Sector, 1988; Worthy & Ventura-Merkel, 1982).

It seems that a commonly accepted assumption, and part of the basic definition, is that volunteering is not done primarily for monetary compensation or material gain, but even this condition may not be absolute. Can volunteers be compensated in any way and still be considered volunteers? The Senior Companion and Foster Grandparent programs, which are federally sponsored, both have stipends and income requirements for volunteers; that is, the volunteers must be low-income older persons. In our interviews with the directors of several of these programs, we were told that the stipend, although small, is financially important to many of their volunteers, who use the money for necessities. So, are Senior Companions and Foster Grandparents volunteers or not? On the one hand, it is likely that their motivation is, at least in part, economic. On the other hand, the stipend they receive is well below "market value" or even minimum wage. Moreover, it is also clear that without stipended programs, very poor people often cannot afford to contribute their time and talent (see Cahn, 1988; Romero, 1986; Smith, 1982).

There are other sources of confusion, as well. Volunteering often is seasonal work that may vary, systematically, depending on the time of year. So methodological problems develop when surveys are conducted at different times of the year (Chambre, 1989).

One final definitional issue needs to be mentioned. There is an implicit assumption that volunteering is "good" or for the common good. But some forms of volunteering might be viewed as serving self-interests. Active workers in unions and neighborhood organizations, for instance, are providing service to others but also are benefitting themselves. Moreover, not everyone agrees about what "doing good" is. As a case in point, the members of the Ku Klux Klan might see themselves as "volunteering" to help their communities (Van Til, 1987).[3]

How Many Volunteer?

The range of estimates on the numbers of volunteers is astonishingly broad. According to various surveys, among people ages 18 and over, somewhere between 18% and 55% volunteer. For older adults the estimates range from 11% to 52%.

Table 2.1 presents a summary of findings from a number of studies on rates of volunteering. Some of the differences might be accounted for by variation among samples, while some of the discrepancy reflects differences in questions on volunteering. Despite the differences across surveys, the trend appears to be that *rates of volunteering have been increasing over time for both younger and older volunteers.*

TABLE 2.1 How Many Adults and How Many Older Adults Volunteer?

Date	Study	Percentage of adults volunteering[a]	Percentage of older adults volunteering
1965	*Americans Volunteer* (U.S. Department of Labor, 1965)	18	11 (age 65+)
1974	National Council on Aging (Harris & Associates, 1975)	35	28 (ages 65-69) 20 (ages 70-79) 12 (age 80+)
1974	*Americans Volunteer* (U.S. Bureau of the Census, 1974)	25	14 (age 65+)
1981	National Council on Aging (Harris & Associates, 1981)	55	28 (ages 65-69) 23 (ages 70-79) 12 (age 80+)
1981	AARP (Hamilton, Frederick, & Schneiders Company, 1981)	—	28 (ages 60-64) 29 (ages 65-69) 33 (ages 70-79) 13 (age 80+)
1981	Gallup (Independent Sector, 1981)	52	37 (age 65+)
1985	Yankelovich, Skelly, & White, Inc. (Independent Sector, 1985)	47	36 (age 65+)
1986	Gallup (Independent Sector, 1985)	48	38 (age 65+)
1988	AARP (Hamilton, Frederick, & Schneiders Company, 1988)	—	41 (ages 65-69) 37 (ages 70+)
1988	Gallup (Independent Sector, 1988)	45	40 (ages 65-74) 29 (age 75+)
1988	*Older Minnesotans* (Fischer, Mueller, & Cooper, 1991)	—	52 (age 60+)
1989	Current Population Survey (Hayghe, 1991)	20	17 (age 65+)
1989	Americans Changing Lives (ACL) Survey (Herzog, Kahn, Morgan, Jackson, & Antonucci, 1989)	45	40 (ages 65-74) 26 (age 75+)
1989	Gallup (Independent Sector, 1990)	54	47 (ages 65-74) 32 (age 75+)
1991	Marriott Senior Volunteerism Study (Marriott Senior Living Services and the Administration on Aging, 1991)	—	42 (ages 60-64) 46 (ages 65-69) 45 (ages 70-74) 39 (ages 75-79) 27 (age 80+)

NOTE: a. Includes persons age 18+.

The various studies are also consistent in one other way: There does not appear to be any increase in volunteering in old age. The relationship between volunteering and age is an inverted U-shape. People in their 30s and 40s are the most likely to volunteer. Both younger people and older people have lower rates of volunteering (Herzog et al., 1989; Independent Sector, 1988; Lackner & Koeck, 1980). We might expect that retirees would have more time for volunteering than younger people. But various studies have shown that most elderly volunteers do not spend large amounts of time in their volunteer work. One study, for example, found that only 5% of older adult volunteers spent more than 6 hours a week volunteering (see Worthy & Ventura-Merkel, 1982).

It is clear that there are a number of significant barriers to volunteering by older people. The elderly are much more likely than others to give poor health and lack of transportation as reasons for not volunteering. Another problem is income level. Low income is likely to restrict a person's ability to volunteer time, as well as to give money to charity. According to national surveys, older people are much more likely than working-age adults to have only enough money for basic necessities (see Fischer et al., 1989, 1991; Hamilton, Frederick, & Schneiders Company, 1988; Independent Sector, 1988; Kieffer, 1986).

On the other hand, most elderly are not too sick to volunteer, and having lower incomes does not prevent older persons from giving to charity. In fact, people age 65 and over give the highest proportion of their income to charity. A recent report on charitable giving in the United States noted: "Among the 56% of contributors who worried about having enough money in the future, *only respondents 65 years of age or older gave an average of 2% or more of their household income to charity* [italics added]" (Independent Sector, 1988, p. 3). Even if rates of volunteering decline with age, substantial numbers of elderly, even among the very old, continue to volunteer. About an eighth of Americans over age 80 are volunteers (Worthy & Ventura-Merkel, 1982; see also Fischer et al., 1989, 1991; Lackner & Koeck, 1980).

Interestingly the age curve may be changing so that *the decline in volunteering occurs at much later ages.* Previous surveys indicated a substantial decline in volunteering at around age 60. In

more recent surveys, the drop-off in rates of volunteering seems
to happen much later—after age 75 or 80 (Chambre, 1989, n. d.;
Harris & Associates, 1974, 1981; Herzog et al., 1989; Kieffer,
1986; Marriott Seniors Volunteerism Study, 1991).
If postretirement careers (including volunteer careers) last for
many years, the implications are intriguing.

- *Retired volunteers should have ample time for "career development."*
  If retirees look forward to 10, 20, or 30 productive years, this span
  of time is not very different from a person's work life. Retiree volunteers may need opportunities for growth and advancement to sustain a long-term involvement in volunteering.
- *Periodic retraining may be important.* As we discuss later in this
  book (see Chapter 6), retirees are often stable, long-term volunteers.
  Just as paid employees in many fields require ongoing training,
  older volunteers may need further training to maintain their skills,
  at least for certain forms of volunteer work.
- *The problem of "aging in place" may be a concern for older volunteers.*
  This term has been used in reference to senior housing. That is,
  long-time residents of senior housing experience the effects of aging
  while continuing to live in their apartments; consequently they may
  begin to have service needs like residents in long-term care facilities.
  In a similar way, long-time older volunteers may experience a loss
  of physical capabilities, associated with the hazards of aging (e.g.,
  problems with vision, hearing, or frailty). Volunteer programs
  need to develop strategies for accommodating age-related physical
  changes.

Who Volunteers: A Demographic Profile

Demographic factors seem to influence who volunteers. For example, people with more education, higher incomes, higher occupational status, and better health are more likely to volunteer
than other people. Research findings on demographic characteristics of volunteers are summarized in Table 2.2. However, as this
table shows, the findings are not entirely consistent across studies.

Social Class. Among demographic factors associated with rates
of volunteering, social class seems to be the most significant. People

TABLE 2.2 A Demographic Profile of Volunteers

Number of studies	*Summary of findings*
	Education
12 studies	As educational level increases, the likelihood of volunteering increases.
1 study	As educational level increases, time spent on volunteering increases.
	Income
10 studies	As income increases, the likelihood of volunteering increases.
1 study	There is no relationship between income and rates of volunteering.
	Occupational Status
4 studies	As occupational status increases, the likelihood of volunteering increases.
	Gender
7 studies	Women are more likely to volunteer than men.
2 studies	Women volunteers spend more time volunteering.
2 studies	Men and women do different types of volunteer work.
2 studies	Men are more likely to volunteer than women.
3 studies	There is no gender difference in rates of volunteering.
	Marital Status
6 studies	Married people are more likely to volunteer.
1 study	Single people are more likely to volunteer.
2 studies	Single volunteers spend more time volunteering.
1 study	People who are currently married or never married are more likely to volunteer than those who are widowed or divorced.
2 studies	There is no marital status difference in rates of volunteering.
	Health
3 studies	People in poor health are less likely to volunteer.
	Employment Status
5 studies	Employed people are more likely to volunteer than unemployed people.
1 study	Unemployed people are more likely to volunteer than employed people.
5 studies	Part-time workers are the most likely to volunteer.
1 study	Unemployed and retired volunteers spend more time volunteering than employed volunteers.
1 study	Full-time employed men and part-time employed women are the most likely to volunteer.

TABLE 2.2 Continued

Number of studies	*Summary of findings*
	Religion
4 studies	Most volunteer work, especially by the elderly, is "church work."
1 study	Members of religious congregations are more likely to volunteer than nonmembers.
1 study	The highest rates of church work are by blacks.
2 studies	Protestants are more likely to volunteer than Catholics or Jews.
2 studies	Jews are more likely to volunteer than Catholics or Protestants.
1 study	There is no difference among Protestants, Catholics, and Jews in rates of volunteering.
	Race
6 studies	Whites are more likely to volunteer.
2 studies	Black volunteers spend more time volunteering.
1 study	There are no racial differences in rates of volunteering.
	Regional Differences in the United States
2 studies	People in the Midwest are the most likely to volunteer.
1 study	People in the West are the most likely to volunteer.
2 studies	People in the central and western parts of the country are the most likely to volunteer.
1 study	Volunteers in the Northeast spend the most time volunteering.
2 studies	Volunteers in the West spend the most time volunteering.
1 study	There are no differences by region in rates of volunteering.

with higher incomes, with more education, and with professional types of occupations not only are more likely to give money to charity but also are more likely to volunteer their time to organizations. Moreover, among volunteers, the more affluent and the better educated are the most active and give the most time. One researcher observed: "We also know from an earlier study asking about all volunteer work—for organizations or relatives—that income dominated the explanations, so much so that, surprisingly, the single best predictor was the number of modern appliances in the home" (Morgan, 1986, p. 76). Among the elderly, income and education also affect the amount of volunteering. Various studies suggest, in fact, that social class has much more of an impact on volunteering than age. It is possible that older persons are less likely to volunteer than working-age adults, in large part, *because* the elderly tend to have less education and lower incomes (see, for example, Chambre, 1984, 1987; Edwards, White, & Owens, 1977; Fischer et al., 1989; Herzog & Morgan, in press; Independent Sector, 1988; J. C. Penney Company, 1988; Kieffer, 1986; Lemke & Moos, 1989; Reddy, 1980; Romero, 1986; Sundeen, 1988; Vaillancourt & Payette, 1986).

Gender. Do women volunteer more than men? Certainly the perception is that volunteering is an avocation for women as housewives. In fact, a major reason for rising concern about the supply of volunteers and the need to recruit older volunteers is that women have been entering the paid labor force in increasing numbers. Research findings on the effect of gender on volunteering, however, are somewhat mixed. Some studies have found that women volunteer more. Others have found no gender difference in rates of volunteering but have reported that women spend somewhat more hours volunteering than men. According to some research, women no longer do more volunteering than men, so that much of the growth in volunteering has come from increased participation by men (see, for example, Chambre, 1984, 1989; Herzog et al., 1989; Morgan, 1986; Vaillancourt & Payette, 1986).

Whether men or women are more likely to volunteer, it appears that volunteering, like the paid labor force, tends to be "gendered"; that is, men and women often do different kinds of jobs as volunteers. These differences largely conform to gender role expectations (Fischer et al., 1989, 1991; Gallagher, 1991).

Marital Status. A number of studies have found that married people are more likely to volunteer than nonmarried people. This situation has been found both in general populations and in studies of the elderly. Married people tend to have more income than unmarried people, and the gap in income level may be enough to explain the difference in volunteering by marital status (see Fischer et al., 1991; Hayghe, 1991; Independent Sector, 1988; Sundeen, 1988; Vaillancourt & Payette, 1986).

Health. Many studies have found that health is a major factor in well-being—perhaps especially for the elderly. It is not surprising that poor health is a significant barrier to volunteering. This finding has been reported in a number of studies of volunteering among the elderly. In fact, when nonvolunteers are asked why they do not volunteer, poor health is given as one of the two most common reasons; lack of time is the other (see Cohen-Mansfield, 1989; Fischer et al., 1989; Herzog & Morgan, in press; Hooker & Ventis, 1984; Independent Sector, 1988; Ozawa & Morrow-Howell, 1988; Rosenblatt, 1966).

Work and Retirement. An important rationale for recruiting older volunteers is that retirees ought to have more time to do volunteer work than workers. We might expect, then, that older retirees would be more likely to volunteer than older adults who are still working. In fact, the reverse appears to be true; that is, the elderly who remain in the labor force are more likely to volunteer than retired elderly. Surveys have found that older persons who are working part-time are more likely to volunteer than either full-time workers or those who have retired completely. But research also indicates that among older volunteers, those who are retired spend somewhat more time in volunteering than those still in the paid work force (see Chambre, 1984, 1987; Fischer et al., 1989, 1991; Hayghe, 1991; Morgan, 1986).

Furthermore, when we make comparisons between retirees and older workers, we have to keep in mind the substantial age and health differences between these groups. Older workers, on average, are considerably younger than retirees and are much less likely to have health and functional problems.

Religion. A large proportion of volunteering and charitable giving in the United States is through religious organizations. Church members are considerably more likely to give to charity and to volunteer than nonmembers. Among church members, those who are the most active (attend services at least once a week) are the most likely to volunteer their time. Survey findings are mixed, however, on how specific religious affiliation affects volunteering (see

Hamilton, Frederick, & Schneiders Company, 1988; Hodgkinson & Weitzman, 1989; Hodgkinson, Weitzman, & Kirsch, 1990).

Race and Ethnicity. The research on how racial and ethnic factors affect volunteering is very limited, and the conclusions are controversial. Some data show that certain minority groups have substantially lower rates of volunteering than Whites. Other studies, however, have found no difference or even the converse of these trends. It is clear that income and education are confounding factors in assessing the relationship between volunteering and race or ethnicity. Middle and upper income Blacks are more likely to volunteer than poorer Blacks. In fact, some research suggests that when social class is controlled, Blacks have *more* involvement in voluntary action than Whites[4] (see Carson, 1990a; Chambre, 1987; Hayghe, 1991; Height, 1989; Independent Sector, 1985, 1988, 1990; Smith, 1975; Sundeen, 1988).

The discussion of race and ethnicity requires a caveat. The diversity across minority communities is considerable, so research on one ethnic minority may not apply equally to all ethnic groups. We discuss older minority volunteers in some detail in Chapter 9.

Region. We might expect to find regional differences in volunteering, to reflect "cultural" variation from one part of the country to another. We found only a few studies that offered regional comparisons. The 1988 Gallup survey on giving and volunteering indicated that Midwesterners are the most likely to volunteer (Independent Sector, 1988). The findings from the 1990 Gallup survey, however, suggest that a substantial increase in volunteerism has occurred in all regions *except* the Midwest, so the regional differences are much narrower (Independent Sector, 1990). The Marriott Seniors Volunteerism Study (1991), which divides the regions somewhat differently, found the highest rates of volunteering among older people in the West.

We also might expect more volunteering in small towns and rural areas than in large metropolitan communities. We found only two studies that are suggestive of such a trend. Sundeen (1988) reported more volunteering in moderate-sized cities than in inner-city areas. The Minnesota Seniors Study found small differences in rates of volunteering between greater Minnesota (which is largely rural) and the metropolitan Twin Cities area. Older volunteers in greater Minnesota are especially likely to do church work and to help with transportation (Fischer et al., 1989, 1991).

* * *

Why and how do these demographic and social factors influence whether someone volunteers? The most logical explanation is that virtually all of these factors represent resources of various types. Income and health are obvious resources. Education is another kind of resource in terms of knowledge and skills (education also is connected to status, which is another resource). Marital status is a personal resource in that being married means having a spouse—a roommate, a financial partner, a confidante, and a companion in leisure activities. Other variables, such as being employed and living in a small city or town, also indicate personal resources—that is, having ties with other people. *These various resources affect both the costs and the opportunities for volunteering in a variety of ways.*

Deficits in these resources raise the cost of volunteering. For example, a volunteer who does not have good health must expend a much larger portion of his or her available energy on volunteering tasks than otherwise would be required. For a person whose income is very low, the direct and indirect expenditures associated with volunteering (such as transportation or foregone wages) might be an insurmountable obstacle.

Conversely, having resources expands opportunities for volunteering in many ways. For example, having many social contacts increases the likelihood that a person will be invited to volunteer. Thus, for example, being employed (in contrast to being retired or being a housewife) exposes an individual to many relationships and opens up possibilities for a variety of activities, including volunteering.

Education is a particularly important resource. It is likely that well-educated persons have the most interesting and attractive volunteer opportunities. Among older volunteers, retired executives and other professionals may be in a uniquely advantageous volunteer position when their skills and expertise are valued and they are able to offer volunteer services that are both useful to others and meaningful to themselves.

To what extent do these demographic factors "determine" whether someone volunteers? A recent survey on volunteering (the J. C. Penney study, 1988) found that "volunteers and non-volunteers are very similar with respect to sex, age, marital status, annual household income, presence of children under the age of 18 in the household, and region of the country in which they live" (p. 2). We might infer from the research evidence to date that demographic factors operate as predispositions in volunteering. But demography by itself cannot explain who volunteers—or why (see also Caro & Bass, 1991).

Who Volunteers for What?

We began this chapter by discussing the diversity of volunteering and the difficulty of defining this complex phenomenon. Paradoxically, many of the studies we have reviewed for this chapter have examined giving and volunteering in general, as if all volunteering were the same. Surveys such as the Gallup survey and the Marriott survey tend to ask global questions about volunteering. Even if some attempt is made to report different types of volunteer activities, most analyses are based on comparisons of people who volunteer versus those who do not volunteer at all.

A few studies have looked at predictors of involvement in different types of volunteer activities. Interestingly these studies have found different sets of predictors for different types of volunteer activities (see, for example, Okun & Eisenberg, n. d.; Sundeen, 1988; Townsend, 1973). This finding suggests that to understand why and when people volunteer, we need to examine the complexity and diversity of volunteer behavior. In the next chapter, we discuss differing types of volunteer roles and volunteer organizations.

Summary of Findings

- Estimates of rates of volunteering range from 18% to 55% for people ages 18 and over and from 11% to 52% volunteer for older adults.
- It appears that the drop-off in rates of volunteering occurs at much later ages now than previously. Twenty years ago, rates of volunteering decreased for people in their 60s. Now the decline in volunteering occurs after age 75 or 80, according to several surveys.
- Several demographic variables appear to be associated with higher rates of volunteerism:
    higher education
    higher income
    higher occupational status
    being employed, especially part-time
    good health
- Findings are less consistent on several other demographic variables:
    gender
    marital status
    race
    religion
    region

Summary of Key Themes

- Estimates of rates of volunteering vary so widely, in large part, because there is no standard definition of volunteerism and because different surveys ask different questions.
- If volunteering does not decline until very old age, This suggests that there is ample time for career development among retired volunteers, that retiree volunteers may need opportunities for growth and advancement to sustain a long-term involvement in volunteering, that periodic retraining may be important, and that volunteer programs need to develop strategies for accommodating age-related physical changes.
- People with resources (money, education, social status, health, and social ties through family and work) are more likely to volunteer than those who lack such resources. These resources affect both the costs and the opportunities for volunteering.

- Research evidence to date suggests that demographic factors influence, but do not determine, volunteering behavior.

- There is much variability in types of volunteering, and any explanation of when and why people volunteer needs to take into account these differences. It appears that different demographic, personal, and social characteristics may be associated with different forms of volunteer work.

THREE

Politics to Bake Sales:
Types of Volunteering

Everyday about 8,000 people visit a certain museum on the West Coast. This museum is quite new—only about 7 years old. But it has a large number of attractive and interesting exhibits and many educational programs, and new ideas constantly are being developed. This museum has 300 or so paid staff and more than 600 volunteers (about half of them are seniors) who serve as guides and teachers and work in every department. It is not easy to become a volunteer at this museum. The application, selection, and training process is elaborate. Potential volunteers receive glossy, multicolored brochures; the newsletter for volunteers and other contributors is professionally printed; and an assortment of perks is offered, such as special buttons, uniforms, and parking spaces for volunteers. There is a waiting list for volunteer positions.

▼

In a small Northeastern town, a new volunteer program is reaching out to people who are newly widowed. The volunteers are all themselves widowed. Some of the volunteers read through obituaries and develop a list of widowed persons. Others make phone calls, and, if they find a widow or widower who is interested, they meet and offer support. The program is small, with only 20 or 30 active volunteers, no paid staff, and almost no money to fund their operation. Their newsletter is typed and photocopied.

▼

A Retired Senior Volunteer Program (RSVP) in a Southeastern metropolitan community began almost 20 years ago with only 25 volunteers; now 4,200 volunteers are in this program, which refers senior volunteers to more than 250 different nonprofit agencies. The organization has grown so large that it now has three offices in three counties.

Volunteer programs differ from each other in many ways—for example, in size, structure, sponsorship, age, and type of membership. The most complex way that volunteer programs differ is in the types of activities and services they offer. Many thousands of jobs are available for volunteers, including senior volunteers. In fact, a single volunteer organization may have a large diversity of roles and positions for volunteers. Some types of volunteering are episodic; others require a long-term commitment. Some kinds of jobs seem to be especially attractive, and there may be waiting lists for these; other types of volunteering seem to be less desirable, and it may be difficult to attract and/or keep good volunteers.

The three organizations in the examples at the beginning of this chapter are all very different from each other. They have very different missions, and they range in size from 20 to more than 4,000 volunteers. They also differ in how long they have been established. The second vignette describes a very new organization with a relatively "simple" structure: a small number of volunteers doing only a few jobs (providing support to widowed persons) and with very little financial support. The other two not only are much larger but also are much more complex organizations with large budgets, many volunteers, and many different volunteer jobs. But these two organizations are nonetheless very different from each other. Volunteers for the museum tend to be college educated, and virtually all of their activities relate to cultural and educational functions. Volunteer roles for RSVP are much more diverse, and often these volunteers have no more than a high school education.

In this chapter we describe several ways to compare "types" of volunteering. To do this, we outline dimensions of volunteer roles and organizations and examine the natural or logical categories within each of these dimensions. As will become apparent in the following pages, the process of classification is multilayered. Not only are there many different types of volunteer services and volunteer organizations, but there also are many different yardsticks for measuring variability.

A Typology of Volunteer Roles

If we made a list of the different types of voluntary services, it would be a very long list. How do we make sense of this variety? One way to think about the types of volunteering is to group volunteer jobs or roles according to the following criteria (see Table 3.1):

- Is the voluntary service formal (arranged through an organization) or informal (arranged by individuals)?
- Does the activity require a regular (ongoing) time commitment or an occasional (once or twice) commitment?
- What is the nature of the activity—working with the public, working with objects, or helping individual people?

Formal Versus Informal Volunteering. Formal volunteering refers to services arranged through or for organizations—churches, social welfare agencies, museums, hospitals, and so forth. In informal volunteering no organizational affiliation is involved. Informal volunteering includes services for friends, neighbors, and other individuals in the community. As Table 3.1 shows, many of the same activities may be arranged either formally or informally.

Time. The time commitment issue is important because of the fundamental differences between regular and occasional volunteering. In formal volunteer organizations, volunteers who have ongoing responsibilities have jobs that are often similar to paid jobs. In informal volunteering, regular voluntary service is similar to responsibilities typically done in families.

Serving the Public. Some kinds of volunteering require interactions with the community or with large organizations or groups of people. Leadership roles—for example, the president or treasurer of a charitable organization—fit this type. But some other volunteer

TABLE 3.1 Conceptual Categories for Classifying Volunteer Roles

Type of service activity	Formal volunteer work		Time commitment	Informal volunteer work	
	Regular[a]	*Occasional*[b]		*Regular*	*Occasional*
Serving the public	Long-term volunteer in public role *Examples:* Officer of charitable organization, unpaid editor of newsletter	Temporary volunteer in public role *Examples:* Chairperson of ad hoc committee, unpaid usher for cultural event		—	—
Working with objects	Core volunteer for general services to organizations *Examples:* Envelope stuffer for political campaign, church handyperson	Temporary volunteer for general services to organizations *Examples:* Cake baker for church bazaar, decoration maker for fund-raising event		Long-term helper for general tasks for neighbors or friends *Examples:* Bookkeeper for neighbor or friend, person who regularly shovels neighbor's driveway for no pay	Temporary helper for general tasks for neighbors or friends *Examples:* House-watcher for traveling neighbor, handyman who helps neighbors
Helping individuals	Core volunteer for personal service work *Examples:* Driver for a senior center, language tutor, personal companion sent by church group	Temporary volunteer for personal service work *Examples:* Red Cross volunteer who helps victims during a *natural disaster*		Long-term helper for personal care *Examples:* Spouse-caregiver for someone who is disabled, person who drives neighbor to church weekly	Temporary helper for personal care *Examples:* Caregiver for someone with the flu, person who drives neighbor on one or two errands

NOTES: a. Refers to an ongoing commitment;
b. Refers to a voluntary service that is done once or twice, associated with an episode or event.
SOURCE: Adapted from "Older Volunteers: A Discussion of the Minnesota Senior Study" by L. R. Fischer, D. P. Mueller, & P. W. Cooper, 1991, *Gerontologist*, 31, p. 193.

jobs largely entail contacts with people in the community—for example, an usher at a cultural event, the editor of a newsletter, the salesperson at a hospitality shop, or a performer at a charity concert. We can note that public roles, almost by definition, involve formal rather than informal arrangements.

Working With Objects. In some kinds of volunteering, although the service is intended to help a person or group, the actual work centers on manipulating objects. This type of work includes stuffing envelopes for a charitable organization or political campaign, bookkeeping, baking a cake for a bake sale, housecleaning for a church or neighbor, fixing a car, or mowing a lawn. The service may or may not lead to contact with others (one can stuff envelopes alone or with others), but the performance of the work is oriented toward contact with objects rather than people.

Helping Individuals. Some types of volunteering require private and face-to-face involvement with other people. This type of service work may be arranged on an informal basis or may be organized through a church or other organization. One obvious example of this type of service is caregiving. Caregiving can be formal or informal, regular or occasional. Person-to-person services are not necessarily as intimate as caregiving and also include personal services, such as providing transportation, serving food (not preparing the food), baby-sitting, and tutoring.

*   *   *

For a person who is considering volunteering, it is useful to think how each of these types matches his or her individual preferences. People who like to spend their time interacting with other people are not likely to be very satisfied with jobs that mainly involve working with objects, or vice versa. Someone who is unwilling to make a regular commitment for a volunteer job can volunteer for occasional events. Conversely a retiree who wants an ongoing commitment needs to look for regular volunteer opportunities.

Volunteer organizations often have multiple roles. For example, in the museum described in the first vignette at the beginning of this chapter, many volunteers serve as docents (serving the public), but other volunteers have essentially clerical functions (working with objects). This museum requires volunteers to make a commitment of at least 4 hours per week, so most volunteers are regular rather than occasional. Even so, some of the volunteers might work on fund-raising for special events, which would be episodic volunteering.

Types of Volunteer Programs

A classification of volunteer roles is different from a categorization of volunteer organizations. In a typology of volunteer organizations, the dimensions would be characteristics of organizations rather than of individuals or roles. It would be convenient if we could describe a small number of types of volunteer organizations. We might use the three chapter-opening vignettes, for example, to represent three "typical" organizations: a cultural, a self-help, and a referral organization. We could add a few more portraits, and in this way we could generate our list of volunteer organization types. But such an approach, we believe, would be misleading.

At the beginning of this chapter we made the point that volunteer organizations differ from each other in many ways. To adequately represent variability across volunteer organizations, we need multidimensional yardsticks. Table 3.2 shows five broad dimensions of volunteer organizations: *organizational functions, structure, "demographics," composition,* and *sponsorship.* These five broad dimensions cover the parameters of volunteer organizations: what they do, how they are structured, their characteristics, who belongs, and how they are connected to other organizations and institutions. Each of these is comprised of a number of separate components.

In later chapters, we discuss findings from the case studies to see how these features of organizations might affect recruiting, retaining, and working with older volunteers. What are the

TABLE 3.2 Attributes of Volunteer Organizations

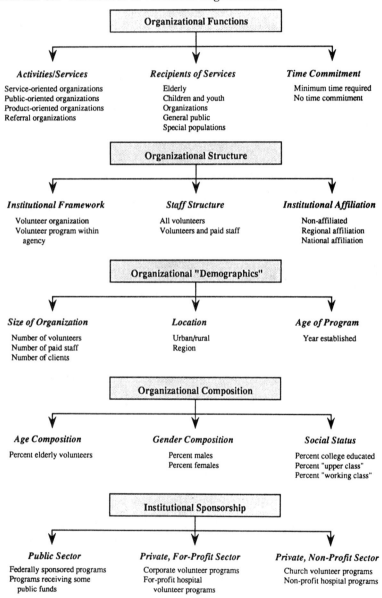

Organizational Functions

Activities/Services

Service-oriented organizations
Public-oriented organizations
Product-oriented organizations
Referral organizations

Recipients of Services

Elderly
Children and youth
Organizations
General public
Special populations

Time Commitment

Minimum time required
No time commitment

Organizational Structure

Institutional Framework

Volunteer organization
Volunteer program within
    agency

Staff Structure

All volunteers
Volunteers and paid staff

Institutional Affiliation

Non-affiliated
Regional affiliation
National affiliation

Organizational "Demographics"

Size of Organization

Number of volunteers
Number of paid staff
Number of clients

Location

Urban/rural
Region

Age of Program

Year established

Organizational Composition

Age Composition

Percent elderly volunteers

Gender Composition

Percent males
Percent females

Social Status

Percent college educated
Percent "upper class"
Percent "working class"

Institutional Sponsorship

Public Sector

Federally sponsored programs
Programs receiving some
    public funds

Private, For-Profit Sector

Corporate volunteer programs
For-profit hospital
    volunteer programs

Private, Non-Profit Sector

Church volunteer programs
Non-profit hospital programs

differences among the types of volunteer organizations and programs? How do these factors affect the process of recruiting and working with volunteers? Do organizations that require minimum time commitment have more or fewer problems with recruiting and retaining volunteers than other volunteer organizations? Are organizations that work with older volunteers or older minority volunteers different, in any systematic ways, from other kinds of volunteer organizations? How do status factors (such as the education and income levels of participants) affect volunteer organizations?

Organizational Functions. This dimension refers to what volunteer organizations do: the types of activities or services offered, the individuals or groups who are the targets of services, and how the organization operates. Although volunteer organizations typically offer multiple roles to volunteers, often one type of activity defines the mission or purpose of the organization.

Three types of organizations correspond to the *types of service activities* shown in Table 3.1: *public-oriented organizations, product-oriented organizations,* and *service-oriented organizations.* A few examples will illustrate these types.

The functions of *public-oriented organizations* include cultural events, classroom education, and leadership training—all activities in which volunteers interact with communities or groups in a more or less public setting. For example, we categorized the museum described in the first vignette as a public-oriented organization.

In *product-oriented organizations* the central function is to produce something tangible. One volunteer organization, for instance, records technical books for blind students. This category would include both fund-raising organizations and programs in which volunteers prepare special reports, because the main purpose of such organizations is to create and deliver tangible "products."

In *service-oriented organizations* the central activities entail services to individuals. The widow-to-widow support program described in one of the opening vignettes fits into this group. Examples are numerous: a peer counseling program in California, an interfaith caregiver program for the elderly in a small town in New York, a hospital-auxiliary program in Boston, and so forth.

In our case studies, we found a number of organizations that did not fit any of the three categories. Organizations like the Retired Senior Volunteer Program (RSVP) refer volunteers to different agencies for hundreds or even thousands of positions. It makes no sense to classify these organizations by type of service activity because their function is to develop volunteer opportunities and to refer volunteers to other organizations and agencies. Therefore we added a fourth category—*referral organizations*. These include programs like RSVP and a number of corporate retiree programs.

A second way to classify the functions of volunteer organizations is in terms of *who is helped* or served by the activities of volunteers: the elderly, children and youth, special populations (ethnic minorities or persons with specific disabilities), the general public, or organizations (or agencies). This way of grouping organizations overlaps in some ways with the "type of activity" classification just discussed. For example, the actual recipients of services for referral organizations are organizations. However, the converse is not true; that is, not all organizations that provide services to agencies and organizations are referral organizations. Similarly many elderly targeted programs are service-oriented organizations, but some are not.

The third functional component of volunteer organizations concerns how they operate; that is, do they require at least a minimum *time commitment* from volunteers? Time commitment is an important aspect of the functioning of an organization. A program that requires a minimum investment of time can know how many volunteers it has. Conversely, for organizations with no time expectations, a list of volunteers is just that—a list.

Organizational Structure. Table 3.2 depicts three components of organizational structure: the *institutional framework,* the *staff structure,* and the *institutional affiliation.* The *institutional framework* differentiates between volunteer organizations and programs. *Volunteer organizations* are separate institutions whose work is done primarily by volunteers; *volunteer programs* are part of larger agencies or institutions. Some volunteer programs represent a very small voice in large institutions; therefore, many of the paid staff have little involvement with volunteers. A central function for the director of a hospital volunteer program, for example, may be to serve as a link between paid staff and volunteers. Sometimes volunteer programs within larger agencies are treated as marginal departments.

Staff structure is another important component of both volunteer organizations and programs. Volunteer organizations or programs may have no paid staff, a small number of paid staff, or a large paid staff.

Organizational structure also differs by *institutional affiliation*. Local volunteer organizations and programs may have no affiliations, or they may be the local program of a regional or national organization, such as the American Association for Retired Persons (AARP) or the Retired Senior Volunteer Program (RSVP). The reporting and resource structure of organizations with regional or national affiliations is different from that of non- affiliated organizations. Affiliated organizations sometimes must contend with issues of adapting national or regional guidelines to local settings and circumstances.

Organizational "Demographics." Demographic characteristics usually refer to individuals—age, gender, marital status, and so on. But if we are interested in the "population" of volunteer organizations, we can think of their characteristics also as demographics. An organizational demographic profile would include such factors as the *size of the organization* (number of volunteers, number of clients, number of paid staff, ratio of volunteers to paid staff, size of budget), *location* (region of the country and whether the program is in an urban/suburban community, a small town, or a rural area), and the *age of the program*.

Organizational Composition. Another way to characterize organizations is in terms of their participants. Some volunteer organizations have special types of participants—either by design or because the organization's activities selectively attract certain groups of people. In some organizations all (or almost all) of the volunteers are seniors, men, women, or members of particular religious or ethnic groups.

Many types of volunteer activities, organizations, and programs selectively attract either men or women. Most of the volunteer organizations in our case studies have women as the majority of their volunteers. A number of directors of these organizations said they would like to recruit more men but that somehow men do not seem as interested. Only eight organizations in our case studies reported that most of their volunteers are men. All of these organizations are either public-oriented or product-oriented organizations. A volunteer program for retired executives, for example, does not exclude women from joining; nonetheless most of its volunteers (like most business executives) are men. Conversely staff at all of the service-oriented organizations said that their volunteers are primarily (and often overwhelmingly) women.

Institutional Sponsorship. The fourth dimension of volunteer organizations refers to the environmental context. Many volunteer programs are sponsored by or affiliated with institutions of various types—from the private sector (corporations, for-profit agencies), the public sector (government), or the "third sector" (nonprofit foundations or agencies, religious organizations).

The institutional sponsorship influences volunteer programs in a number of ways, including the mission of a program. For example, church-sponsored programs often have a spiritual component. The director of a church-based program commented: "[Our volunteers] really see volunteering as a part of church life—as part of their service to God."

Three programs for the elderly are federally sponsored: the Retired Senior Volunteer Program, the Senior Companion Program, and the Foster Grandparent Program. All of these are under the ACTION Office; the last two are stipended programs for low-income seniors. The federal government provides a portion of the funding for local programs, which have to raise other funds in their own communities. In addition to these programs, many other volunteer programs receive public funding. Typically, government funds come with regulations and stipulations.

The institutional arrangements also define who can volunteer. In many corporate retiree programs, only the corporation's retirees or the spouses of retirees are eligible to participate. Sometimes the institutional affiliation also determines what services are provided and who should benefit from these services. Perhaps most significantly the institutional framework determines the culture and style of programs. Thus eldercare services (care for older persons at risk) might be provided through a number of types of programs. It is likely, however, that programs affiliated with religious organizations will have an orientation different from that of secular programs. Other types of affiliations have comparable distinctions. For example, volunteers providing eldercare through a social service agency might be trained to emphasize needs for socialization, whereas an eldercare service arranged through hospitals or other health care facilities might focus more on health needs.

Service Exchange Programs

One special type of volunteering needs its own explanation and discussion—a service exchange program. A few such experimental programs have been tried. For example, in some programs volunteers earn "service credits" by providing respite care, babysitting, and other services (Cahn, 1988; Coughlin & Meiners, 1990; Pynoos, Hade-Kaplan, & Fliesher, 1984). The incentive system for this type of program is rather different from that of most other volunteer activities.

Cahn (1988), a major proponent of the service credit system, asserted that an exchange program can generate a considerable amount of service for a modest set of administrative costs and is attractive to legislators, who can satisfy service needs without having to raise large revenues. He estimated that service credits cost about $1.50 per hour of service. Four states have enacted service credit laws, and nine other states are considering such legislation (Coughlin & Meiners, 1990).

The *service credit* concept is especially interesting as a way to provide long-term care at home for frail elderly who are at risk of institutionalization. Long-term care is expensive and does not necessarily require a high level of skill. The use of volunteers through a service credit program (or through other types of volunteer programs) both serves the needs of the elderly, who usually want to continue living in their own homes, and potentially can reduce public expenditures on long-term care.

Unfortunately, administrating service exchange programs can be complicated. An exchange program is only valuable if it has an adequate tracking system and if the program continues. Otherwise a donor risks getting no "payback" for time volunteered. An exchange program becomes increasingly valuable as the range of services grows. But, of course, the larger the program, the more complex it is to administer and the greater the administrative costs.

Cahn (1988) noted that until service credits establish a track record, their extrinsic value will be regarded with skepticism. Thus a catch-22 type of problem exists: An exchange program has little value unless it is functioning, but it can only attract participants—volunteers, clients, and stable sources of funding—if it has value!

Summary of Key Themes

- Volunteer programs differ from each other across a number of dimensions. Understanding these dimensions can help us categorize particular volunteer organizations and also understand variability across organizations.
- We have identified three dimensions for categorizing volunteer roles: (a) whether the voluntary service is formal or informal, (b) whether the activity entails a regular or episodic time commitment, and (c) the type of service activity: serving the public, working with objects, and helping individuals.
- We have identified five broad dimensions of volunteer organizations:
  organizational functions—type of service, recipient of service, and time commitment
  organizational structure—institutional framework, staff structure, and institutional affiliation
  organizational "demographics"—size of organization, location, and age of program

organizational composition—age, gender, and socioeconomic status of volunteers

institutional sponsorship—public, private for-profit, and private non-profit sectors

These five broad dimensions cover what volunteer organizations do, how they are structured, who belongs, and how they are connected to other organizations and institutions.

• A special type of volunteer program is a service exchange or service credit system. An exchange program becomes increasingly valuable as the range of services grows, but it also becomes more complex to administer.

FOUR

Why Volunteer?

"I've always wondered, why do I do these things; I don't always enjoy them. But somehow I invite them, I do them." But Jack admits this line of reasoning leaves him with more questions than answers. Sometimes his compulsion to help has even led him to do dangerous things, such as the time he rescued the woman from the lake. "I shouldn't have gone out without a life jacket; it was a stupid thing to do." But still he somehow cannot deny his impulses to help; he sacrifices himself even when it is not necessary. "So I wonder why," he ponders. "I don't know." (Wuthnow, 1991, p. 25)

Ordinary people do extraordinary things as volunteers. Some people commit many hours every week as volunteers: They tutor children, deliver meals to homebound elderly, serve on the boards of charitable organizations, and use their particular talents to help individuals and organizations. Why? What motivates people to volunteer their time?

In this chapter, we discuss the complex issue of motivation. How do volunteers themselves explain their motivations? How much should we believe what they say? Even when volunteers say they are motivated by a desire to help others, do they also have more selfish reasons? Do people really know or understand their own motivations? Do older people and younger people volunteer for the same or for different reasons? Why are some people more willing to volunteer than others? Is there a volunteering type of personality? How do social conditions affect whether people volunteer? In what ways does religion provide a spiritual rationale for volunteering?

What Are the Motivations?

Understanding motivation is relevant to virtually all aspects of volunteer programs—from recruiting to maintaining the commitment of volunteers. Several studies have suggested that recruitment and retention of volunteers are more effective when volunteer programs appeal to the specific needs and motivations of their volunteers (Clary & Miller, 1986; Clary & Orenstein, in press; Clary & Snyder, 1991a; Francies, 1983).

Table 4.1 presents an overview of theory and research on motivations to volunteer. We have identified eight categories of motivations: altruistic, ideological, egoistic, material/reward, status/ reward, social relationship, leisure time, and personal growth motivations. These categories represent a synthesis of research findings and theoretical concepts from a number of sources (although these sources use somewhat different terms). The categories are not absolutely distinct; in any case most volunteers seem to have multiple reasons for volunteering.

Altruistic Motivations. Most studies of volunteer motivation have found a majority of volunteers to give altruistic types of responses when asked why they volunteer; that is, they talk about wanting to help, wanting to be useful, having a sense of social responsibility, or wanting to do good. In a recent national survey (J. C. Penney, 1988) 97% of volunteers gave "I want to help others" as a reason for volunteering.

Some scholars, however, are skeptical about these stated reasons for volunteering, and they insist that even when people say they want to help others, their real motivations are much more complex (Smith, 1982; see also Cialdini et al., 1987; Clary & Snyder, 1991a; Francies, 1983; Henderson, 1984). There is a somewhat convoluted debate about altruistic versus egoistic motives. David Horton Smith (1982), for example, argued that there is no such thing as "pure altruism." There are intrinsic psychic rewards for altruistic acts, he said, because helping others makes the helper feel good. Conversely some scholars assert that there is a "self-deprecating bias" in that people are reluctant to admit having

TABLE 4.1 Motivations for Volunteering: From Theory and Research on Volunteerism in General

References	Research and theory

Altruistic Motivations

Clary & Snyder, 1991a	Surveys show that "helping," "doing
Francies, 1983	good," and "having a sense of social
Gillespie & King, 1985	responsibility" are the most common
Grieshop, 1985	reasons for volunteering.
Independent Sector, 1990	
J. C. Penney Company, 1988	
Smith, 1982	

Ideological Motivations

Clary & Snyder, 1991a	Volunteers often are motivated by
Eisenberg, 1986	specific causes, ideologies, or values.
Grieshop, 1985	"Purposive" motivations for volunteer-
J. C. Penney Company, 1988	ing include, but are not limited to,
Smith, 1982	altruistic purposes.
Wuthnow, 1990	

Egoistic Motivations

Clary & Snyder, 1991a	People may volunteer to serve their
Francies, 1983	ego needs—e.g., to cope with inner
	conflicts or to gain approval.

Material/Reward Motivations

Grieshop, 1985	Material motivations include benefits
Smith, 1982	to self or family. According to some
	scholars, much voluntary effort is
	motivated by the anticipation of
	material rewards.

Status/Reward Motivations

Chapman, 1985	The desire to gain professional knowl-
Clary & Snyder, 1991b	edge, skills, contacts, and recognition
Francies, 1983	are especially likely to motivate
Grieshop, 1985	students and working-age adults to
Independent Sector, 1990	volunteer.
J. C. Penney Company, 1988	

Social Relationship Motivations

Clary & Snyder, 1991a	Many volunteers (though a minority on
Daniels, 1985	surveys) list "meeting people" or
Francies, 1983	"making friends" as one motivation for
Gillespie & King, 1985	volunteering. It appears that friend-
J. C. Penney Company, 1988	ship is an important factor in sustain-
Smith, 1982	ing volunteer work.

References	Research and theory
Leisure Time Motivations	
Gillespie & King, 1985	Volunteering is a form of leisure time
Henderson, 1984	activity.
J. C. Penney Company, 1988	Some volunteers say they are volunteering because they have "free time."
Personal Growth Motivations	
References	Research and theory
Chapman, 1985	Learning, personal growth, and spirit-
Isley, 1990	ual development are important moti-
Luks with Payne, 1991	vators for volunteerism. People experi-
Wuthnow, 1991	ence a "helper's high" from giving to others. The great majority of volunteers believe that there are personal/ spiritual rewards from giving.

*   *   *

Multiple Motivations	
Clary & Orenstein, in press	When asked why they volunteer, people
Clary & Snyder, 1991a	tend to give multiple reasons. More-
Pitterman, 1973	over, motivations may change over
Schram, 1985	time, and there may be different
Wuthnow, 1990	reasons to begin volunteering than to continue in a particular volunteer job.

altruistic motives (Batson, Fultz, Schoenrade, & Paduano, 1987; see also Miller, 1982).

Roberta Simmons, in her research on kidney and bone marrow donors, reported that people are often suspicious of altruism. One transplant donor commented: "I would say across the board everybody said I was crazy" (Simmons, 1991, p. 14). Referring to experimental research on helping behavior, Simmons (1991, p. 10) wrote: "In my opinion, altruism is trivialized in many of these experiments. Helping behavior is called egoistic simply because it raises happiness and self-esteem. But helping to save a life is, in fact, an important act and warrants the helper's resultant good feelings."

Ideological Motivations. Even when people have an altruistic impulse, inevitably an ideological component is involved in determining what is "doing good." Ideology is an important motivator

for volunteerism because people volunteer for particular organizations or to work on specific issues (see Chin, 1989; Eisenberg, 1986).
A volunteer for an AIDS crisis center is responding to a very specific situation in his or her environment. People are unlikely to volunteer unless they agree with the values represented by a volunteer organization and/or by a particular cause. Some voluntary
organizations overtly recruit volunteers on the basis of political
or religious beliefs and values. Volunteers for pro-life or pro-choice
organizations, for example, are driven in large part by the intens-
ity of their beliefs. Interestingly these volunteers may have oppos-
ing values, but they often engage in remarkably similar political
activities.

Egoistic Motivations. Potentially volunteers are motivated by
diverse emotional needs: wanting to avoid feelings of guilt, wanting
approval, wanting to cope with anxiety, and so forth. Some theories
on motivations for helping behavior make a distinction between
helping that is other-oriented and helping that is motivated toward
serving the helper's psychological needs. Clary and Snyder (1991a,
p. 130), for example, differentiated between the following responses
to a question on motivation for volunteering: "I am concerned about
those less fortunate than I" is an *altruistic* motivation, while "It
gives me a good feeling or sense of satisfaction to help others" is an
egoistic motivation. Abraham Lincoln has been quoted as explaining an act of kindness as the "very essence of selfishness" because
"I did it to get peace of mind, don't you see?"

Material/Reward Motivations. Sometimes tangible perks are
associated with giving and volunteering, including gifts, tax deduc-
tions, and other privileges. Some forms of volunteer work provide
direct material benefits for the volunteer. The man who volunteers
in a cooperative neighborhood group, which represents the interests of residents, is protecting his own property and quality of life.
He and his family, as well as his neighbors, are the beneficiaries
of his efforts. Similarly the woman who works for the Parent Teacher
Association at her child's school also is providing a service to her
own family, in addition to serving others. Of course, the fact that this
man and this woman have material motivations for volunteering

does not entirely answer the question about why these particular people have chosen to volunteer—and not others who equally benefit from their services.

Status/Reward Motivations. Status rewards for volunteering are much like material rewards but are less direct. Volunteers may be motivated by the hope of gaining entrée to paid jobs or skill training that can be translated into both salaried dollars and social mobility. Similarly a business executive who donates time and money to a charity or an arts organization might be motivated, at least in part, by the prospect of indirect rewards: publicity, public goodwill, status in the community, the possibility of influencing public policies (which could affect the business climate), opportunities to network with other influential persons in the community, and so forth. If this person were asked "Why do you do this?" the response might focus on altruistic motivations—caring about the community, doing good for a worthy cause—but there is also an important element of "enlightened self-interest," in the sense that doing good happens to be good for business (see Galaskiewicz & Schaffer, 1989).

Social Relationship Motivations. Volunteering is often, if not always, social because volunteers frequently interact with others when they volunteer. They may make new friends with fellow volunteers, the people they help, and other staff with whom they work. In most surveys, when people are asked why they volunteer, one type of response is "to socialize," "to meet people," or "to make friends." Some research suggests that social motivations may be even more important in retaining than in recruiting volunteers. Friendship motivates volunteers to continue in their roles because of both their loyalty to particular people and the pleasure of their social interactions (see Chapter 6; Daniels, 1985).

Leisure Time Motivations. Whereas social motivations concern attachments to people, leisure motivations concern time. Having leisure time is sometimes given, by itself, as a motivating factor—a reason to volunteer. Conversely, being "too busy" is a disincentive to volunteering.

Personal Growth Motivations. Intangible benefits that appear to motivate volunteering include having an opportunity to learn and to grow personally, gaining a sense of meaning and purpose, and feeling a "helper's high." In his book, *Acts of Compassion,* Robert Wuthnow (1991) reported that the great majority of volunteers agree with the following statement: "When you help someone in need, you get as much as they do" (pp. 55-56; see also Isley, 1990; Luks with Payne, 1991).

The Motivations of Older Volunteers

Most research findings and theoretical concepts about volunteer motivation seem to apply to volunteers of all ages. For example, older volunteers and younger volunteers are about equally likely to say that they volunteer to "help others" or to "do something useful" (Independent Sector, 1990).

Table 4.2 presents an overview of research findings specifically about older volunteers. Some of the studies reviewed in this table are based on samples of older volunteers; others compare the motivations of younger versus older persons to volunteer. The data in Table 4.2 suggest several distinct features of volunteer motivation for older persons.

- *Older volunteers are much less likely than younger volunteers to be motivated by material rewards to themselves or their families.* In itself, this finding should not be surprising. Many volunteer opportunities are associated with family responsibilities—for example, serving on the PTA, being a Scout leader, and working for a church youth group. It is rather rare for older persons to be responsible for small children. Their own children have grown, and their ties with their grandchildren are more likely to be social than obligatory. It appears to be very uncommon for grandparents to be recruited for the PTA or other such organizations (Independent Sector, 1990).
- *Older volunteers are less likely to indicate having status/reward motivations.* This finding is logical. Most older volunteers are retired or close to retirement. Although a small percentage may be interested in volunteering to develop postretirement careers, career development is not nearly as salient an issue for retirees as it is for

TABLE 4.2 Motivations for Volunteering: From Research on Older Volunteers

References	Research findings
Altruistic Motivations	
Hellebrandt, 1980	Helping others is important in the adjustment to old age.
Herzog & House, 1991	Older people tend to believe that retirees should contribute to the community.
Marriott Seniors Volunteerism Study, 1991	The great majority of seniors surveyed said they volunteer to feel useful and to help others.
Seguin, O'Brien, Berton, Hummell, & McConney, 1976	Helping others is a major motivation for older volunteers.
Ideological Motivations	
Cohen-Mansfield, 1989	Ideological and philosophical reasons are important for older volunteers.
Hulbert & Chase, 1991	Most retiree volunteers surveyed said the primary reason for volunteering was that the cause is worthwhile.
Independent Sector, 1990	Older volunteers were somewhat more likely than younger volunteers to give "religious concerns" as a motivation for volunteering.
Material/Reward Motivations	
Independent Sector, 1990	Older volunteers are less likely than younger volunteers to cite benefits to family or self as a motivation for volunteering.
Status/Reward Motivations	
Gidron, 1978	Older volunteers are less likely than younger volunteers to have expectations for learning and self-development.
Independent Sector, 1990	Older volunteers are less likely to say getting "experience" is a motivation.
Seguin, O'Brien, Berton, Hummell, & McConney, 1976	Maintaining professional skills is a motivation for older volunteers.
Social Relationship Motivations	
Seguin, O'Brien, Berton, Hummell, & McConney, 1976	Meeting other people is a major motivation for older volunteers.
Leisure Time Motivations	
Independent Sector, 1990	Older volunteers are more likely than younger volunteers to say that having "free time" is a motivation to volunteer.
Seguin, O'Brien, Berton, Hummell, & McConney, 1976	Making good use of spare time is a motivation for older volunteers.

(Continued)

TABLE 4.2 Continued

References	Research findings
Personal Growth Motivations	
Chambre, 1987	According to a recent survey of older volunteers, the most common reason for volunteering is "self-fulfillment."
Charner, Fox, & Trachtman, 1988	About half of union retirees are interested in further education.
Cook, 1991	Senior companion volunteers feel "vali-
Fogelman, 1981	dated" and "needed" by their work with elderly clients.
Gidron, 1978	Older volunteers are less likely than younger volunteers to have expectations for learning and self-development (but this includes career development). Older volunteers find volunteer work "meaningful."
Kelley, 1981	Study of retirees: Giving to others is
Midlarsky, 1990	positively related to well-being.
Petty & Cusack, 1989	Older volunteer peer counselors with little formal education said that "learning" was one of the things they "enjoyed most about the program."
Johnson & Schiaffino, 1990	Older volunteers report a "good feeling" from helping others.

students, young adults, and others who are in career transitions (Gidron, 1983; Independent Sector, 1990).

- *Although most older people are not concerned about education for the sake of career development, many older people are interested in education as a form of personal growth.* An interest in learning and self-improvement is found both among elderly with high levels of education and among those with little formal schooling (Arella, 1984; Chambre, 1987; Charner et al., 1988; Chapman, 1985; Petty & Cusack, 1989; Seguin, O'Brien, Berton, Hummell, & McConney, 1976).[5] The attraction to educational opportunities for older people can be inferred from the outstanding success of the Elderhostel program, which grew from 200 participants in 1975 to hundreds of thousands of elderly who now attend classes every year all over the world (see Romaniuk & Romaniuk, 1982).

- *Older volunteers are more likely than younger volunteers to say that they volunteer because they have "free time."* Clearly this finding reflects the rhythm of postretirement life, compared to the working years.

- *Older volunteers are somewhat more likely than younger volunteers to say that they volunteer because of religious concerns.* Older people tend to be more active in their churches and synagogues than younger people and are more likely to volunteer for churches and other religious organizations. It is not surprising, then, that older persons are especially likely to be motivated by religion.

The Mystery of Motivations

We began this chapter by noting that motivation to volunteer is complex. A catalogue of volunteer motivations does not really explain why some people volunteer and not others. As numerous surveys have shown, many more people believe that they "should" volunteer than actually do so (see Clary & Snyder, 1991a). What moves people to action?

Studies have found that most volunteers give multiple motivations when asked why they volunteer or why they continue to do volunteer work (see Table 4.1; Clary & Miller, 1986; Clary & Orenstein, in press; Clary & Snyder, 1991a, 1991b; J. C. Penney, 1988; Marriott Seniors Volunteerism Study, 1991; Romero, 1986). Perhaps it is a "package" of motivations, not a single motivational impulse, that drives behavior. Potentially the more separate reasons for volunteering, the more likely a person is to volunteer. In this sense egoistic, altruistic, and other motives might be viewed as additive, rather than as competing explanations for voluntary action.

As with all kinds of behavior, there is a cost-benefit calculus, an assessment of costs (time, inconvenience, hazards) and benefits (Smith, 1982, p. 39). With an "altruistic calculus," benefit to others is part of the calculation. But there is a catch: Motivations can be mutually contradictory and do not necessarily add together in a simple way. Research has shown that if extrinsic (or material) rewards are superimposed on intrinsic motivations, there actually can be a decrease in the motivation to volunteer (see Organ, 1988; Pearce, 1985.)

At least one authority on volunteerism has suggested that it may be futile to try to understand motivations for volunteering. Jone Pearce (1985, p. 211) wrote: "Perhaps we should accept the inherent mystery of volunteer motivation—recognizing its benefits as well as its costs—rather than searching for an 'explanation' that will never really fit." This is a note of caution to take seriously. For certain topics, such as love and religious belief, scientific research can only nip around the edges. We cannot expect to understand fully why humans love one another or why humans help one another.

*   *   *

The "why volunteer" question seems to lead us through a philosophical maze and to trip us up with logical inconsistencies. A more appropriate question, perhaps, is not why but *when*—or under what circumstances—do people volunteer? The "when" question suggests a more concrete approach, more accessible to counting and measurement. Over the next several pages, we examine two sources of variability to explain different inclinations to volunteer: variability among people and variability in social conditions. This review addresses two questions about the circumstances and conditions of volunteering: What types of people are especially inclined to help others and to volunteer? and What types of social situations are particularly conducive to helping and volunteering?

People Who Help

We all know people who are helpers, who seem to have a natural talent for doing good. There is the man who cleans driveways for all his neighbors with his snowblower; he never allows them to pay him, and he is embarrassed when they bring him Christmas gifts as a way of saying thank you. There is the woman who has been cooking for her church for years and years; at every special event, at holidays or for personal celebrations, she is in charge of the kitchen. There are the people who volunteer for a dozen worthy causes and who always say yes when they are asked to make a charitable donation. Why do some people help and volunteer more than others? In Chapter 2 we looked at how demographic factors predict whether or not people volunteer. Research findings on the impact on volunteering of demographic factors such as, income, gender, race, and religion have been inconsistent. It seems that demographic factors, by themselves, give us only small hints to predict when or whether people volunteer.

Several recent reviews of research on helping, volunteering, and other forms of prosocial behavior have concluded that there is an altruistic personality; that is, some people are inclined to be helpers because of their moral character, their capacity for empathy, and their particular configuration of personality traits. Laboratory experiments reveal that people with altruistic or other-oriented personality traits, according to psychological test scores, are more likely to help others if presented with opportunities (Eisenberg et al., 1989; see also Batson, Bolen, Cross, & Neuringer-Benefiel, 1986; Batson et al., 1988; Clary & Miller, 1986; Clary & Orenstein, in press).

Empathy is an important component of the altruistic personality. People behave altruistically when they feel empathy for a person in need of help (see Clary & Miller, 1986; Clary & Orenstein, in press; Piliavin & Charng, 1990). Salovey and his co-authors (Salovey, Mayer, & Rosenhan, 1991) suggested that some people have a "high emotional IQ"; that is, they have a well-developed capacity for empathy, understanding, and caring about others.

Clearly *empathy is a critical factor for at least certain forms of volunteerism.* Leigh and his co-researchers (Leigh, Gerrish, & Gillespie, 1986), in an evaluation of a program for volunteers working as "buddies" for alcoholics, reported that empathy, insight, and concern were among the most important factors in predicting whether a volunteer would stay with the program. This is an interesting example because the buddy system represents a particularly difficult condition for volunteering. Many volunteers leave the program out of frustration because the clients they work with seem intractable and often unreliable; that is, the clients do not show up at meetings and/or drop out of the program. When their efforts seem wasted, volunteers often want to give up. It is hard to imagine, in fact, that a volunteer without empathic concern could survive these conditions.

It also appears that when people have an *altruistic identity*— that is, if they believe they are altruistic—they are more likely to behave generously. In an intriguing study of helping behavior in childhood, children who were told that they were "kind and helpful" performed better on altruism tests than children who were socially reinforced for their sharing by being told they had done a "kind thing" (Grusec, 1991). In the first condition, the children were given an altruistic identity; in the second, the label was only for the act, not the person.

Similar identity issues pertain to adult volunteers. For example, people who give blood begin to identify themselves as "donors," and this identity motivates future donations year after year. Conversely, being rejected as a blood donor negatively affects the potential giver's self-image. People who are rejected, for whatever reason, develop an identity as "nondonor" and tend not to try again (Piliavin & Callero, 1990).

An association seems to exist between good feelings and doing good. Thus people who feel good about themselves are more likely to help and give to others. And people are more likely to help others when they are in a good mood than when they are in a bad mood (see Clary & Snyder, 1991a; Midlarsky, 1984; Organ, 1988; Wuthnow, 1990). Potentially there is a positive reinforcement loop: Good feelings create a positive identity—which is both created and reinforced by altruistic behavior.

An accumulation of experimental and field research shows that personality is an important factor in helping and volunteering. Personality, of course, is in some ways like a black box, part of the "mystery" of motivations. It is very difficult to know to what extent an altruistic personality is a result of nature or nurture or some combination. This review suggests several practical implications for volunteer professionals. Interestingly, however, these suggestions are in some ways mutually contradictory.

- *Recruit selectively.* Screening potential volunteers for personality factors such as their capacity for empathy and their altruistic values should reduce turnover, thus prompting a greater payoff from the investment in each volunteer.

- *Avoid situations in which volunteers or potential volunteers experience rejection.* If people feel that their offer to help is not valued, they are disinclined to develop a volunteer "identity." Obviously this advice controverts the first point because selective recruitment inevitably entails choosing some and not choosing (rejecting) others. It may be important in many situations to offer alternatives to potential volunteers and to frame recruitment decisions as a matter of matching rather than rejecting "bad" volunteers. It is likely that a high emotional IQ is important for some, but not all, forms of volunteering. Also episodic volunteering requires less of a commitment, for example, than certain forms of regular, frequent volunteering.

- *Use volunteer training programs to enhance an altruistic identity.* This suggestion also mutes the contradiction between the two points above. People are socialized in adulthood, not only in childhood. With effective training, volunteers can enhance both their empathic and their social skills.

The Social Context of Helping

Personality is not the entire explanation for when people volunteer. Situational factors also are involved. It appears that certain conditions encourage and inspire helping behavior. In effect, the more favorable the social conditions, the larger the numbers of people who would be inclined to help.

Imagine the following scene:

It is evening, and you are taking a walk in your neighborhood. You see a woman lying in the road. She seems to have been hit by a car. In the moonlight you think you notice blood staining the road, and she seems to be moaning in pain. It is a quiet neighborhood, and although lights are on in some of the houses, you see no one else on the road. What do you do?

And here is another scene:

In the early evening, you are walking along a city street. The street glitters with neon lights, and many restaurants and a few shops are open. You pass a woman and a child squatting in a doorway. They are both dirty and shabbily dressed. An old blanket and a pair of adult-sized crutches are lying on the sidewalk beside them. The woman, looking up at you, asks for money. "We need money to eat," she says. What do you do?

These are both situations in which an individual might help someone in need. But they seem quite different. Emotionally, morally, and legally they elicit different levels of responsibility. It is likely that your response to these two scenes is not the same.

In the first situation, it is hard to imagine not helping. In fact, simply to notice and walk on might be considered morally, if not legally, as negligence—because there is no assurance that someone else would help, and the woman could die. Interestingly the woman and child in the second vignette also may be in peril. Presumably they are lacking a basic necessity—food—without which they also could die. Even so, many people who pass them probably will turn away and give nothing.

Experts on altruism contrast two kinds of conditions that elicit helping behavior: strong situations and weak situations. In strong situations the following conditions apply: (a) a pressing need, (b) no alternative source of help, and (c) a strong likelihood of a direct and positive impact. All of these conditions are met by the first scenario; they are arguable in the second. In the case of the woman lying injured on a lonely road, the vulnerability is clear: There is an ostensible risk of immediate death. Because the road seems to be empty, there is no one else to take responsibility for this woman's life. The strong probability also exists that intervention by a passerby will be useful—at the very least, an ambulance can be called. Moreover, what is called for is a one-time service. The passerby has no reason to suppose that, after this one act, he or she will be called on for any ongoing responsibility or rescue service. A quick and spontaneous altruistic calculus will show that the cost (to the helper) is relatively modest, while the benefit (to the woman in the road) is substantial.

With the situation of the woman begging on the street, the first condition is partially met: The woman asking for help appears vulnerable and in need. Even so, the need is not so immediate that she actually would die if the passerby does not help her. In fact, one of the most critical factors here is the presence of alternative sources of help. A large number of bystander studies have shown that the number of people nearby strongly affects the choice to help or not. In this case a passerby can rationalize that there are many others on the street to give her money and/or other sources of help (government funds and private charities), and/or perhaps she could help herself (get a job). Finally we come to the issue of the impact of help. At best the benefit will be temporary. In a short while this same woman and child will again need money for food. Moreover, donating to these two people will make virtually no dent in the overwhelming problem of hungry and homeless people in our cities. The risk, in fact, is that a passerby who gives to one person with a tin cup will be seen as a "mark" by others on the street, and the demands could be limitless. Therefore the cost-benefit assessment in this case is very different from that in the first situation (see Batson et al., 1986; Clary & Orenstein, in press; Clary & Snyder, 1991a; Simmons, 1991).

Regular volunteer work for organizations is more likely to approximate a weak than a strong helping condition. In regular volunteering, the need for help is more likely to be muted than critical. In most kinds of volunteer work, the impact tends to be more subtle than obvious. And most important, it is very rare for a potential volunteer to believe that he or she is indispensable for a needed and necessary service to be provided.

Interestingly studies of natural and human-caused disasters have found that in such situations there are often more volunteers than needed (Dynes & Quarantelli, 1980). These are situations with obvious vulnerability and a clear benefit to those in need. When a situation is viewed as a crisis, then inherently a shortage of volunteers is perceived because there is little time to recruit helpers. Similarly personal crises also function as strong helping situations. Simmons (1991) reported that kidney donors are more likely to volunteer if there are no other possible donors. Moreover, she found that donors, particularly if they are relatives, tend to decide instantaneously, without having to think about the decision. Such situations meet all the conditions of strong helping situations: immediate vulnerability (risk of kidney failure), no alternative helpers (the relative has, by far, the best tissue match), and a direct, positive impact (the probability of saving a life). Even if regular volunteering constitutes a relatively weak helping situation, there are still matters of degree. All three components of strong situations can be simulated, at least to some approximation. For example, volunteers might be recruited in ways that stress their unique contributions, suggesting that alternative sources of help are not available or could not be nearly as effective. A volunteer organization, moreover, might be able to recruit volunteers on the basis of an immediate and critical need (e.g., AIDS, teenagers using drugs, elderly at risk of losing their independence). A case study of volunteers who hosted poor, inner-city children for summer vacations provides an interesting illustration of the importance of vulnerability and need in recipients of help. The study found that the volunteer "hosts" tended to feel disappointed when a child arrived with new clothes. Of course, the parents and the children very much wanted to present themselves positively, so they dressed their city children in new clothes. But many of the hosts then looked at the children and thought they did not "look deprived" (Phillips, 1982).

But by far the most important motivational factor that can be affected by the social conditions of volunteering (and also sometimes can be influenced by volunteer organizations) is the probable impact of a volunteer's efforts. A number of studies suggest that prosocial or altruistic behavior is increased by competence and success. Organ (1988, p. 30), in his studies of altruistic behaviors in industrial settings, described the "warm afterglow of success" that reinforces prosocial behavior and induces further effort. Conversely, he said, the experience of failure results in a decrease in prosocial behavior. He added, "Rigging a task or game so as to ensure that a person experiences 'success' is one of the most reliable operations recorded in the experimental social-psychology literature for inducing prosocial behavior" (p. 97). As Wheeler (1986-1987, p. 6) noted: "People do not volunteer if they perceive that their time and efforts will be wasted."

There is no reason to suppose that the economic logic of altruism is different for older and younger volunteers. Before a potential volunteer engages in a volunteer role, he or she is likely to pose the following question: How much good can I do? To some degree, age may influence the costs and benefits of volunteering. For example, health problems are more likely in old age, so the energy costs of volunteer efforts may be relatively higher for older persons. But older volunteers, like all volunteers, do not want to waste their time.

If success motivates volunteers, including older volunteers, a number of practical implications should be considered.

- *Older volunteers, like younger volunteers, are motivated by the significance of their work.* This implication suggests that busywork—or volunteering for the sake of making the volunteer feel good (the inoculation idea)—should have much less appeal than outcome-oriented volunteering.
- *Evidence of success and effectiveness may be an important motivator for all volunteers, including older volunteers.* Perhaps one way to "measure" success is through recognition ceremonies, certificates, and plaques for volunteers. It is likely that such symbols probably do not, in themselves, motivate volunteering, but they do provide an indirect acknowledgment that the volunteer has had an impact. Potentially, however, more direct documentation would be a more powerful motivator. Such documentation can be obtained in two ways: through supervision of volunteers (giving specific feedback about what works) and through evaluation of volunteer programs (showing how the program has an impact).
- *Environmental factors are important in facilitating volunteer success.* The success of volunteer efforts is affected by circumstances beyond the control of either volunteers or volunteer programs. For example, when funds are cut back and programs are strained, potential volunteers may lose their motivation to help if their efforts are likely to be wasted.

Religion and Volunteering

A large proportion of volunteering, especially by older volunteers, is for or through religious organizations. Therefore we cannot understand the motivation to volunteer without examining the role of religious ideologies and religious communities (Hamilton,

Frederick, & Schneiders Company, 1988; Hodgkinson & Weitzman, 1989; Hodgkinson et al., 1990; Wuthnow, 1990).

Why are churches so important in fostering volunteer work? One reason may be that volunteer work is simply a part of everyday church work. Churches, as nonprofit organizations, are bound to rely heavily on unpaid labor. Thus it ought not to be surprising that a large portion of church members say they are volunteers. But other factors may be at work as well. Religions are likely to encourage altruistic values and behavior. Religious values also tend to foster a sense of community cohesion and responsibility for others in the community. This influence may be why church members are more likely to volunteer, in general, not just for church-sponsored activities (see Hodgkinson & Weitzman, 1989; Reddy, 1980; Wuthnow, 1990).

It is also possible that churches offer another, indirect impetus to volunteer work; that is, they provide a focal organization and network of potential volunteers. In the 1960s, churches, especially black churches in the South, were the organizational linchpin of the civil rights movement. Leadership for the civil rights movement came from the churches; mass meetings happened in the churches; spiritual guidance came through the religious teachings of the churches; and legitimacy for the movement was enhanced by the authority of the churches. In a similar way, religious establishments may be the organizational focal points of volunteering activities. This possibility may be particularly true for the elderly population, which tends to have high rates of church membership. Older volunteers are particularly likely to do "church work" (Fischer et al., 1991; Hayghe, 1991; Marriott Seniors Volunteerism Study, 1991).

To motivate increasing numbers of older volunteers, a logical starting point could be through churches, synagogues, and other religious organizations. Religious organizations could serve the same energizing functions for an "older volunteer movement" that black churches gave to the civil rights movement. In fact, churches may be especially important in reaching out to black and other minority elderly for both service and volunteer recruitment. Religious organizations are in a particularly advantageous position to locate and recruit older volunteers: They can provide potential volunteers with a spiritual rationale for providing their services, they can offer recognition within their congregational community, and they also can help develop a lay leadership among older volunteers. For all these reasons, church work has important implications for volunteering that go well beyond services provided to or through individual churches or particular religious organizations (see Fischer et al., 1991; Wuthnow, 1990).

Summary of Key Themes

- We identified eight categories of motivations to volunteer: altruistic, ideological, egoistic, material/reward, status/reward, social relationship, leisure time, and personal growth motivations.
- When volunteers are asked why they volunteer, the most common responses are altruistic: wanting to help, wanting to be useful, and having a sense of social responsibility.
- Most volunteers have multiple motivations for volunteering.
- Older volunteers, compared to younger volunteers, are less likely to be motivated by material rewards to themselves or their families, are less likely to indicate having status/reward motivations, are more likely to say they volunteer because they have free time, and are somewhat more likely to say they volunteer because of religious concerns.
- Two sources of variability explain the variability in why or when people volunteer: variability among people because some people are especially inclined to help and volunteer, and variability in social condition because certain social situations are particularly conducive to volunteering.
- People who are inclined to be helpers seem to have a high emotional IQ; that is, they have a well-developed capacity for empathy.
- People are more likely to behave altruistically if they believe they are altruistic—that is, if they have an altruistic identity. In this sense, people can be socialized (or trained) to be altruistic, as children or adults.
- People are most likely to volunteer their help if they perceive a strong helping situation; that is, there is a pressing need, no alternative source of help, and a likelihood that their help will have a direct and positive impact.

- It appears that the most important motivational factor associated with the social conditions of volunteering is the impact of a volunteer's efforts. How much good will be accomplished? What is the ratio of costs to benefits? Older volunteers, like all volunteers, do not want to waste their efforts and time.

- Church work provides a spiritual rationale for altruism, especially for the older population, which has a high rate of church membership.

Part II

Working With Older Volunteers

FIVE

Recruiting Older Volunteers

We always have problems getting enough recruits. It used to be that there wasn't so much for older persons to do. Now there are many activities that compete for retirees, and there are also no housewives around. And, at the same time, there are more and more elderly that need Meals on Wheels. So it's a problem.

▼

Our biggest problem is getting more people involved on a continuing basis. We have no problem if we have a one-time event—like we have a camp-day for children, and we get plenty of volunteers. But to get people to volunteer once a week—like in a child-care center— that's a big problem. It seems like people don't want to be tied down. We have tried ongoing programs but not with a lot of success.

▼

Every time we have a PR piece in the newspapers—which is maybe three or four times a month—the first thing we get are requests for services, and then we get people volunteering, and then we get checks. That order is always repeated, every time there is a PR piece. We have a lot of people volunteering, but the need for our services is so great that we will never have enough people to keep up.

▼

One of my jobs is Director of Volunteers, and I have never recruited a volunteer. I have no time for that, and there is no need. We are not hurting for volunteers in any program. If I did recruiting, there would be too many for us to cope with.

For volunteer programs, recruitment is often a challenge. Some volunteer organizations can never find enough people who are willing to make a commitment of their time and talent. Others have the opposite problem: There are "too many" recruits, and the challenge is in finding enough jobs for volunteers to do before they lose interest. Some volunteer organizations have elaborate techniques for attracting and processing new recruits, while for others recruitment is a minor activity either because the turnover of volunteers is low or because volunteers are recruited easily by word of mouth.

In this chapter, we examine research on volunteering to address a number of questions about recruiting volunteers: What are the best techniques for recruitment? How important is personal (word-of-mouth) recruitment versus other methods (such as public advertising)? Should volunteer recruitment be targeted to particular types or groups of people? How difficult is it to recruit people who have never volunteered before? What features of volunteer programs do people find especially attractive?

We also discuss our case studies of high-quality volunteer programs. What problems and challenges do these organizations confront in recruiting older volunteers? What techniques and approaches have they found to be effective in recruitment? Why do some programs, and not others, have problems in recruiting older volunteers?

Older Volunteers

In many ways the process of recruitment is essentially the same for younger and older volunteers. Yet several specific issues need to be considered in recruiting older persons as volunteers. First are the concerns related to aging, especially when recruiting and working with a population of very old persons as volunteers. Second is the concern that older people are potentially less accessible to volunteer recruitment in the sense that they have fewer work and family ties. Third are the scheduling issues related to the time frame of postretirement lives. Fourth is the experience factor; that is, older persons have accumulated many years' worth of experiences that potentially affect their interest in volunteering and the value of their contributed time.

Aging. In working with older volunteers, volunteer organizations explicitly or implicitly confront issues associated with aging. Older volunteers or potential volunteers, especially those age 75+, are much more likely to have health and functional problems than younger persons (see Independent Sector, 1990). Some programs have a turnover of volunteers—and a need for new recruits —because of aging. Volunteers may become frail, or, even without serious health problems, they simply may have less energy as they enter older and older ages. Their eyesight may become impaired, and they may no longer be able to drive a car safely. We are not suggesting, of course, that all or most older volunteers are incapacitated. But, quite simply, there are more risks of health problems and functional deficits for volunteers in their late 70s and over. Some organizations may "solve" the aging problem by recruiting and working almost exclusively with young-old volunteers—people who are recently retired and who are unlikely to be frail or to have serious health deficits. But this "solution" requires an ongoing attention to recruiting new generations of young old volunteers as aging volunteers are "retired."

Access. Age affects access to volunteering in a paradoxical way: Older people potentially are more accessible as volunteers because they have diminished responsibilities in work and family roles and therefore have more time for volunteering. But without these roles, older persons are less accessible for recruitment because they are not associated with the institutions and organizations from which volunteers are commonly recruited. Many volunteer programs are associated directly or indirectly with occupations or with family roles. Two of the most common types of voluntary associations to which individuals contribute their time are trade groups and civic organizations; both of these tend to attract memberships through their occupations and professions. Many programs also are associated with family roles, such as Parent Teacher Associations, Boy Scouts, Girl Scouts, and church youth programs. Older volunteers are far less likely than volunteers in their middle years to say they volunteer because they have a "child, relative or friend who was involved in the activity or would benefit from it" (Independent Sector, 1990, p. 149).

Scheduling. Access to older volunteers also is related to scheduling issues. According to a recent survey, older persons were much less likely to give "personal schedule too full" as an excuse for not volunteering (Independent Sector, 1990, p. 152). Retirees are potentially more accessible because they do not have work commitments during daytime hours. Nonetheless many older volunteers are unable or unwilling to volunteer after dark either because of problems with night driving or fear of crime. The implication is that not only are many older volunteers available during the day but they also may be available only during the day. In the winter months this constraint may cause some scheduling problems for volunteer programs. Winter also presents another problem: In January and February, volunteer programs in cold-climate states sometimes lose many of their regular volunteers who go as "snow- birds" to Florida, California, Arizona, and other states with temperate climates. Older persons are able to be snowbirds because they lack time commitments imposed by work or school schedules. It is their relative freedom from such schedules that makes retirees both accessible and, in some ways, not consistently available as volunteers.

The Experience Factor. There is at least one other age-related issue: Persons in later life have accumulated many years of experience, and in a number of ways these past experiences affect the recruitment of older volunteers. Surveys have shown that both young persons and the elderly have relatively lower rates of volunteering than people in their middle years. But these patterns have different meanings. We might view a very young adult as not-yet-a-volunteer rather than a nonvolunteer. But if by age 70 an individual has never volunteered, he or she has "missed" various "opportunities" for volunteering in the peak middle years. Moreover, older persons have had many experiences over their lives—in family, work, friendship, and so forth. *Older volunteers are especially valuable to volunteer programs when they are given opportunities to use the particular skills and abilities they have gained over their lives.*

How Important Is Personal Recruitment?

Agreement is virtually universal that the "best" way to recruit volunteers is through word-of-mouth or personal contacts. Many of the volunteer directors and coordinators that we interviewed for our case studies insisted that they rely primarily on word-of-mouth contacts:

> The most successful recruiting comes from the excitement of those who are currently involved. If they know someone with skills that we can use, then that's really the way we get people.

> Eighty to 85% of the new recruits come from other members.

> The main kind of recruitment is neighbors telling neighbors. If the things are successful, then the word gets out.

Even with programs that use advertising, public speaking, and other methods for recruiting volunteers, there tends to be an acknowledgment that personal contact is effective and is virtually *always* relied on as one, if not the only, way of recruiting new volunteers.

Table 5.1 presents a summary of research findings on techniques for recruitment. A number of studies have found that personal contact is more effective than other techniques for recruiting volunteers. Several of these studies also have suggested, however, that personal contact is only one of several effective methods for recruiting new volunteers.

One way to assess the importance of personal recruitment is through inference. Several studies have found that a large proportion of volunteers, at least for certain types of volunteer work, have been recruited personally. For example, a study of a neighborhood volunteer program in the Midwest found that recruitment by personal solicitation is more effective than advertising and that most volunteers were *asked* to join; that is, they did not volunteer on their own initiative (responding to a public announcement), but rather volunteered because a neighbor approached them (Morrow-Howell & Mui, 1989). Similarly a survey of younger and

TABLE 5.1 What Are the Best Techniques for Recruiting Volunteers?

Type of study	Finding	Reference
Interviews with agency or program directors	Direct solicitation is the most effective technique for recruitment.	Chambre, 1987 Farkas & Milligan, 1991 Schiman & Lordeman, 1989 Smith & Gutheil, 1988 Watts & Edwards, 1983
Interviews with volunteers	The most frequent way volunteers are recruited is through word of mouth.	Morrow-Howell & Mui, 1989 Goldberg-Glen & Cnaan, 1989
Literature review	Personal requests and social pressure are the most important reasons for volunteering time.	Piliavin & Charng, 1990
Interviews with volunteers and nonvolunteers	An important reason that nonvolunteers give for not volunteering is "no one asked me."	Kieffer, 1986 Marriott Seniors Volunteerism Study, 1991 Perry, 1983
Interviews with volunteers and nonvolunteers	People who participate in formal organizations are more likely to volunteer.	Herzog & Morgan, in press
Interviews with volunteers, potential volunteers, and/or program directors	Mass media can be effective in recruitment. Volunteer programs that grow and/or expand their population of potential volunteers tend to use media-based recruitment techniques.	Chambre, 1987 Goldberg-Glen & Cnaan, 1989 Schiman & Lordeman, 1989 Watts & Edwards, 1983 Wyant, 1991
Laboratory experiments	The effectiveness of recruitment ads depends on whether messages appeal to the specific motives that are important to potential volunteers.	Clary & Snyder, 1991b

Implications of research findings
- Developing a systematic way of recruiting new volunteers through personal solicitation is vital for *all* volunteer programs. This includes both using current volunteers to generate lists of potential volunteers and recruiting through existing organizations.
- Programs that recruit *only* through personal contacts are unlikely to grow and/or will tend to recruit only from a narrowly defined population.
- Media-based recruitment can be effective, especially if the messages are tailored to fit the particular interests and motivations of potential recruits.

older volunteers in Philadelphia found that volunteer agencies most frequently use word of mouth to recruit new volunteers. "Most volunteers who were interviewed were not familiar with recruitment methods such as telephone calls, letters, and billboards. Less than 10% of the sample had been recruited through the above methods" (Goldberg-Glen & Cnaan, 1989, p. 10; see also Farkas & Milligan, 1991; Independent Sector, 1990; Schiman & Lordeman, 1989; Smith & Gutheil, 1988; Watts & Edwards, 1983). The implication of these various surveys and studies is that the impetus for volunteering comes from personal solicitation. Conversely surveys of nonvolunteers suggest that one reason for not volunteering is "no one asked" them (Independent Sector, 1990; Kieffer, 1986; Marriott Seniors Volunteerism Study, 1991; Perry, 1983).

Another perspective on the importance of word-of-mouth contacts is suggested by the association between volunteering and membership in organizations; that is, people who belong to formal organizations are more likely to volunteer than are nonmembers (Herzog & Morgan, in press; Marvit, 1984). Being a member of an organization brings people in contact with a network of friends and associates who might solicit them as volunteers.

Why does personal recruitment seems to work so well? Some research suggests that personal recruitment is effective because it is difficult for people to say no when asked directly to help: The more direct the appeal, the more difficult it is to refuse. It may be that a request for help triggers an altruistic response. It is also possible that refusal creates a problem of "loss of face" (see Simmons, 1991).

Another implicit factor in personal recruitment is modeling. Because the recruiter is often a volunteer, he or she is not only asking for help but also is providing an example of acting as a volunteer. Studies show that people are more likely to engage in helping behavior soon after watching someone else behave in a similar situation (see Organ, 1988, p. 29). Interestingly, personal recruitment as a form of volunteer work is its own publicity; the message is, "I am helping others by talking to you [potential volunteer] about helping others."

From the case study data, as well as from several other studies, we can draw several inferences about how volunteer programs can successfully recruit new volunteers through a word-of-mouth process.

- *Successful recruitment is tied to, and is a consequence of, a successful volunteer work experience.* A number of volunteer directors emphasized the enthusiasm of their volunteers.
- *Word-of-mouth recruitment is effective (a) when volunteers understand whom to recruit and (b) when they are involved in developing programs.* One program director pointed out that volunteers are committed to recruiting new volunteers when they believe that it is "their" organization. He described it is a matter of "ownership."
- *Volunteers are good at recruitment to the extent that they are tied into social networks.* Volunteers recruit their peers. We noted above that people who belong to organizations are more likely to volunteer than nonmembers. People who participate in social clubs, church groups, and other organizations have regular contact with groups of people who represent a natural pool of potential volunteers. Conversely persons whose social worlds are more constricted or whose lives revolve around their families may be less able to attract new recruits.

Some Caveats About Word-of-Mouth Recruitment

Personal or word-of-mouth recruitment is important for virtually all volunteer organizations. But relying almost exclusively, or even primarily, on this approach is effective only under certain conditions and circumstances. For very small programs and organizations, it may make no sense to try any other methods of recruitment. A neighborhood-based volunteer program, for example, might rely successfully on personal recruitment because the universe of potential volunteers (everyone in the neighborhood) ought to be reachable this way. For recruiting volunteers with very specialized skills or from special populations, no other approach may be as effective as recruiting by word of mouth.

Sometimes programs rely exclusively on personal recruitment because they have very limited resources. Poorly funded organizations, even if they could afford to conduct media campaigns, would have no way to support new volunteers. For example, stipended programs in some regions—such as the Senior Companion and Foster Grandparent programs—rely on word-of-mouth recruitment, at least in part, because this technique limits the number of applicants for their stipended volunteer positions.

For many volunteer organizations, reliance on word of mouth has two major disadvantages. First, and perhaps the most serious problem, *personal networking limits the population of volunteers.* People generally associate with others who are similar to them. Through word of mouth, volunteers tend to recruit peers who are much like them, for example, in income and educational level, gender, race, and religion. People who are different from the original or core group of volunteers—because of life-style, ethnicity, and so forth—are never reached, so outsiders systematically (even if inadvertently) are excluded from the pool of volunteers.

The second problem is that *reliance solely on personal recruitment tends to limit the potential for growth and development.* In our case studies we found a number of examples of organizations that have used their achievements to expand their programs, their funds, and their numbers of volunteers. To do this, they have found ways to reach out to their communities, using a variety of methods: advertising, articles in newspapers, television and radio coverage, public speaking, brochures, posters, and so forth. On a small or large scale, these efforts are part of a recruitment campaign.

Interestingly, many organizations that say they only recruit volunteers by word of mouth actually use a pyramid-type of process. A number of programs in our case studies select volunteers out of classes that their organizations offer. These programs typically do some public advertising or announcing for their classes, but not for their volunteers. Indirectly, however, in pyramid fashion, they have recruited the "top" (the volunteer teachers, leaders, etc.) from the larger "base" (the students or others who have attended their programs).

Running a Recruitment Campaign

When a volunteer organization launches a campaign to recruit volunteers, the purpose is to reach a broad audience, and the method almost always involves some form of public advertising. This advertising can take a number of forms. Some forms require few or no out-of-pocket expenses. Many local newspapers list ads for volunteer positions without charge, volunteers or staff can make brief presentations at public meetings, and sometimes local libraries help with volunteer referral (for instance, by posting announcements). But many forms of advertising entail costs—for printing, postage, and so forth. In our case study interviews we were cautioned that recruitment campaigns sometimes can be costly failures. We were told of one program, for example, that advertised on television and had a lot of other publicity in the media. Their campaign brought them a great deal of visibility, and they received 500 responses from people interested in volunteering. From these responses, they sent out 100 applications. In the end only one person actually came to work as a volunteer, and that person quit within 3 months. There were other, similar stories of disappointments: "I have given talks to over 250 people at a time and not gotten one volunteer." "Sometimes when I set up speaking engagements, only two people show up. Another thing —we attend some of the fairs around the city and although this is good PR, they are not really good for recruiting." "We've had a big push to get new people who have technical skills. . . . Out of every five or six people who express some interest, maybe one actually stays."

Table 5.1, which presents summaries of research literature on techniques for recruiting volunteers, confirms what we suggested in the introduction to this book: Not much research has been conducted on specific recruitment techniques, especially for older volunteers. Not one of these studies provides detailed and specific evaluations on methods of recruitment. Nonetheless the research to date does offer some guidance for developing volunteer recruitment strategies. This research also suggests *a strong potential for increasing the numbers and types of volunteers through effective media-based recruitment.*

The actual impact of mass media advertising on volunteer recruitment is difficult to assess. According to a recent survey by Gallup (Independent Sector, 1990), volunteers are far more likely to say they learned about a volunteer opportunity through personal contact or through participating in an organization than through any other method. In fact, only 6% said they found out about volunteering through an advertisement. This finding suggests that mass media efforts account for a very small portion of volunteering. On the other hand, Clary and Snyder (1991b), in a study of volunteers working in six organizations in one community, found that advertisements seemed to attract a much larger portion of volunteers: Over a third of their sample said they volunteered in response to some form of public advertising. Although their study also showed that personal contact (or word of mouth) is cited more often as the form of recruitment, their research does suggest that publicity may attract a substantial number of volunteers.

Another study, by Watts and Edwards (1983), provides even more dramatic evidence of the importance of publicity and advertising campaigns for volunteer recruitment. These researchers surveyed 261 human service agencies about the recruitment and retention of volunteers. They found that among agencies that employ volunteers, virtually all (94%) use word of mouth, while 56% use mass media in their recruitment. More significant, Watts and Edwards reported that agencies that had grown 20% or more in the last year had used mass media for recruitment. The implication of their findings is clear: *To the extent that volunteer programs want to grow and increase their numbers of volunteers, they need to devise some ways of recruitment using mass-media-based campaigns.*

Another recent report, moreover, suggests that a recruitment campaign not only can increase the numbers of volunteers but also can expand the volunteer pool by reaching people who tend to be less likely to volunteer. Wyant (1991) described a massive campaign to recruit volunteers for hospitals and nursing homes in New York City. The campaign was supported by a small grant and by a large number of volunteer contributions, including time contributed by an advertising agency. The recruitment effort included posters for citywide distribution, advertisements that appeared on buses, radio announcements featuring Tony Randall, and a series of newspaper ads. Each ad described the rewards of volunteering and provided a telephone number that interested individuals could call for more information. After the first phase of the campaign—the bus posters—they received about 20 calls a day. But during the peak of the campaign, Wyant wrote: "Our phones started to ring off the hook. We jumped from 20 to more than 100 calls a day" (p. 15). What is most significant about this recruitment campaign is that three fifths of those who responded had never volunteered before. Moreover, many of the responses came from groups that have relatively low rates of formal volunteering—young adults and blacks. It appears, therefore, that the campaign was successful in expanding the pool of potential volunteers. Nonetheless we need to be somewhat cautious about assessing the achievements of this recruitment campaign because the full impact has not yet been evaluated. Those who responded to the advertisements were calling for more information; they had not yet volunteered. The report was published in the fall of 1991. As of this writing, we have no data on the numbers or characteristics of people actually volunteering because of this campaign.

Two Minnesota psychologists, Gil Clary and Mark Snyder (1991b), used laboratory experiments to examine how potential volunteers might react to advertisements for recruitment. Their subjects were all college students whose motivations to volunteer were measured by the Volunteers' Functions Inventory (VFI). In two separate experiments, the students viewed either video ads or brochures, and they rated these materials on their appeal and persuasiveness. Clary and Snyder (1991b) reported that recruitment materials that were "motive-appropriate" (matched to the subject's specific VFI score) were rated by respondents as higher quality and more motivating than were "non-motive-appropriate" messages. For example, according to the VFI, if a potential volunteer is motivated by a career function ("to enhance one's job and career prospects, to gain experience and contacts"), then a message about how volunteering helps career goals would be more appealing than a message appealing to altruism. The researchers found that the strength of the motivation is also important, so a message is rated as effective when the motive is strong, and is rated as less effective when the motive is weak.

Experimental research, such as this work, offers a way to study systematically volunteer motivations and behavior. Even so, these experiments by Clary and Snyder have an important limitation:

They do not show whether messages that are motive-appropriate actually lead to volunteerism. What they have tested is that motive-appropriate messages are rated as more appealing than motive-inappropriate messages.

The studies reviewed in Table 5.1, along with our case studies, suggest several conclusions about strategies for recruitment.

- *Recruitment campaigns could be made more effective with target marketing and market research.* Clary and Snyder's (1991b) research provides support for an important point: Effective recruitment needs to appeal to the specific motivations of potential volunteers. It would be difficult, of course, to know a priori the motivations of possible volunteer recruits, but focus groups and other methods of testing the motivations of target populations could be used to design effective recruitment materials.

- *Volunteer recruitment is a multiphased process and requires a combination of approaches.* In some ways recruiting for volunteer positions is similar to other forms of marketing. An important element in any marketing strategy is exposure—that is, making potential clients/customers aware of a product, service, or opportunity. Huge advertising and marketing industries are premised on the idea that advertising serves this purpose. In our case studies a number of directors of successful volunteer programs, while insisting that "word of mouth works best," also noted that "no one recruitment or media effort works best all the time." It is likely that a variety of recruitment efforts is effective together—not only because different approaches are targeted to different potential volunteers but also because the same people may be reached multiple times. Salespeople know that a sale requires multiple contacts through mailings, meetings, brochures, letters, or personal contacts before a customer is "sold." Similarly recruitment of volunteers is also likely to require multiple approaches before a commitment is made.

- *If there were more extensive and effective recruitment campaigns, it is likely that many more volunteers could be recruited.* Our case studies, as well as other research, indicate that most volunteer programs rely largely on networking and personal contacts for recruiting new volunteers. Of course, many organizations do not use other methods of recruitment because they do not have the resources to work with more volunteers. Nonetheless several studies indicate that media-based recruitment can be effective in helping volunteer organizations grow and expand the numbers and types of their volunteers. This conclusion is somewhat tentative, given the limited amount of research to date. Even so, these findings suggest that the volunteer potential in our society, perhaps especially of older volunteers, may be substantially underused.

Whom to Recruit

They are twin issues: how to recruit and whom to recruit. We have just discussed techniques for recruitment—word-of-mouth and media-based methods. But the method selected cannot be separated from the pool of potential volunteers to be targeted for recruitment. A mass media approach is intended to reach a broad population, particularly to appeal to those who would not be easily found among networks of people already volunteering. Before embarking on an extensive recruitment campaign, it is important to address a basic question about the feasibility of recruiting volunteers from the general population. Specifically *is it possible— or reasonable—to recruit people who have never volunteered before?*

Research relevant to this question is summarized in Table 5.2. These studies cover a variety of settings and activities; a few focus on participation in voluntary associations, rather than on volunteering. Many of these studies lead to a single conclusion: *People who have volunteered before are by far the most likely to be recruited.* As we discussed in Chapter 4, it is likely that there is a personality factor; that is, some people are perennial volunteers. People who volunteer tend to be active in general—they are "joiners" who belong to numerous organizations, they tend to have high levels of empathy and altruism, and they have positive attitudes and moods. In our case study interviews we were told by volunteer directors that many of their "core" volunteers are active in a number of volunteer organizations. This finding suggests that volunteer programs may find themselves competing with other volunteer programs or organizations for the time and commitment of a limited pool of active volunteers.

People who have volunteered before and are accustomed to volunteering are relatively easy to recruit. They understand the process of approaching a volunteer organization and making a commitment. Probably even more important, experienced volunteers often

TABLE 5.2 How and to Whom Should Recruitment Efforts for Older Volunteers Be Targeted?

Type of study	Finding	References
Interviews with volunteers and nonvolunteers	Older people who have volunteered before are more likely to volunteer currently.	Bosse & Ekerdt, 1981 Cohen-Mansfield, 1989
Literature review	People of all ages who have volunteered before are more likely to volunteer currently.	Rushton, 1984
Interviews with volunteers	Active volunteers tend to be those who have volunteered before.	Faulkner, 1975
Interviews with volunteers and nonvolunteers	Volunteers are most effectively recruited from existing groups and organizations.	Herzog & Morgan, in press Marvit, 1984
Interviews with program directors and/or potential volunteers	Certain volunteer programs are able to recruit people who have special skills but who have never volunteered before.	Farkas & Milligan, 1991 Wyant, 1991
Survey of volunteers and nonvolunteers	People who have a sense of "community rootedness" are the most likely to volunteer and/or to participate in voluntary associations.	Faulkner, 1975 Florin, Jones, & Wandersman, 1986 Hougland & Shepard, 1985 Perkinson, 1980 Wandersman, Florin, Friedmann, & Meier, 1987
Interviews with volunteers and nonvolunteers	A majority of blacks, of all socioeconomic backgrounds, volunteer primarily for organizations run by and/or providing service to black persons.	Carson, 1990a

Implications of research findings
- Older people who have volunteered in the past for formal organizations are relatively easy to recruit.
- Nonetheless volunteer organizations with effective mass media recruitment campaigns and/or with volunteer programs that match the skills and interests of a targeted population can be successful in recruiting older persons who have had no previous experience in formal volunteer work.
- Older people who are affiliated with formal organizations are relatively easy to recruit.
- Persons who have a strong sense of "community rootedness" are relatively easy to recruit.
- People are likely to be responsive to efforts to recruit them as volunteers if they feel similar to and bonded with those they are asked to help.

know other volunteers. They are accessible to volunteer organizations. Conversely nonvolunteers may be much less accessible, especially older persons. For older persons with no previous volunteer experience, the whole process of becoming a volunteer might seem rather daunting.

In light of this context, a finding from a recent evaluation of Family Friends projects is striking: *Almost half of the volunteers for this program had never done formal volunteer work before.* This program matches elderly volunteers with children in troubled families. The client families are poor, and their problems vary: Some of the children have physical or emotional deficits; sometimes the problem is abuse or neglect. The great majority of the volunteers are women. Their role is to provide the children with affection and to offer support and a positive role model to the families. It is notable that although many of the volunteers had no formal volunteer experience, virtually all of them had appropriate role experience; that is, they were mothers and grandmothers. Most of the volunteers had heard about the program either informally through conversations with friends or through a speaker who gave presentations at various meetings and support groups. Both the client families and the volunteers rated the program very positively (Farkas & Milligan, 1991). Given the positive evaluation of this volunteer program, we might conclude that, at least under certain conditions, older persons without previous volunteer experience can and should be recruited.

Community Ties

In previous chapters, we identified demographic and personality profiles of volunteers and nonvolunteers. But another factor also seems to be important in volunteer recruitment: *community rootedness.* This term refers to the sense of attachment and commitment that people feel for their neighborhoods and communities. Table 5.2 includes a review of a number of studies that illustrate in different ways the importance of community rootedness for volunteering and voluntary participation.

A relationship exists between community rootedness and previous volunteer experience, but they are not really the same. People who feel tied to their communities are likely to have volunteered in the past. But community rootedness refers to current attachments to a particular community. It is possible for a person who has volunteered often in the past to move to a new community where he or she feels alienated and where there is no pull to help one's neighbors. Conversely a person who is a novice to volunteering might readily become a volunteer in the appropriate social environment.

A case study of a community of retired ministers provides an interesting example of how a community environment can foster volunteerism (Perkinson, 1980). This community has a norm of self-government and self-help; everyone is expected to participate in committees. Virtually everyone volunteers, formally or informally, within the retirement community or in hospitals or churches in the neighboring towns. The members describe themselves as being "one big Christian family here." Clearly this is an unusual community. Its population is homogeneous, and its residents are all retired ministers who, presumably, have ideological and spiritual values that support volunteerism. Under these conditions, there is clearly social pressure for community involvement—and everyone volunteers.

Other studies have shown that, in more diverse societies, people who feel the strongest ties to their communities are the ones most likely to be involved in voluntary activities. A number of studies, for example, have found that people who have lived in the same community for a long time are more likely to participate than new residents (Dailey, 1986; Daniels, 1985; Faulkner, 1975; Florin, Jones, & Wandersman, 1986; Hougland & Shepard, 1985).

One study compared participants and nonparticipants in voluntary associations in two very different societies—Tennessee and Israel (Wandersman, Florin, Friedmann, & Meier, 1987). The researchers conducted surveys in both regions and found that, in neighborhoods in both Tennessee and Israel, people who participate in voluntary associations, compared to nonparticipants, tend to have lived in their neighborhoods longer, have a stronger sense of community and citizenship duty, and have a greater sense that they could have an impact on solving problems in their neighborhoods. What is remarkable about this study is that the findings were similar in such diverse communities. Community rootedness does not necessarily mean feeling connected to neighbors. A community can be geographically dispersed. Research shows that people tend to help others to whom they feel similar (Simmons, 1991). For example, black volunteers of all socioeconomic backgrounds tend to target their help to other black persons (Carson, 1990b). What is important is that individuals feel strong ties with an identifiable social group—a block or neighborhood, a church, an ethnic group, and so forth.

The research outlined in Table 5.2 has several implications for volunteer organizations.

- *It is much easier to recruit persons with "natural" community ties than persons without such roots in a community.* The logical targets for volunteer recruitment are people who have volunteered before, who have participated in other social organizations, who have lived in their communities or neighborhoods a long time, and/or who have strong attachments to their communities through their churches or other organizations.

- *An effective recruitment strategy should emphasize and build on the community attachments of potential volunteers.* This strategy requires understanding the specific community ties of potential recruits and developing recruitment messages that stress these ties. To some degree it may be possible to enhance community attachments through effective messages. Thus a campaign might focus on strengthening community attachment because recruitment of volunteers is facilitated when individuals feel rooted in their communities.

- *Volunteer programs may be most effective when they are established in natural communities.* This research is supportive of volunteer programs that are based in neighborhoods or other community groups. Our case studies included a number of such programs. One of the remarkable characteristics of all such programs is that the volunteers and the recipients of services tend to be very similar in social class, ethnicity, religion, and values. Although ideally we might want to encourage diverse social contacts, it seems that the most effective structures for helping relationships are when people feel similar to one another. Conversely help imposed from "outsiders" is likely to be resisted (see Faulkner, 1975). Interestingly, although there are a number of community-based volunteer groups, it seems that charity work is more typically unidirectional—the fortunate sectors of society helping the unfortunate. The research on the importance of community ties suggests that this type of structure may be ineffective. Community-based organizations may be more successful in recruiting committed volunteers and in providing effective services.

Recruitment for "Strong Helping" Situations

In Chapter 4 we discussed the differences between strong and weak helping situations. In strong helping situations the following conditions apply: (a) a pressing need for help, (b) no alternative sources of help, and (c) a likelihood of a direct and positive impact. Conversely, weak helping situations lack all or some of these conditions. We pointed out that formal volunteer work is much more likely to resemble weak than strong situations, especially because volunteer organizations usually are focused on chronic social problems where volunteers may constitute one, but not the only, source of help. But we also noted that under certain conditions, components of strong helping situations may be approximated by volunteer programs. Table 5.3 presents examples of how the conditions associated with strong helping situations can promote the recruitment of volunteers. This table shows how each condition may apply to certain kinds of programs.

A Pressing Need. Some programs provide help to people in critical need, such as people dying of AIDS or homeless families. Other types of volunteering are "pressing" because of time constraints; that is, if help is not "immediate," then it will be "too late." Service-oriented programs are the ones most likely to fit the condition of "pressing need."

No Alternative Help. The condition of "no alternative sources of help" can apply if the supply of people able or willing to help is extremely limited. For instance, a program that needs Chinese-speaking volunteers to work with immigrant hospital patients can approach

TABLE 5.3 How Conditions of "Strong Helping" Situations Promote Volunteer Recruitment

---

Conditions of "strong helping" situations

There is a pressing need.

Most volunteer service organizations address important social needs. These needs can be defined as "pressing," or critical, if the following apply:
- The help needed is urgent (lack of assistance could imperil health or survival).
  Examples: AIDS programs   Assistance to natural-disaster victims
              Help to homeless   Programs to prevent child abuse
- There are time constraints on delivering help (help "too late" is no help).
  Examples: Tutoring for high-   Programs to prevent teen pregnancy
              risk children   Peer counseling for persons at risk
              Hospice programs   of suicide

There are no alternative sources of help.

Alternative sources of help are unavailable if the following apply:
- Specialized help is required (few people have the needed skills).
  Examples: Executive retiree   Spanish-speaking hospital volunteers
              programs   Recording technical books for blind
              Home restoration   students
              projects
- Other resources are unavailable (if people "fall through the cracks").
  Examples: Eldercare for   Volunteer work with prisoners
              isolated, frail
              elderly
              Programs for   Tutoring for new immigrants
              homeless families
- The work requires unusual commitment (other people will not do this work).
  Examples: Mentoring for   Caregiving for "crack babies"
              troubled children
              "Befrienders" for   "Buddies" for alcoholics in treatment
              people in crisis

There is a real likelihood of a direct, positive impact.

Volunteer programs can recruit volunteers on the basis of their impact if the following apply:
- They can demonstrate their effectiveness (there are measures of success).
  Examples: Tutoring programs with a track record of performance
              improvement
              Programs that have received strong, positive evaluations

- There is strong community recognition of the importance of the program.
  Examples: Museums with high public visibility
  Civic programs that have received strong public
  endorsement for their efforts

Implications for volunteer recruitment
- Many programs have some of these qualities; very few have all of these characteristics.
- Media-based recruitment messages can emphasize these qualities.
- These characteristics can be emphasized in training of volunteers, who subsequently will recruit other volunteers.
- An evaluation of a volunteer program can serve both to improve the program and to measure the effectiveness. This information can be used for recruiting and retaining volunteers.

---

a special target population of prospective volunteers with the message: If you do not help, there will be no one to communicate with these patients.

Direct Impact. The condition of a "direct, positive impact" applies when the effect of volunteer work can be demonstrated, especially if the reward (or feedback) is relatively immediate. The evidence for impact can include recognition ceremonies and positive publicity. A civic organization was raising funds for a local hospital to establish a bone marrow donor unit. Their efforts became much more successful after newspapers reported that the first patient —a 9-year-old girl—had come home after her treatment in the new unit.

> It really helped our fund-raising. . . . She would have died from leukemia, and so this was her last hope. . . . None of us wanted this kind of effort. It has been like a half-time job, but the payoff was [this little girl] last week, and it was a letter from the mother thanking [our] organization that saved her child. That is the payoff that has meaning.

A few volunteer programs can show measurable evidence of what a volunteer or the volunteer program has accomplished. For example, if children from poor families are tutored by volunteers and then their test scores improve, the clear inference is that the volunteer investment was well spent. Often, however, the effectiveness of a volunteer service is not easy to demonstrate. In many forms of volunteer work the outcomes are neither observable nor measurable. For example, in service-oriented organizations whose recipients are elderly, it may be difficult to assess "success," especially if success is supposed to mean some change in the recipient of services. The very old, frail, and homebound elderly who receive eldercare services do not recover from their chronic health problems; in fact, over the course of receiving volunteer services, they are more likely to get worse than better. For such programs it is important to define appropriate outcomes—by showing, for example, how an eldercare volunteer helps a frail, elderly person in specific ways to compensate for functional impairments.

*   *   *

Many volunteer programs have some of the qualities associated with strong helping situations. Almost none have them all. Table 5.3 offers some ideas for promoting volunteer recruitment by enhancing and emphasizing these conditions. These factors can be part of a recruitment campaign through either word-of-mouth or media-based recruitment. For example, a recruitment message for an intergenerational program might emphasize (a) that there is a pressing need for helping high-risk children because if these children are not given appropriate attention in their early years, it will be "too late" to help them when they are older; (b) that only a limited, targeted population has the requisite skills, time, or ability to help; and (c) that the volunteer program actually has improved students' performance on standardized tests (so volunteering will have an impact).

An important implication of this analysis is that evaluation of volunteer programs can be useful for volunteer recruitment. Evaluation provides a way to demonstrate effectiveness and impact, and a positive evaluation can help recruit and retain volunteers. Formal evaluation, however, appears to be rare, even for the "exemplary" volunteer programs in our case studies.

Problems in Recruiting Older Volunteers

We noted in the beginning of this chapter that recruiting enough volunteers may or may not be a problem for a volunteer program. Why do some volunteer organizations, but not others, have problems with attracting volunteers? What accounts for problems with recruitment? In our case studies we noticed two types of distinctions between programs with and without recruitment problems: differences in organizational composition and in organizational functions (see Table 3.2, in Chapter 3).

In terms of the composition or membership of volunteer organizations, several indicators of "status" differences occur among organizations: *high status* is indicated by having volunteers who are primarily college educated, whose social background is largely upper class (or upper middle class), and/or who are men. *High-status organizations are* **less** *likely than other volunteer programs to have both resource and recruitment problems;* that is, they do not report that they lack adequate funds or paid staff. They are also considerably less likely to have problems with recruiting volunteers. Several volunteer program directors in organizations that attract mostly high-status volunteers pointed to the strong reputation of their programs and commented that their volunteers are "proud" to be part of their organization.

Conversely *low-status organizations are* **much more** *likely to have both resource and recruiting problems.* One volunteer director from a municipal hospital complained: "Because we have a 'low prestige' program, we don't get much money or support." Moreover, some programs that say they have no problems in recruitment actually are very restricted in their ability to recruit new volunteers because of limited resources. In particular a number of service organizations that help poor elderly or poor children report no problems in recruitment because they have no resources to support more volunteers. Even so, it is clear that these programs could readily find more clients to serve if they had more resources and more volunteers.

In terms of organizational functions, our case studies suggest that *organizations that require time commitments from their volunteers are less likely to have recruitment problems* than organizations that require no minimum commitment of time. This finding might seem counterintuitive: It ought to be harder to recruit volunteers when there are expectations and restrictions. And yet the opposite appears to be true. Possibly volunteers who make commitments may perceive their work as more meaningful and important because they know that people are counting on them. We also suspect that organizations that require volunteers to commit a fixed amount of time are able to have more control over the quality of their products and services. It has to be easier to manage effective programs if they can count on their volunteers' time. In this sense they offer their volunteers an important incentive: that their time will be well spent.

For some programs the problem is not too few recruits, but rather too many. This might seem like a "good" problem—something for a volunteer director to be pleased with rather than to worry about. Yet having too many volunteers—and not enough jobs—can create morale problems and can have negative consequences for recruiting future volunteers. For example, the chair of a new corporate volunteer program described his frustration when

a radio station that was organizing a telethon had asked for too many volunteers and had overrecruited. Our volunteers were sitting around waiting for maybe an hour or two, and then they were told that they didn't need them. And these were people who looked forward to and planned their day around this, and then were told that they weren't needed and they had to go home. So, ever since that incident, we have tried to be careful to work with the organizations and make sure that things are more properly set up because otherwise you would turn off volunteers pretty quickly.

Other programs have reported similar problems—that sometimes they have more volunteers than positions and that a good way to lose volunteers is to have nothing for them to do.

When we do mailings, on the outside flap we have something that says, "Yes, I would like more information about volunteering." Then if people send that in, we can recruit them. The last time we did that was about one year ago, and we got between 300 to 400 responses back. But we are cautious about doing that because we don't want

to recruit and then have no positions for someone who is eager to
volunteer.

A number of programs also reported that although they do not
have problems in general recruiting volunteers, they do have
some difficulties getting volunteers to serve in leadership roles.
"We can get volunteers to say they will do whatever we want. But
we have a really hard time getting one person to be the manager
of it all because people don't seem to want to take the responsibility." What may need to be taken into account, however, is the
cost—in dollars, as well as in time—of assuming a leadership role.
As an extreme example from our case studies, in one program the
president of a cultural organization has out-of-pocket expenses
amounting to $10,000 a year! "The presidents have been women
that spend 30 to 40 hours a week in their volunteer role, and there
are a lot of out-of-pocket expenses. These include travel, lunch-
eons, and tickets for all the events; these are not covered, and
there have been fairly major expenses." Obviously, being the chair
of a program committee would almost never be so costly. Even so,
there are often hidden or overt costs. There may be entertainment,
travel, and telephone costs, and few organizations provide any
reimbursement for these.

The cost issue is particularly likely to be a barrier for older
volunteers who live on fixed incomes (Allen, 1981; Lackner &
Koeck, 1980). Many older volunteers also have a related problem:
transportation. A few programs provide reimbursement for transportation; most do not. A volunteer director for an intergenerational service program in a rural community commented:

> Considering the lack of transportation, I feel we have been quite
> successful. There is no public transportation anywhere in this county.
> We have had some seniors who are interested, but if they don't
> drive, they really can't participate. I sometimes pick up volunteers
> for meetings, and we have arranged some transportation with the
> local Head Start program. But it is very hard to arrange involvement
> with families if the seniors don't drive.

Interestingly there is no obvious way to assess whether a
volunteer program has a "problem" with recruitment. In the case

quoted above, the program director acknowledges that the program has not recruited nearly as many volunteers as originally expected by their funders: They were supposed to recruit 35 volunteers; after a year, they have only 13. Yet she believes their program to be successful, given their rural setting and the limited resources. Although we have treated recruitment as a separate issue in this chapter, it really is intertwined with other issues. In particular the recruitment and retention of volunteers are interwoven, both in practice and in research: Recruitment of new volunteers is a "problem" if they do not stay, and if retention of volunteers is a problem, then there is an ongoing need for new recruits. Many of the issues to be addressed in the next chapter (on keeping older volunteers), such as matching volunteers with appropriate positions, also might be discussed under the topic of recruitment.

Summary of Key Themes

- The literature review and case study data show that word-of-mouth recruitment is important and effective for virtually all types of volunteer programs.
- Nonetheless relying on word-of-mouth recruitment limits the population of volunteers and the potential for growth.
- A tentative conclusion from this review, based on a small number of studies, is that volunteer organizations could recruit substantially more volunteers by using media-based recruitment campaigns, target marketing, and market research.
- Older volunteers who have volunteered before are easier to recruit than inexperienced volunteers. Nonetheless programs that match the skills and interests of a targeted population can effectively recruit elderly persons who have virtually no previous formal volunteer experience.
- Older volunteers who have strong community ties are more likely to volunteer than people without such roots, especially if their volunteer work serves their natural community.
- Conditions associated with strong helping can promote the recruitment of volunteers; that is, volunteers are likely to be attracted to programs if they believe that (a) there is a pressing need, (b) their

help is needed because there is almost no one else to help, and (c) their work will have an immediate and beneficial impact.

- Evaluations of volunteer programs appear to be quite rare but can be very useful. Evaluations can help recruit and retain volunteers by demonstrating the impact and effectiveness of volunteer services.

- Our case study data suggest that high-status programs (those with volunteers who are well educated, upper class, and/or males) are less likely than other programs to have problems in recruiting volunteers.

- Our case study data also indicate that programs that require time commitments from their volunteers are less likely than other programs to have problems in recruiting volunteers. This finding has an important practical application: Programs may be more effective in recruiting and working with older (and perhaps younger) volunteers if they make more, rather than fewer, demands on those who volunteer their time.

SIX

Keeping Volunteers

Brown County (Wisconsin) Department of Social Services recruited 104 volunteers in 1979. But they also lost 102 volunteers and so tallied a net gain of two! (Francies, 1983, p. 17)

▼

In volunteer administration, there is a lot of focus on keeping volunteers. But I think it is important to say to a volunteer that it's okay to leave. Many volunteers struggle with that issue for a long time. But it is important to say to them, "You can move on."

Retaining volunteers may be even more critical than recruitment for the survival of volunteer organizations. Reliable volunteers can be counted on both by their organizations and by those who receive their services. Conversely, volunteers who quit after a short time are costly. Costs are incurred for training and supervising them. Typically, ex-volunteers or almost-volunteers take away their acquired learning and leave little behind. Another problem is disrupted service—the person who was counting on help either has to be assigned to someone else or, at worst, gets no help at all. But there are other problems as well. Turnover, especially high turnover, can create havoc in the administration and management of volunteer programs. A vicious cycle may be set up: There may be no point in training or spending time with volunteers if most of them are going to quit shortly anyway. However, if volunteers are given no training or guidance, the quality of their work is not likely to be very good. If their work is not good, they will feel incompetent and frustrated, and soon they will quit. Morale is another problem. When a program seems like a "revolving door"— volunteers come, volunteers go—both paid staff and volunteers easily can feel that their efforts are just not worthwhile (see Stevens, 1989-1990, 1991).

Even so, as the second quote above suggests, turnover is a natural component of volunteer management and is not necessarily a problem. This astute volunteer coordinator, who directs a large and successful volunteer program in a museum, points out that it is all right to say to volunteers: "You can move on." In her program, all volunteers receive education and training, they are required to work at least 4 hours per week, and it seems that most of the volunteers stay with the program for several years. But organizations vary widely in their expectations for volunteer retention. *High turnover is especially a problem when the following conditions apply:* (a) a need for extensive investment in volunteer training and supervision, (b) jobs that require long-term commitments, (c) clients who can be harmed when volunteers leave, and/or (d) a shortage of qualified volunteers.

In this chapter we address a number of separate but related questions concerning the retention of volunteers. To what extent is turnover a problem in volunteer organizations? How does the selection of volunteers affect whether or not they stay; that is, is the issue of retention really a matter of recruiting and selecting the "right" people? What are the best techniques for matching volunteers with appropriate volunteer jobs so that they are satisfied with their work and are committed to continuing? What kinds of rewards account for whether volunteers stay or leave? How do volunteer motivations change as volunteers move from being new recruits to more established volunteers? What are the most effective techniques for addressing the problem of burnout?

How Much Turnover?

In our case studies the directors of exemplary voluntary organizations and programs were far more likely to tell us that they have problems with recruitment than with retention. Three-quarters of the sample indicated having virtually no problems with retention. In fact, most of the volunteer directors that we interviewed spoke about the remarkable commitment of their volunteers:

> Our turnover rate has been less than 6% [per year], and our volunteers average 8 or more hours of service a week!

> Our volunteers are amazingly committed, and they really feel like they are part of the organization. Many of our volunteers help to raise funds for the organization. . . . We have a crunch right now because some of the volunteers are on vacation. But, then, there are a lot of other volunteers who put in extra time. . . . It is because people have been here for such a long time and they are so committed—especially the older volunteers.

> Some volunteers leave because of health or family illness. But there was one couple—people called them "Mr. and Mrs. AARP". . . . Well, Mr. AARP had a massive stroke, and he has worked very hard to get well so he can get back on his committee.

Older workers and older volunteers are less likely to quit than their younger counterparts (see Miller, Powell, & Seltzer, 1990). Most of the volunteer coordinators said that their older volunteers stay in their programs a very long time. If they stop volunteering, it is only because they move away, have serious health problems, or die. A number of them asserted, in fact, that older volunteers are more likely to remain in their programs than younger volunteers. This finding is consistent with research on retention rates for both paid workers and volunteers.

However, the assessment that retention is not a problem has a caveat: Most of the organizations that insist they have no problem with retention also acknowledge that *they gather no data on rates of attrition.* In fact, only about 30% collect any information at all on the numbers of volunteers who leave, and usually these data are very limited.

Most of the organizations in our case studies neither collect formal data nor have their volunteers contract for a minimum time commitment. For organizations requiring no time commitment, attrition would seem to be especially difficult to measure. A "volunteer" could remain on a list but never, or very rarely, contribute time. Is such a person a dropout or not? Virtually all of the programs have a core group of highly committed volunteers. We suspect that many of the volunteer directors, when answering questions about retention, were thinking about this volunteer core.

The issue of turnover has different meanings for different types of volunteer work. Some of the volunteer directors said that they had a substantial dropout rate but that this was not really a problem because they were always able to replace dropouts by recruiting more volunteers. Some of these programs specialize in short-term assignments for special projects, so they expect volunteers to make only short-term commitments. In episodic volunteering, the issue may not be turnover so much as reliability; that is, does the volunteer show up for a scheduled event? Conversely, for volunteer jobs that require special skills and detailed training, such as certain types of service-oriented volunteering, turnover can be both costly and disruptive to clients.

Some retention problems are related to transitions in the lives of volunteers. For example, the director of a cultural program that has some older volunteers but also many working-age volunteers and is in a large Eastern metropolitan community said that retention is not really a problem because it is quite easy to recruit replacements. But she noted: "We have an exit poll, and the majority leave because they are moving out of the area. [This city] is a very transient city, so that is a major reason for leaving." Another program, a service exchange in a Midwestern city, that has volunteers of all ages has to have a continuous recruitment process because

> turnover can be a problem. What happens is that the volunteers improve their self-esteem, and then they go out and get a job. Some people move out of the neighborhood; some of the older people get frail. People tend to stay a year or two in the program. That's why we have to keep developing our sources.

For a few programs, a retention problem is associated with the aging of their volunteers. The director of Senior Companion and

Foster Grandparent programs in a Northwestern rural area reported:

> In the Foster Grandparent Program, after the 10th year, we lost a lot of volunteers in one year. We had to recruit heavily that year, and that was because people sort of aged all of a sudden. The Senior Companion Project is still rather young, but I think that's going to happen there too. As the volunteers get older, there may be quite a few that quit at the same time.

What this quote suggests is that volunteer programs sometimes confront an "aging-in-place" issue that is similar to the problem faced by senior housing projects. The term *aging in place* refers to the changes in residents who move into senior housing when they are in their early 70s and then remain living in these apartments as they survive into their late 80s and 90s and become increasingly frail and in need of services. A senior volunteer program (just like a new housing project) may attract a "cohort" of older volunteers. These volunteers may be young-old when they enter the program, but they age together. Then suddenly an age effect triggers as a whole cohort reaches a later life stage. Of course, we can observe from the above quote that this aging-in-place effect occurred after 10 years. This time span hardly constitutes evidence for the quick turnover of older volunteers.

From our case study data we can draw several conclusions about volunteer turnover.

- *Ensuring volunteer commitment seems to be a less common problem than attracting and recruiting volunteers,* particularly for very successful volunteer programs. Volunteer coordinators often have high praise for the commitment of their volunteers.
- Nonetheless *it is somewhat difficult to assess when or whether there are attrition problems,* because most volunteer organizations do not have adequate data.
- From the research to date, it is apparent that *older volunteers are often highly committed and remain in their volunteer positions for a very long time.* No evidence suggests that the age factor should be used to discriminate against older volunteers. To the contrary, evidence suggests that older volunteers are more stable and committed than younger volunteers.

Picking the Right People

In Chapter 5 we asked the question: How difficult is it to recruit people who have never volunteered before? We now turn to a related issue—not whether people can be induced to volunteer, but rather *who are the best volunteers to recruit?* At least to some degree retention may be a natural consequence of effective recruitment. Should the recruitment of volunteers be selective—to screen out people who are likely to quit? How do people's reasons for volunteering affect how long they stay? Table 6.1 presents an overview of research literature on how the selection of volunteers affects retention.

A study by David Horton Smith (1986) compared 45 voluntary organizations that were rated by expert judges as "outstanding" with a random cross section of 52 "average" organizations.[6] One of the important findings from this study is that *outstanding volunteer organizations are more likely than average organizations to be selective in recruiting their membership.*

Smith found that in a number of ways the outstanding and average voluntary organizations do not seem to differ. For example, the two samples were about equally likely to have a newsletter and to have yearly elections; their size and their budgets were not significantly different; and there were no significant differences in the age of the organizations (when they were established). Smith found, however, a number of interesting differences in recruitment.

- The effective organizations were more likely to recruit selectively rather than just take anyone who applies.
- The outstanding organizations were less likely to use a newsletter for recruiting and more likely to use personal, face-to-face recruiting.
- The members of the outstanding organizations were more committed and had more loyalty than members in the average organizations.

Smith (1986, p. 31) wrote:

The outstanding organizations' leaders estimated that a higher percentage of members are active participants, attending over half

TABLE 6.1 Selection of Volunteers and Retention

Type of study	Finding	References
Comparison of outstanding and average voluntary associations	Outstanding organizations are more likely to recruit members selectively. The members of outstanding organizations are more active, committed, and loyal.	Smith, 1986
Comparison of "stayers" and "leavers" in a longitudinal study of volunteers for community centers in Israel	Experienced volunteers (people who have volunteered before) are more likely to continue volunteering. It is easier to characterize "stayers" than "leavers."	Gidron, 1985
Longitudinal studies— surveys of volunteers in service-oriented organizations	Volunteers who are motivated by nonaltruistic reasons (e.g., to get out of the house) tend to drop out.	Houghland, Turner, & Hendricks, 1988 Clary & Orenstein, in press
Comparison of the values of crisis center volunteers who stay, volunteers who drop out, and a matched sample of nonvolunteers	The study did not find value differences between volunteers who stay and those who drop out. But volunteers for a crisis center have more altruistic values than nonvolunteers.	Mahoney & Pechura, 1980
Study of volunteer "buddies" in recovery program for alcoholics	Volunteers who were high on altruism and who accepted the mission of the program were more likely to complete the project.	Leigh, Gerrish, & Gillespie, 1986
Experiment using the Volunteer Needs Profile	The Volunteer Needs Profile improves the match for volunteers. Well-matched volunteers are the most satisfied with their volunteer work. Volunteers with the best matches are the most likely to remain active.	Francies, 1983

Implications of research findings
- A selective process of recruitment can help screen out people who are likely to drop out of the program.

- Targeting recruitment efforts toward people who have volunteered before may help enhance the quality and commitment of volunteers.
- If people are recruited primarily for nonaltruistic reasons, they are more likely to be unreliable and uncommitted than those motivated by a desire to help others.
- Much more research is needed to identify what criteria to use for matching the "right" volunteers with appropriate assignments.

of the regular meetings and other activities. . . . Thus, it is not the number of members or length of membership but rather the degree of activity of the membership that distinguishes the outstanding organizations. . . . It is likely that the outstanding organizations are generating much more organizational commitment and loyalty in order to obtain the higher levels of participation.

From this research on effective organizations we might infer that *when members are recruited carefully and selectively, they are more likely to be involved, active, and committed to their voluntary organizations.*

Several studies have compared committed (or long-term) volunteers with volunteers who quickly drop out (see Table 6.1). These studies suggest that committed volunteers who continue volunteering are different in a number of ways from less committed volunteers. For example, a longitudinal study of young volunteers for three community centers in Israel compared "stayers," "leavers by choice," and "leavers for objective reasons" (e.g., youth who were drafted into the Israeli army). The study found that the stayers were more likely to have volunteered before than those who chose to drop out. Although this sample was comprised primarily of young people (teenagers), the findings are suggestive—that *targeting recruitment efforts toward more experienced volunteers may be effective* not only because such people are more likely to be receptive to recruitment but also because they may be more committed volunteers (Gidron, 1985).

Hougland and his co-researchers (Hougland, Turner, & Hendricks, 1988) did a study of retiree volunteers in public service agencies. A finding pertinent to this discussion is that those whose motivation to volunteer was "primarily as a means of getting out of the house or to find new activities actually decreased the time they committed to volunteer activities over the course of the project"

(p. 26). That is, *people who volunteer for extraneous reasons (not related to the volunteer work itself) do not make good (or committed) volunteers.*

Research by Clary and Orenstein (in press) of volunteers for YES, a telephone crisis referral program, has similar implications. This study compared the motives of volunteers who fulfilled their 9-month commitment with volunteers who either left the program on their own or were screened out. The study found that volunteers who dropped out of the program were less likely to have altruistic motivations than volunteers who either completed their service or were screened out. Again the implication is that *people who are not primarily motivated by a desire to help others are less likely to sustain their commitment* (see also Leigh et al., 1986).

Research findings, however, are not entirely consistent. For example, Mahoney and Pechura (1980) examined the values and attitudes of crisis center volunteers with a three-way comparison: committed volunteers (who completed a training program and worked for at least 2 months), noncommitted volunteers (who dropped out before 2 months), and nonvolunteers. The volunteers were all college students; the nonvolunteers were drawn as a random sample of students, matched by gender with the sample of volunteers. The researchers found significant differences in values between the crisis center volunteers and the nonvolunteers; that is, on a self-administered attitudes form, the crisis center volunteers appeared to be more altruistic, emotionally sensitive, and emotionally stable. The volunteers also tended to place greater emphasis on personal integrity and personal openness. But *the researchers found almost no value differences between those who remained and those who dropped out during the study period.* The authors concluded that the differences in values between the volunteers and the nonvolunteers are reasonable and logical. This type of (service-oriented) volunteering should selectively attract people with altruistic values. But the authors found nothing in this study to help explain why some volunteers were successful (went forward with the program), while others were not. They commented: "The results of the present study suggest that value differences are critical in the volunteer selection but are generally unimportant in retention. Unfortunately, there is little research on patterns of volunteer retention. Further work in this area appears warranted" (Mahoney & Pechura, 1980, p. 1011). Our review of research on the importance of selective recruitment and picking the right people suggests the following conclusions.

- *A selective process of recruitment is effective in improving the quality of volunteers;* that is, selective recruitment can help screen out people who are likely to be uncommitted volunteers and drop out of the program.
- *Targeting recruitment efforts toward people who have volunteered before may help enhance the quality and commitment of volunteers.*
- *Volunteers who are motivated by a desire to help tend to sustain their commitment.* Conversely those who volunteer for reasons unrelated to the work itself tend to lose their commitment easily.
- We need to treat all of these findings and conclusions with some caution because *much more research is needed* to identify what criteria to use for selecting the right volunteers.

Making a Match

Is matchmaking science or art? The romance business has different approaches to making matches, and it is not clear what works better—the personal touch (like Yente, the matchmaker in *Fiddler on the Roof*) or technology (computer dating services). Similarly volunteer programs have various options for matching potential volunteers with appropriate positions.

Some programs have a systematic process for matching volunteers with jobs. One report (Francies, 1983) described the development, implementation, and evaluation of a matching system for volunteers in human services. The researcher tested the following hypothesis: Volunteers are more likely to stay, and less likely to quit, if their volunteer job meets their individual needs. He outlined seven types of needs: (a) need for experience, (b) need to express feelings of social responsibility, (c) need for social contact, (d) need to respond to the expectations of others, (e) need for social approval, (f) need for future rewards, and (g) need to achieve. He then developed the Volunteer Needs Profile and tested this tool in volunteer recruitment and matching. The volunteers were recontacted 10 weeks later. The evaluation of this system found the following.

- Using the Volunteer Needs Profile improves the match in volunteer assignments.
- Volunteers whose assignments must closely meet their individual needs are the most likely to be satisfied with their volunteer work.
- Volunteers with the best matches are the most likely to remain active (69% of the high-match group remained active, compared with 29% of the low-match group).

This report is unusual, perhaps unique, both because it provides a systematic evaluation and because it presents an innovative, formal procedure—a new tool—for improving volunteer placement.

In our case studies of exemplary volunteer programs, we found that none use a testing procedure as described in the above report. Even so, some of the programs use a formally developed process for assigning volunteers. This formality means written guidelines, so almost all potential volunteers undergo comparable procedures. A formal interview usually is scheduled in advance and entails specified questions or items to cover. Sometimes an applicant's name and other data are entered into a computer data bank. For many organizations with formal procedures, potential volunteers are given several choices of volunteer placements.

A formal matching process is especially likely for relatively large volunteer programs and organizations. It also appears that *the more formal the process, the more likely that recruitment is selective*—that is, that many people who apply are not chosen as volunteers. The director of a highly regarded health care volunteer program in a West Coast city commented:

Sometimes I can't match. I can't always find a position for a potential volunteer, and I refer them someplace else. Not everyone who comes to interview is ready to really be a volunteer. Sometimes they hear the expectations, and they don't want to make that kind of commitment. About half the people who come for an interview actually get into a volunteer job. I think this is a decent rate, based on our own experience and other volunteer organizations. There are some people who are just exploring.

This program provides extensive training and insists that volunteers make commitments. The program's mission is clearly defined as offering a service to clients, not as providing benefit or something interesting to do for the volunteers. Similarly a program for upper level retired executives also is concerned about the quality of the volunteer work:

> It is one thing to say that a person has been an executive, but they are not necessarily excellent consultants. We are looking for quality. We have some people that we would love to clone because they can just do anything, and there are some we just don't ask to do as much because we are concerned about the quality. . . . Occasionally one of our members will say, "You don't keep me busy." And I tell them, "That is not my job." My job is to be able to utilize talents, and if there aren't enough jobs for a particular person, then they may have to find other things to do. I might help them, but that is not really my job.

Virtually all of the programs that rely on a formal matching process require skilled, and often specially trained, volunteers. These organizations are client oriented in that the success of the program is determined by the quality of the service provided to clients (whether individual or agency). In this sense these organizations are managed more as business enterprises than is common for many volunteer programs.

We found that most of the volunteer organizations in our case studies have a much more informal or intuitive approach that takes into account the individual interests, needs, and characteristics of both the client (individual or agency) and the volunteer. Although prospective volunteers usually are interviewed, the format and atmosphere are loose.

An informal process seems to be particularly adaptive in small communities. The director of a church-based eldercare program in a small town commented:

> We know the people here. One of my part-time volunteer coordinators used to trim dogs, and she knows a lot of people through that. We had a request from somebody who was a professor at one of the colleges around here. Her aunt was visiting and was going to be staying

with her until she went into some kind of facility. This woman didn't speak any English. Well, Lisa, one of my coordinators, found somebody who could speak Italian.

Interestingly this approach works well because of the special knowledge of the volunteer coordinators; that is, they know their community, their volunteers, and their clients. In such situations a formal placement process would seem to be unnecessary.

Whether the process is formal or informal depends on circumstances. In small programs and in small communities, matching can be done with an informal, intuitive process. Using a computerized data bank in a town where everyone knows everyone else probably would be a waste of resources. But a more bureaucratic process becomes necessary when

the target population of volunteers is very large,

there is a need for very specialized skills, and

there is no other efficient means for locating people with appropriate skills.

A careful screening or matching process (as well as quality training) sends a message to potential volunteers: The work is important. This also is likely to help build commitment. It is possible, however, that in the process of becoming more formal, something is lost. The director of an RSVP that has grown from 25 to more than 4,000 volunteers commented: "The bigger RSVP grows, the less personal it is."

Why Do Volunteers Stay? Why Do They Leave?

Consider the following hypothetical situations:

Mrs. W's husband died recently, and she feels lost without him. One day she is called by a volunteer from a widow support program. She likes having someone to talk to and finds the support helpful. Later she is asked whether she would like to do this kind of volunteering. Because she feels grateful for the help she received, she decides that maybe she can call other widows and offer support in the same way. So she goes through a training program and is given a list of people who are newly widowed. As luck would have it, the first four people she calls are all rude. One hangs up on her. One demands: "How did you get my number?" The other two widows just tell her they are not interested. Feeling shaken, she puts the list in a drawer and decides not to do any more volunteering, at least for a while.

Mrs. M has done very little volunteering before. She was always too busy with her children, her grandchildren, and her jobs. She sees a notice about volunteer positions as teachers' aides in a grade school nearby. She is not sure she wants to make a big commitment because she and her husband go to Arizona for at least a month every winter. But she loves children, and she decides to give it a try. Now she spends every Thursday in a first-grade class. As soon as she walks through the door, about a dozen children run up to her, shouting, "Grandma Sally! Grandma Sally!" She makes up stories for them, and she also listens to them read. She helps them with arithmetic. She plays the piano for them. She gives them lots of love. She had been worried, before she started, that she would not know enough to be a teacher's aide. But she has discovered that she has lots of skills and experiences that are useful for this volunteer work. Thursday is her favorite day of the week.

What are the differences between these two experiences? These are, of course, different kinds of volunteer work. In one the service is primarily to help older people; the other involves working with children. But the type of work, by itself, does not explain why the first is an aborted volunteer experience, while the second is so successful. It may be that personality accounts, in part, for the differing outcomes. Mrs. M seems to be an active and sociable person with many talents and a natural ability to get along with children. Possibly Mrs. W, the widow, has a low level of self-confidence and is easily deterred by rejection. But these outcomes were not inevitable. One could easily imagine that if Mrs. W had had better luck and if she had happened to call someone who was more receptive, she might have continued in this volunteer role. Even if she were somewhat shy, experiencing success would build her confidence. And it was by no means certain that Mrs. M's experience would have been so successful. Children are not always so friendly to volunteers coming into their classrooms. Mrs. M might have had a bad experience on her first day or later that would have made her walk out of the classroom door and never come back.

Studies have shown that psychological factors in the volunteer experience affect whether or not a person becomes a committed volunteer (see Table 6.2); that is, the way a volunteer feels about his or her experience affects whether or not the person remains committed. The psychological factors include feelings of competence, job satisfaction, and ideological congruence.

Competence. What really distinguishes between Mrs. W and Mrs. M is that Mrs. M (Grandma Sally) feels competent as a volunteer. Out of her positive experience, she believes herself capable of helping the children in the class to which she has been assigned. It is her success that keeps her going. Studies have shown that feeling competent and successful is tied closely to continued service as a volunteer. Clary and Orenstein (in press), in their research on volunteer motivations, found that both motives and ability are important in helping behavior and that effective help depends on both. Similarly Midlarsky (1984) noted that confidence in one's own competence is a critical factor in driving helping behavior.

Leigh and his co-researchers (1986), in a case study of volunteers working in an alcohol rehabilitation program, found that volunteers who seemed to be successful (their "buddies" made progress in the program) tended to continue volunteering, while those with recalcitrant clients were more likely to drop out. One might argue that the "success" of the "buddies" might or might not be caused by the volunteer (it might be luck—which volunteers get the better clients who are more invested in working for their own cure). But the point is, *if volunteers perceive their work as successful, they will feel competent, and if they feel competent, they will make further commitments of their time* (see also, Brummel, 1984; Hougland et al., 1988; Morrow-Howell & Mui, 1989; Payne, 1977).

Findings from our case study data are similar. In almost all of our case study interviews, we were told that volunteer programs are successful when volunteers believe that their work is important and has an impact. To give just one example, the coordinator for a volunteer program in a police department commented:

TABLE 6.2 What Psychological Factors Account for Volunteer Commitment and Retention?

Type of study	Finding	References
Surveys of volunteers/ Literature reviews	If volunteers feel competent and successful in their volunteer efforts, they are more likely to continue volunteering than volunteers who feel rejected, incompetent, and/or frustrated.	Brummel, 1984 Clary & Orenstein, in press Houghland, Turner, & Hendricks, 1988 Leigh, Gerrish, & Gillespie, 1986 Midlarsky, 1984 Morrow-Howell & Mui, 1989
Surveys of volunteers	Volunteers are more likely to continue volunteering if they find the job interesting.	Brummel, 1984 Dailey, 1986 Jenner, 1982 Pearce, 1983
Case studies of voluntary associations	The most active members are those who are most committed to the ideology of the organization.	Chin, 1989 Katz, 1981
Longitudinal studies of volunteers	Volunteers reach a critical transition time during the first few months of volunteering.	Arella, 1984 Gidron, 1978

Implications of research findings
- To sustain the commitment of volunteers, it is important to provide for successful experiences so that the volunteer feels competent.
- Intrinsic rewards (designing jobs so that they are interesting to the volunteer) are critical for volunteer retention.
- Volunteer organizations need to recruit people who share their ideology and/or they need to offer training to inculcate appropriate values and ideology.
- New volunteers require careful attention and monitoring, especially after 3 to 6 months of service.

What seems to account for how long a volunteer stays on a job is that they feel that they are doing something important and because the job is a core function of the police department. This work is truly vital, and the volunteers know that and understand how important their work is.

Job Satisfaction. A second psychological factor associated with volunteer commitment is how much the volunteer likes the specific type of work. A survey of women volunteering for the League of Women Voters (Jenner, 1982) found that a major reason volunteers give for continued volunteering is that they find the work interesting. What is notable is that the appeal of interesting work was much more likely to be given as a reason for staying active than for joining the organization.

The volunteer directors in our case studies also were often sensitive to the needs of volunteers for interesting jobs. An RSVP director, for example, commented, "We are careful to place volunteers in challenging positions. We don't want them to have just routine work." The director of a volunteer program in a cultural center said that their volunteer work is "really fun for the people. They get to know what's going on behind the scenes. And there are a lot of educational opportunities—different seminars and training sessions that people can go to."

Intrinsic rewards—finding the job interesting, being able to use one's skills, having opportunities for professional growth—are important for both volunteer jobs and paid jobs. An unusual study (Pearce, 1983) compared volunteers and paid employees who were doing essentially the same kinds of work. This study found no significant differences between employees and volunteers in terms of their intrinsic motivations, but volunteers reported more job satisfaction. The author pointed out, however, that the study had a "sampling bias" because paid workers may stay at a job even if they feel dissatisfied, while volunteers do not have the same kind of extrinsic (or material) incentive to stay if they do not like a job.

Ideological Congruence. Finally we list at least one other psychological factor in commitment—how much the volunteer believes in the goals or values of the organization. One study of participants in a food cooperative examined how ideology is related to voluntary participation. This study found that members who believe strongly in the goals of the organization (beliefs such as building community-based enterprises or supporting cooperation) are considerably more active in contributing their time and labor than are members who lack such strong beliefs. The finding is not surprising. One would expect that ideological commitments would be related to commitments of time. Yet this ideological factor often is overlooked in

assessments of volunteerism. The author of this report noted that
almost no research has been done on the "relationship or 'fit' between
the stated goals of the organization and those of its membership
and its effect on member participation" (Chin, 1989, p. 29; see also
Katz, 1981).[7]

*   *   *

From the research reviewed in Table 6.2 and the discussion on
the last several pages, we can draw the following inferences.

- *The most effective way to sustain the commitment of volunteers is
  to provide for successful experiences.* Volunteers who believe that they
  are capable of helping and that their investment is worth their efforts
  are much more likely to continue their work than those who feel
  frustrated, rejected, and incompetent.
- *Intrinsic rewards are more critical for volunteers than paid workers* in
  the sense that it is easier for volunteers to quit. If a job is intrinsically uninteresting (or worse, repugnant), it is difficult to attract,
  and even more difficult to keep, volunteers.
- *People are willing to commit their time when they believe that the cause
  and the goals are worthy.* Ideology is important. The more people believe in the purpose of an organization, the more committed they will
  be to committing their time and continuing their work. This inference suggests that (a) volunteer organizations need to recruit people
  who share their ideology and values, and/or (b) organizations need
  to offer training in values and ideology, not just in skills.

How Volunteering Changes the Volunteer

Both volunteer professionals and researchers have commented
that the reasons why people start volunteering may be different
from why they continue. Clary and Snyder (1991a) noted that
"the volunteer experience may change the volunteer and his or
her motivations, and rather than motivations influencing volunteering, it may be a case of volunteering influencing motivations"
(p. 136) (see also Isley, 1990; Moore, 1985; Piliavin & Charng, 1990).
Beyond making this general point, however, little research directly addresses the question of specifically *how* volunteering

changes the volunteer. In the discussion that follows, we draw inferences from several studies suggesting two types of changes that seem to happen to volunteers: (a) a volunteer transition process that happens within the first few months of volunteering and (b) a long-term change as a volunteer becomes committed to a specific activity.

The First 6 Months. Some research suggests a "critical" time for volunteers—after a few months of service, when the likelihood of dropping out is strong. Such a trend is indicated, for example, by an evaluation of RSVP volunteers in Greene County in New York. This study used "appeal ratings" (the ratio between the importance of a feature of a volunteer organization and the success of the organization in fulfilling this mission) as an indicator of volunteer satisfaction. There appeared to be "critical points" when the appeal rating seems to drop; that is, the appeal rating drops after 6 to 12 months of service.

> Immediately after these results were compiled, the Greene County RSVP project administrators began a campaign to personally follow-up volunteers nearing the "critical points" either in length of membership or reported volunteer hours/weeks. When probed, nearly every volunteer approached expressed some unfulfilled expectation: some asked for different assignments; some have even suggested rather creative ways to better use their talents; others would simply like to be assigned more hours each week.[8] (Arella, 1984, p. 60)

Similar findings also were reported in another study. Gidron (1978) surveyed volunteers in four social service, health, and mental health agencies in Baltimore and examined "negative discrepancies"—that is, the gaps between expected versus actual rewards from volunteering. He found fewer negative discrepancies for longer term volunteers. Gidron (1978, p. 23) reported:

> In terms of average numbers of negative discrepancies, volunteers on the job between 9 and 11 months more closely resembled volunteers with more than 11 years services than they do volunteers with 4-6 months tenure on the job. *The volunteer coordinators in all four institutions reported that "dropping out" usually occurs during the*

*first 6 months of volunteer work and, especially, during the first 3
months.*

What we might infer from these studies is a process that can
lead to a *post-honeymoon blues* effect:

- When volunteers are recruited, their motivations are general and
abstract. Their reasons for volunteering may be altruistic (helping
others), or utilitarian (serving their own interest), or some combination. But whatever their reasons, it is likely that some gap exists
between what they hope to accomplish and what is possible. Such
a gap is likely because before people actually become involved in a
particular volunteer activity, their specific knowledge is likely to be
rather limited.
- When a person first starts to volunteer, however, he or she may have
no sense of this gap. In fact, at first the volunteer probably is filled
with good feelings about being a helper. Friends and others may
praise the volunteer, so this stage is a "honeymoon" stage of euphoria and self-congratulation.
- As volunteers begin to do their work, they begin to understand what
the organization does, actually and concretely (rather than ideally),
and what they as volunteers realistically might accomplish. They
may find that what they thought they knew about a volunteer
organization no longer seems accurate.
- The gap between what they expected and what they find is not
necessarily negative. New volunteers might be pleasantly surprised.
But if their expectations were idealistic, there is likely to be some
degree of disappointment. And the larger the gap between expectations and reality, the greater the frustration for volunteers. The
volunteer has now arrived at the post-honeymoon blues.

The findings from these studies are intriguing, though not con-
clusive. They suggest a process of transformation as volunteers
move from being new recruits to becoming socialized into a specific
volunteer role. These studies offer a warning to volunteer programs: *It is not sufficient simply to recruit. Volunteer programs have
to monitor and work carefully with their new volunteers to help
them through the ups and downs of this early transition in the
volunteer role.*

Long-Term Commitments. A small amount of research points to longer term changes in volunteers. What is suggested by these studies is that *volunteer commitments become more specific over time;* that is, a committed volunteer develops an enduring attachment to, and a responsibility toward, a particular cause and organization. Some studies have found that with continued volunteering, a switch occurs from more external to internal motivations. Thus, for example, for a first-time volunteer, a reason to help might be that the person was asked or encouraged by a friend. But the volunteer, once committed, develops her own personal sense of "moral obligation." At that point it does not matter much if a friend or anyone else asks her to do this; she feels a responsibility to a particular organization (for a review of this literature, see Piliavin & Charng, 1990).

Over time, volunteers also become committed to their fellow volunteers and to the cause(s) that these people represent. Daniels (1985) described this process in an interesting article on "high society" women who volunteer. An important theme of her analysis is that "sociability" is used to serve altruistic functions because friendship helps sustain volunteer work. "Women volunteers who stand at the juncture of philanthropy and 'high society' organize community service within a framework of *sociability:* a party-like ambience that encourages others to attend and participate in the activity" (Daniels, 1985, p. 363). Daniels observed that elaborate dinners are important and are used to persuade people to participate in the campaign. She pointed out that the sense of fellowship that arises from these events contributes to the sense of community responsibility.

New Versus Established Volunteers. The research to date, although sparse, offers a compelling portrait: *The experience of being a volunteer changes over time, so new volunteers are very different from committed volunteers.* New volunteers have to undergo a period of adjustment. It was clear from our case study interviews that volunteer managers in high-quality programs do not expect all new volunteers to remain in their organizations. In fact, some said that when they think of retention rates, they do not even count those who drop out while they are in training or when they first start. They expect people to drop out then.

We can offer several applications from this analysis.

- *New volunteers require a much closer form of management than committed volunteers.* There appears to be a substantial risk that new volunteers who are unattended will drop out when they reach the post-honeymoon blues stage. For some volunteers, leaving at this stage simply may reflect a problem in the selection process, so their dropping out may be appropriate. For others, however, effective intervention might allay their frustrations during the first few months of volunteering.

- Conversely, *committed volunteers may require support and fellowship rather than monitoring.* We suspect that a long-term volunteer who feels a sense of moral obligation to an organization would feel offended if he or she were supervised in a way that discounted his or her commitment.

- *Friendship supports volunteerism.* Long-term volunteers are committed not just to an ideology, not just to a cause, and not just to an organization in the abstract. It is particular people who keep them going—their friendships with their fellow volunteers, the other staff, and/or their clients. Such friendships are a backbone of volunteerism and should be supported.

The Problem of Burnout

Volunteers can experience a feeling of burnout from any kind of volunteer work. A volunteer for a fund-raising event might feel that he has done too much and is overused if he has spent night and day on this work for weeks on end. Or a volunteer in a hospice program might experience a sense of burnout from watching her patient suffer and die. When volunteers drop out because of burnout, it is not because they lack commitment. To the contrary, they may be overcommitted; they may care too much and do too much, so they become emotionally and/or physically worn down.

In the next few pages, we use our case studies to illustrate the different forms and causes of burnout and to discuss how volunteer organizations confront problems of burnout. Volunteer burnout appears to have four separate forms or causes:

grief, especially when volunteers work with patients who are very ill
   or dying,
frustration, because volunteers feel thwarted in their efforts,
personal intrusion, when volunteers are called on to help in ways that
   are inappropriate and that intrude on their private lives,
time demands, when volunteers spend so much time volunteering that
   they (or their families) believe that they are giving too much.

These are all separate issues, although sometimes volunteers can
experience more than one form of burnout simultaneously.

Grief. Grief work is an inherent part of managing volunteer organizations that offer services to frail, sick, and dying persons. For
some programs, in fact, it is not only the death of clients but also
the death of volunteers. The director of an eldercare program whose
clients and volunteers both tend to be very old commented: "One
of the big problems is grief, because often there is death. There is
a constant feeling of bereavement among our volunteers."

Some programs have developed methods for dealing with grief
burnout. An organization that helps AIDS victims offers grief and
stress workshops for its volunteers.[9] According to the director of
this program, the workshops have been very effective and have
had a significant impact on retention. He believes that AIDS grief
tends to be different from other kinds of grief and affects everyone
working in this environment—even the volunteers who just answer
the telephone. With AIDS grief, he said, people identify three phe-
nomena: (a) a feeling of physical pain, (b) a feeling of being over-
whelmed (with images of water and drowning, being caught in
the undertow), and (c) a feeling that their lives are detached from
any other kind of reality, as if they were living "on the moon."

He said that a major function of the workshops is to let people
know that "there are other people on the moon with us." He described "an incredible bonding" that happens in these workshops
between volunteers from different parts of the agency who did
not know each other before and between people who come from very
different cultural and economic backgrounds. The workshops last
for 2 ½ days. They rent a comfortable space, serve nutritious meals,
and provide a nurturing environment. The workshop goes on for

20 hours. Then they have a half-day follow-up about 4 months later.

They began their first groups with 21 team leaders. Team leaders are volunteers who have worked for at least 2 to 4 years and are responsible not only for their own clients but also for 5 to 20 volunteer buddies and their volunteers' clients. At least half of these team leaders had been ready to quit. After the workshops, they all said they were willing to stay.

The director of this organization described the process of doing the workshops as

> quite an experience. It has changed our organization, changed the way the staff communicate with each other, changed how team leaders run their meetings. What happened is that the workshops have transformed the way volunteers take care of one another. They have begun to acknowledge that what we do is painful for us, that we have to be there for ourselves, not just our clients. . . . We have to take as good care of our volunteers as they do of their clients.

In our interviews with the directors of other volunteer programs, we found several who offered some grief training and support but none with quite as elaborate procedures. It may be, as this director pointed out, that the type of grief from working with AIDS clients is special. AIDS is a modern-day plague whose victims are almost all young. Even so, it seems that the grief experiences described by many of the volunteer programs—for example, in eldercare—are more similar than different and, therefore, that this kind of workshop ought to be useful in many different settings.

Frustration. The second type of burnout can take a number of forms. Frustration refers to a sense of being blocked. It can be a sense that whatever I do, it is not enough, and nothing seems to help. It can come from not being able to change a person or a situation. Sometimes frustration has ties to grief work because there is a sense of helplessness in the face of an overwhelming problem (including sickness or death).

One eldercare organization that has volunteers serving as companions to families with Alzheimer's patients is particularly sensitive to the problem of burnout. The director of this program said:

> We started a support group for the companions. They really needed it because many of them have very difficult clients to work with. We also watch our volunteers and make sure that they are not depressed and that there aren't problems brewing. Sometimes surprises happen. Occasionally somebody will quit and say, "I'm burned out and can't do it anymore," and we didn't notice it. But we try to keep an eye on this.

In strong helping situations (which are conducive to volunteering), there is a likelihood of a direct, positive impact. The frustration burnout problem reflects the opposite condition. In the case of companions for Alzheimer's patients, for example, what makes the clients difficult is, at least in part, that it is not easy to help them. At best, what a volunteer companion can offer is some respite help to the family. But the problem is overwhelming and cannot be "cured," no matter what the volunteer does.

Often the frustration burnout problem is related to a problem with unreliable or recalcitrant clients (or potential clients). The coordinator of a school-mentoring volunteer program described such a situation:

> Sometimes the student signs an agreement with the mentor, but then they are not really serious about it. So they don't return phone calls, and it can be very frustrating. We might intervene and try to reach the student. We might meet with the student and the mentor. And it might or might not work out.

Similarly the guidebook for a volunteer consulting service for retired business executives tries to confront this frustration problem with the following advice: "A client's calling in a consultant does not guarantee that the advice will be accepted and changes made. It can be frustrating. . . . We can only suggest that you recognize that to some extent it just goes with the territory."

Personal Intrusion. This type of burnout problem happens when clients make inappropriate claims on volunteers either explicitly or implicitly. A personal intrusion problem is especially likely in service-oriented volunteering when the clients being served are very poor and very needy in other ways. In these situations it is sometimes difficult for volunteers to place boundaries around their help. A volunteer coordinator in a shelter for homeless families described this kind of problem:

> We had a problem with one volunteer who was very attached to a family, and the volunteer felt that she had to start supporting the family. The staff at the shelter told her that she couldn't do that. Eventually she did understand that there were limits that she had to set.

In such situations volunteer programs try to protect the volunteer by placing limits on the intrusion of volunteer work into the volunteer's private domain.

A similar situation was described by the chair of an all-volunteer widow-to-widow support service. She said:

> The volunteers write a letter first, and then they telephone. We tell the volunteers that when they send their letters, they might want to use the post office box from the organization as their return address and only sign their first name. That way, if there is some kind of problem, they are protected. There was one newly widowed person who was without housing, and it was a situation of deprivation. This could have imposed a problem on the outreach volunteer. We have to protect our volunteers. Once they have established contact, then they can socialize. But we suggest that they invite this person to meet for the first time at a coffee shop.

This is a common theme for volunteer organizations: "We have to protect our volunteers."

Time Demands. Another issue is protecting volunteers from the fourth source of burnout. The director of an intergenerational volunteer program commented:

> Sometimes volunteers wear so many hats and work in so many different areas that they tend to burn out. So if one of us gets a volunteer to work in one area, we're very protective of that person's name and

do not share it with other people in the organization. We don't want
to lose that volunteer later on. There's a real sense of possessive-
ness around here.

The issue of protecting volunteers is an undercurrent in volunteer management. It is based on the reasonable premise that if
volunteers are unhappy, they will not stay. Even committed volunteers can lose their commitment if they are "abused"—that is, if
too much service and too much time are demanded of them.

*   *   *

Our review of our case interviews suggests that high-quality
volunteer programs confront the various forms of burnout in the
following ways.

- For the problem of *grief,* which affects service-oriented programs
  dealing with clients at risk, programs offer grief training, ongoing
  support groups, and supervision. It appears that a key factor with
  this issue is being able to acknowledge that volunteers feel grief and
  that these feelings are shared by others.
- For the problem of *frustration,* volunteer programs offer several approaches: (a) to provide appropriate monitoring and supervision so
  that volunteers are not working in isolation, (b) to try, if possible,
  to intervene to improve the situation (reduce the cause of frustration), and (c) to anticipate and acknowledge such feelings of frustration (because "things don't always work out").
- To deal with the issue of *personal intrusion,* volunteer programs set
  careful guidelines to place boundaries around what volunteers should
  and should not do. These boundaries help volunteers say no when
  they might feel pressed to help in ways that would create havoc in
  their own lives.
- Programs also are protective of volunteers in terms of the *time
  demands* that are placed on them. Requiring volunteers to contribute
  a minimum amount of time is not the same as expecting unlimited
  contributions of time. To the contrary, effective volunteer programs
  recognize that volunteer time needs to be limited. Sometimes
  volunteer programs tell their volunteers that they are spending too
  much time, and the programs do not allow the volunteers to contribute further hours.

Summary of Key Themes

- Retention of volunteers appears to be a less common problem than recruitment, according to our case studies. However, these organizations do not have very good data on rates of attrition.
- Less turnover appears to occur for older volunteers than for younger volunteers.
- Some evidence suggests that selective recruitment can help screen out people who are likely to be uncommitted volunteers.
- A crucial factor in managing a high-quality volunteer is the ability to match volunteers with appropriate volunteer jobs.
- Volunteers who believe they are competent and successful are more likely to become committed and continuing volunteers than those who feel frustrated and rejected in their efforts.
- Volunteers tend to become committed if they find their volunteer jobs intrinsically rewarding.
- Volunteers tend to become committed if they believe in the ideology of the volunteer organization.
- There appears to be a critical transition time for volunteers—a post-honeymoon blues period, after a few months of service—when there is a substantial risk of dropping out.
- Volunteer commitments become more specific over time, so a committed volunteer develops an enduring attachment to and a responsibility toward a particular cause and organization.
- We have identified four sources of burnout: grief, frustration, personal intrusion, and time demands. Successful volunteer programs deal with burnout by offering support, training, supervision, and intervention, as appropriate. Volunteer leaders are also careful to protect their volunteers by setting limits on both the type and amount of service that is asked of them.

SEVEN

Older Volunteers as Workers

Our volunteers have to read for 2 hours, and for some people, as they get older the quality of their voice declines. We have one man who is 87—he's our oldest volunteer—his voice is not of sufficient quality anymore to use his tape. So we let him read and then we erase what he has read. He comes a couple of times a week, and he doesn't have much else to do. He's the sweetest man. We don't have it in our hearts to tell him, because doing this work is so important for him. But our core group is aging, and we are going to have to find other ways of dealing with this problem.

This story, from an organization that records books for the blind, captures the dilemma of volunteer programs. The work for volunteers in this program is intensive and requires special skills. A reader needs to be familiar with the language in the book. For some books—scientific books or those written in foreign languages —very few volunteers are capable of doing the work. Two volunteers work together in 2-hour sessions—one to read and the other to monitor the taping equipment. After the session another person, either a volunteer or a paid staff, reviews the portions that have been recorded. If the quality is not good, the taping has to be partially or completely redone. Many of their volunteers are quite old now, and the organization is trying, with some difficulty, to recruit younger persons, including young-old. What is particularly remarkable about this story is the cost: another volunteer (the one doing the monitoring) who spends 4 hours a week and whose time is also "wasted" when the tapes are erased.

How can volunteer organizations care about both their volunteers and the quality of the work? In some ways the conflict between compassion and quality may be particularly acute with older volunteers, especially in programs whose mission is to provide meaningful activities for older volunteers. Some volunteer organizations define their older volunteers as their main responsibility, so they may be more concerned with offering opportunities for volunteering than with fulfilling social needs.

In this chapter we discuss how volunteer programs ensure the quality of their products and services. As we show, a delicate balance may exist between treating volunteers as workers and also as special people whose time is a gift and a favor. Volunteer programs offer neither material rewards nor punishments. Under these conditions, how can volunteer programs insist that volunteers perform as reliable workers and get their jobs done well?

The Importance of Quality

A few studies have suggested that volunteers are less reliable than paid workers. For example, fire losses appear to be greater with volunteer fire fighters, as compared to departments with paid staff. Nonetheless, across many types of work, volunteers tend to be rated by agencies, paid staff, clients, and others as making high-quality contributions (Brudney, 1990b, p. 57).

In our case studies of exemplary volunteer organizations, we asked the program directors to describe what is distinctive about their programs. Most of them said that *their programs are exceptionally good because of the quality of their volunteers' work*—what they do or produce. Here are just a few examples. The director of an eldercare program noted:

> Our trained volunteers have actually saved the lives of individuals by contacting the right sources and by getting the services that are needed. On more than one occasion, our volunteers have gone in and found an older person who has been neglected by family members— been allowed to sit in their recliner for 2 full days without having been helped out to go to the bathroom or to be fed.

The director of another eldercare program said that almost two fifths of the people who "receive our services would have to go to nursing homes if they did not have the advantages of [this] program." The director of a local AARP-55 program, which offers driver education classes to older persons, asserted that substantial reductions in traffic deaths have occurred because of their program. A volunteer coordinator for a museum talked about how the well-trained volunteers help "personalize the experience" for children and adults coming to the museum, because they take time with people and also because they can understand a lay person's perspective.

What these responses suggest is that *the quality of the work that volunteers do matters.* The volunteers in these programs offer services that improve their communities, help people in critical need, and sometimes even save lives. These services are not trivial, and, therefore, the quality of their work is an important issue. The director of the museum referred to above commented: "We want to make sure that the volunteers are providing correct information. It's okay to say 'I don't know,' but we don't want to give the wrong information out."

For many programs their credibility and their survival depend on quality. The director of another AARP program noted:

One of the very big problems that we face—and we try to fight it—is this ageism and antivolunteerism. We try to counter this by being the very, very best we can be. That requires building credibility, and that's one of the reasons why poor [volunteer] trainers are not allowed on the program, because we simply can't afford to have our credibility challenged. We keep our people sharp by constantly working and training. But we also want people to realize that they are equal partners, and so the volunteers are not to be given any special treatment. They're supposed to be treated just as staff would be treated —not with kid gloves. We don't want to kill with kindness.

It is not only a question of reputation. There are consequences if volunteers are unreliable or do not do their jobs well. A Meals on Wheels service must take care that the meals they deliver are kept at an appropriate temperature and are safe. A school volunteer program cannot renege on the services promised to teachers and children. For almost all volunteer programs, reliability and quality are important—sometimes critical. Yet special circumstances arise in working with volunteers. The quality issue is complex. From the experiences described in our case studies, we can infer that it is not easy to treat volunteers "just as staff."

Like a Family

Over and over, we heard this word: *family.* Volunteer programs —staff and volunteers—interact as if they were a family.

> People stay at least a year or two and then, if they leave the Meals on Wheels *family,* it's usually because they are sick or they are moving or they have died.

> Most of the shift captains are seniors. Each shift is its own *family.* It is really neat that they are a family and a team, so if somebody is hurting, that they are there for them. One volunteer lost his son and 10 days later lost his wife, and the other volunteers and staff rallied around him. During the earthquake, people who became friends because of the volunteer program were helping each other.

> There's a great deal of caring for each other—a sense of *family.* People send each other birthday cards; they call Joe up because he's not feeling well; they ask how somebody's garden is doing. There's a lot of individual involvement and attention. The sense of family probably is the single biggest benefit.

The family metaphor suggests that a sense of intimacy exists and that particular relationships are important. A family is the opposite of a bureaucracy. Bureaucratic organizations have standard rules, a clear hierarchy of authority, and positions based on qualifications.[10] To portray volunteer organizations as familylike is to emphasize the personal dimension of volunteering, so that people are valued for who they are rather than what they do.

The implication of this metaphor is that a volunteer is different from a paid worker. Of course, we should not exaggerate the difference. Many organizations, including social service agencies and for-profit businesses (even large corporations), portray themselves as family. The metaphor is never entirely apt—either for volunteers or paid workers. The attachments are not as intimate or as enduring, and other factors must be considered—such as can the person do the job?

Even so, the family metaphor is particularly appropriate for volunteer organizations in at least two ways. First, volunteerism connotes a world of caring. As we have discussed in previous chapters, people tend to volunteer, at least in part, because they want to help others. They find fulfillment and meaning because they believe they are helping. It is easy to see how this sense of caring may permeate volunteer organizations. In fact, if the opposite were true—if volunteer organizations cared about the jobs but not about the people—it would seem incongruous. Thus, given the meaning of *volunteerism,* it seems fitting for volunteer programs to be friendly and personable and to operate somewhat more like a family than like a for-profit business. Second, the personal dimension is an important factor in attracting and keeping volunteers. For most programs the tangible incentives are minimal. What induces volunteers to come back are the intangibles: their commitment to the organization and to the people they serve, their enjoyment of the work, and their attachments to their fellow volunteers and the paid staff (see Chapter 6). Volunteer organizations work at creating a friendly and familylike atmosphere. The director of a hospital volunteer program, when asked what is done to keep volunteers, commented: "It's my talking to them every day that keeps them here. There is an atmosphere here—friendliness and interest."

But treating volunteers as quasi-family and insisting on high-quality work can be mutually contradictory when problems arise in the work that volunteers do. In our case study interviews, we were told about a number of instances when problems with volunteers arose. A few volunteer coordinators said that they had "fired" volunteers. But the great majority wavered when asked what they do if problems arise with their volunteers' work performance. They admitted that sometimes problems arise, but they also said that they do not like to fire volunteers. The director of an interfaith program said:

> Occasionally volunteers don't work out. One example is the person
> —a volunteer—who coordinates the minor repair program. He hasn't
> carried out as much of the organizational load for that program as

we expected. . . . We haven't fired him, but I'm thinking of putting a rotation of leadership in—so that might be a kind of solution. . . . We wouldn't fire somebody lightly. This volunteer is a good person. It's just that he's not doing the job very well. You also have to take into consideration that if you have a paid staff and if you fire that person, you have the money to replace that person—to hire somebody else. If you fire a volunteer, you have to find somebody else to fit into that spot, and you don't have the money to replace them.

In part, what this volunteer director faces is a practical problem: If she fires the volunteer, she might not be able to replace him. It is a dilemma both because she has no monetary or material incentive to offer to try to improve his performance and because she has no resources to hire a paid staff to do that job. But the issue goes deeper. From a beggars-can't-be-choosers perspective, she sees herself as having no power or authority to demand minimum work performance. Implicitly the director acknowledges that the volunteer is doing a favor by taking on this position. She pays for this favor with kindness. She implies that she has an *obligation* to be kind to the volunteers. And she is kind, even in her attributions. She insists that this volunteer is a "good person"; she develops a system for working around him and refuses to fire him; and she endeavors to find a way (a "rotation of leadership") so that she can manage the situation without offending anyone.

The perspective of this volunteer director appears to be common. Sometimes the work performance problem relates to aging, as with the story from the beginning of this chapter. The director of an organization in a rural community described an older volunteer who drove for the community outreach program:

She started having difficulty driving. She told me that sometimes her hand shakes. So I started to give out hints to her that perhaps she shouldn't drive. Well, then she told me about having been pulled over by the police while she was driving because she had been swerving. At that point, I said, "Well, you really shouldn't be driving anymore." But she said, "Oh, yes, I simply must. It is, after all, my life, and if I'm not driving, then I will die. It is what is keeping me alive." But the problem got to be much more serious, and we started getting complaints from the station that she was driving for. So I called her into the office, and we talked, and I told her that she had to quit. She cried and cried, and she really didn't believe that she was fired. Finally I wrote her a letter to say that as of August 1 she no longer could drive. I also called the service agency that she had been working for. They, on their own, decided they would nominate her for a large award and bring her to a statewide banquet where she could be recognized. In the meantime, I've tried to find a new placement for her.

In this example a volunteer was fired when a serious liability problem arose and the risk was not just to the volunteer but also to others on the road. But even here the program seemed to tolerate the risk for a rather long time because firing was seen as an extreme measure, to be avoided if possible.

In our 57 case studies, only 5 have policies on firing volunteers. If they are not satisfied with a volunteer's work performance, volunteer directors tend to use an indirect approach. For example, those with short-term projects say they do not fire, but, if problems develop, "we just don't ask them to do it again." One volunteer director quipped that although she almost never fires a volunteer, "I'm really good at talking people into quitting." Most suggested that if a volunteer is "fired" or "retired," it is done "very tactfully and as gently as possible."

In a recent survey of Foster Grandparent programs, the great majority of project directors indicated that bringing about the "retirement" of a volunteer is a very difficult situation for them. The author of this report, who is herself a project director, described her own experience in firing a volunteer: "I still remember her name, her face, her sadness. 'I guess I'm just not good for anything anymore,' she sighed. She went home and died within a week" (Cook, n. d.). For stipended volunteer programs, the problem of firing/retiring is especially complicated. Most of the volunteers in these stipended programs rely on the funds they receive. What is the director to do if he or she realizes that the volunteer he or she fires will no longer be able to afford medicine (Cook, 1991)?

In our review of literature on volunteerism, we found little research that addresses this inherent dilemma in volunteer management. Even so, we can offer several inferences from our case studies.

- *It is useful to recognize the potential tension between quality control and compassion.* Quality of work is important. But volunteer management is a gentle business. Although there may be no simple solution, by acknowledging potential conflicts, it may be possible to avoid serious problems in quality control. A noted authority on volunteerism offered this advice: "It seems to me best to be business-like in the operation of third-sector organizations, but not wholly 'like a business' " (Van Til, 1988, p. 213).
- *In addressing problems in volunteer work, it is important to assess both risks and costs.* It is reasonable, for example, to mandate and implement safety standards (including ability to drive for volunteer drivers) even if the cost is unhappiness for a dedicated volunteer.
- *Finally kindness is not the only operating principle in working with volunteers,* including older volunteers. It is possible to motivate volunteers to improve the quality of their work and also to monitor volunteer work performance, as we discuss below.

How to Motivate Volunteer Workers and Improve Quality

Compared to research on work performance issues for paid workers, there is scant research literature on working with volunteers. In the several studies that we have reviewed, however, is a consistent theme: Work performance is tied to intrinsic rewards. *Intrinsic rewards* refers to the nature of the work—that the jobs are challenging, interesting, and important (see Table 7.1.).

Research suggests that volunteers, including older volunteers, are motivated by challenge and an opportunity for personal growth. Burke and Lindsay (1985), in a review of research, reported that the quality of work and the productivity of volunteers can be increased if they have performance goals, are monitored, and are given feedback about their work. They also assert that "setting difficult or challenging goals is more likely to improve performance than setting easy goals" (p. 97; see also Arella, 1984).

Several studies suggest that volunteers and paid workers are motivated in similar ways. A study of campaign workers (fundraisers for a national charitable organization) found that paid workers tend to be committed (feel identified with their jobs and

TABLE 7.1 How Can Volunteers Be Motivated to Maximize the Quality of Their Work?

Type of study	Finding	References
Theoretical analysis/ research review	Setting difficult goals is more likely to improve performance than setting easy goals.	Burke & Lindsay, 1985
Surveys of volunteers	Volunteers are more satisfied if their jobs require a variety of skills, significant tasks, and feedback about work performance. These factors are essentially the same for paid workers and volunteers.	Arella, 1984 Brown, 1991 Dailey, 1986 Pearce, 1983
National surveys of older persons	Many older persons believe that volunteer work is often busywork.	Harris & Associates, 1981 Lackner & Koeck, 1980
Case study of volunteers in an information and referral service	Formal contracts were used with volunteers, and 84% of the volunteers fulfilled or exceeded their contracts.	Pizzini, 1986

Implications of research findings
- To maximize work performance and to sustain volunteer commitment, it is important to offer intrinsic rewards—that is, jobs that are challenging, interesting, and important.
- To a large degree, volunteer jobs have the same kinds of incentives—in terms of intrinsic rewards—as good jobs for paid workers.
- It appears that a successful strategy for ensuring the quality of volunteer work performance is to design jobs with a formal, joblike structure, including formal contracts.

want to stay) if their jobs entail a variety of skills, significant tasks, and feedback about work performance. Similarly volunteer workers also feel satisfied and committed if their volunteer jobs have these characteristics (Dailey, 1986, p. 86). If their jobs are uninteresting and insignificant and if they get no feedback about how they are doing, volunteers will have little satisfaction with their jobs, they will not feel committed, and they will have no incentive either to perform their jobs well or to continue. In fact, this study found that the characteristics of the job have more impact on satisfaction and commitment than does the personality of the volunteer (see Brown, 1991; Pearce, 1983).

According to surveys of older persons, however, many volunteer jobs are neither interesting nor challenging—especially, perhaps, for older volunteers. Many older volunteers seem to assess volunteer jobs as busywork (Lackner & Koeck, 1980). In a recent Harris poll, nearly a third of the older respondents (age 65+) agreed with the statement: "Most jobs saved for volunteer workers are routine and boring and not very rewarding" (Harris & Associates, 1981). According to some reports, older volunteers often are viewed as "incompetent amateurs" who are not taken seriously enough to be offered interesting jobs (see Rakocy, 1981; White, 1982).

One of the issues in volunteer management is how formal a volunteer program should be. A *formal program* has open recruitment, a prescribed process of applying and training, and "contracts" with volunteers. This kind of system was examined in a case study of a volunteer information and referral program in a metropolitan area (Pizzini, 1986). The study documented, over 5 years, how the service was switched from paraprofessional, paid workers to volunteer workers. The volunteer workers were recruited largely through newspaper advertisement; they underwent an elaborate screening, application, and training process; and they were required to make a commitment to "serve one 5-hour shift a week for 1 year" (p. 69). The researcher concluded that the volunteers' work was better than the work of the paid staff. He found volunteers "to do more interventions than paid staff, to make multiple referrals more often, and to use a broader range of resources than paid staff. All of these are seen as positive indicators of quality service" (Pizzini, 1986, p. 77). The report noted, moreover:

> Of the total 308 volunteers who committed themselves to time contracts, 259 (84%) either fulfilled or exceeded their contracts or are still on-the-line. Clearly these volunteers behaved very responsibly in regards to honoring time contracts. Workers placed a high value on the time contract system. It is a major motivating factor, fostering high morale and sense of esprit de corps. (Pizzini, 1986, p. 71)

This case study has no comparative framework (no example of a volunteer program that was more loosely operated). Nonetheless this report is suggestive that *structuring a volunteer job as a job—with formal guidelines and expectations—is an effective way to manage volunteers and to ensure high-quality work performance.* Findings from our own case studies are similarly suggestive. We examined a number of factors associated with having formal versus informal job structures. Formal job structures for volunteers include

> having a formal recruitment process,
> providing training,
> requiring minimum time commitments, and
> having regular reviews to monitor work performance.

We found that these characteristics tend to come together, so that *volunteer organizations tend to have either formal or informal structures* (see Table 7.2). For example, organizations that require their volunteers to make a minimum time commitment are especially likely to offer training and to regularly review their volunteers' work performance. We observed, moreover, that the formality of a volunteer organization is a matter of choice and is not simply determined by how much money or paid staff are available. Organizations that report a shortage of paid staff were the most likely to offer regular reviews of their volunteers. Possibly organizations that have formal procedures for working with volunteers need more staff than those that offer less supervision.

Our case study data also suggest that *organizations with more formal structures tend to have fewer problems.* For example, organizations that require time commitments from their volunteers are less likely to have problems with recruitment and with retention. Moreover, those organizations with regular reviews are half as likely to have problems with retention. What all of this suggests is that having formally defined jobs for volunteers does not discourage volunteer commitment and work quality. To the contrary, it appears that *the most successful programs may ask the most of their volunteers.* There also may be a reciprocal effect:

TABLE 7.2 Formal Job Structures and Problems With Recruitment and Retention: Selected Findings From Case Studies of Exemplary Volunteer Programs

---

Volunteer organizations tend to have either formal or informal job structures.

- Programs that offer training to volunteers, compared to programs that offer no training, are more likely to require a minimum time commitment from volunteers.
- Programs that do regular reviews of their volunteers, compared to programs that do not have regular reviews, are more likely to have a formal recruitment process and to require a minimum time commitment from volunteers.

Volunteer organizations with more formal job structures tend to have fewer problems with recruitment and retention.

- Programs that require a minimum time commitment from volunteers, compared to programs that require no time commitment, are less likely to report problems with both recruitment and retention.
- Programs that do regular reviews of their volunteers, compared to programs that do not have regular reviews, are less likely to report problems with retention.

The most successful volunteer organizations invest the most in their volunteers. Organizations that require commitments from their volunteers tend to invest in these volunteers by training and supervising them. Volunteers are given the message that their work is important. The formal rules and procedures are indicators of this investment in volunteers.

At the beginning of this section, we acknowledged that research on volunteer work performance is sparse. Therefore the following conclusions, based on our research review and case studies, are somewhat tentative.

- *Intrinsic rewards are a critical factor in working with volunteers, including older volunteers.* When jobs are challenging, interesting, and important, volunteers are motivated to do their best. To a large degree it appears that incentives for paid workers and volunteers are the same, in that intrinsic rewards are important for all workers.
- *It appears that many jobs for volunteers, perhaps especially older volunteers, are neither interesting nor challenging.* Anecdotal evidence suggests that older volunteers are not taken seriously in some organizations and agencies.
- *When volunteer organizations invest in their volunteers by offering training and regular supervision, fewer problems in volunteer management seem to develop.* It appears that volunteer organizations with more formal procedures for working with volunteers tend to have fewer problems in both recruitment and retention.

How Much Do Volunteers Cost?

A recent report on using older volunteers to work with school children noted that "elderly volunteers, like their younger but often unavailable counterparts, generally can help improve learning *without increasing costs* [italics added]" (Tierce & Seelbach, 1987). This statement implies that volunteers are free. But such a conclusion is wrong.

In the last several pages, we have been discussing how volunteer programs "invest" in their volunteers, especially by training and supervising them. These investments have a cost—in money and staff time. But how large are these costs? Knowing that volunteers are not free is not enough. There are many reasons for assessing costs. For example, programs need to make decisions based on their resources: Should they recruit volunteers, and, if so, how many? They also need to plan fund-raising strategies and to determine how much is "enough," given the size of their programs.

We found only a few studies that have tried to look systematically at the costs of working with volunteers. Findings from this research are summarized in Table 7.3. Two of these studies looked at the costs of volunteers in terms of ratios of paid staff to volunteers. One study followed six American Red Cross volunteers over a 4-month period in the Washington, DC, area (Baker & Murowski, 1986). The researchers gathered detailed data on how much time paid staff invested in each volunteer. They presented their information as a ratio—1 hour spent by paid staff to the number of hours contributed by volunteers. On average, 1 hour of paid staff time supported 13.2 hours of volunteer service. But *the ratios varied widely*—from 1:1.4 to 1:33.5; that is, for every hour invested by paid staff, volunteers contributed between 1 and 34 hours. The researchers then estimated the cost in dollars and found that for every $1.00 of paid staff time, the average value of volunteer time was $9.33. But this estimate also showed a broad range—from $1.33 to $14.69. The study suggested that a number of factors decrease efficiency: having high turnover, having individual orientation and training for volunteers (rather than group training), having high-salaried trainers, giving infrequent assignments to volunteers so that they need a lot of retraining, needing many paid staff per volunteer, and recruiting totally unskilled volunteers who need a lot of basic training.

Although this is a small-scale study, both its method and its findings are intriguing. The wide range in ratios, both in staff hours and dollars, suggests that investment in volunteering has a risk of not paying off. Conversely, volunteers can be a very profitable investment. The implication is clear: *Effective use of volunteers can make a major difference in the cost efficiency of a volunteer program.*

Another project that estimated costs in terms of the ratio of staff to volunteers was a study of state long-term care ombudsman programs. The researchers assessed time needed for supervision: The median is 6 hours of volunteer services for every 1 hour of supervision by paid staff. Given this ratio, they concluded that a program needs at least a half-time paid staff position for every 20 volunteers (Schiman & Lordeman, 1989).

One other project, a study of an information and referral service in a metropolitan community, gives us some concrete cost estimates. The study followed the program as it was transformed from paid staff to volunteer staff. One component of this study was to assess the costs of volunteers versus paid workers. The researcher concluded that, indeed, volunteers cost less; that is, a volunteer costs $4.17 per hour, which is $1.83 less than a paid worker. Although this represented a savings, it took the program almost 2 years, after the program had been shifted to a volunteer base, to break even and begin seeing a profit from the use of volunteers rather than paid staff (Pizzini, 1986).

The findings from these few studies are sobering. They suggest that volunteers are not "cheap" and that they are not necessarily even an efficient source of labor. *High turnover and ineffective management can raise costs to the point that volunteers cost more than they give.*

Integrating Volunteers With Paid Staff

Paul Isley, in his book *Enhancing the Volunteer Experience* (1990, p. 119), which is based on case studies of volunteer organizations, observed that the attitudes of paid staff toward volunteers are

TABLE 7.3 How Much Do Volunteers Cost?

Type of study	Finding	References
Study of American Red Cross volunteers	Paid staff spend 1 hour to support 13.5 hours of volunteer service, on average. The ratios range from 1:1.4 to 1:33.5. For every $1.00 of paid staff time, the average volunteer value gained was $9.33 (ranging from $1.33 to $14.69).	Baker & Murowski, 1986
Survey of state long-term care ombudsman volunteer programs	For supervision, paid staff spend 1 hour to support 6 hours of volunteer service. For every 20 volunteers, there needs to be at least 1 half-time paid staff.	Schiman & Lordeman, 1989
Case study of information and referral volunteer program, which was shifted from paid staff to volunteer staff	The cost of a volunteer is $4.17 per hour. This is $1.83 less than the cost of a paid worker. It took almost 2 years to break even and see a "profit" after the program was changed to all volunteers.	Pizzini, 1986
Case studies of volunteer programs	Volunteers can be an extra "burden" for paid staff if time for supervising and training them is not allocated.	Isley, 1990

Implications of research findings
- It is possible to calculate the cost per volunteer or the paid staff time needed for each unit of volunteer service.
- There are substantial costs in running volunteer programs. Volunteers are not free.
- The actual costs of running volunteer programs vary widely.

influenced by the provisions made for integrating volunteers into their work force. Time costs are involved in training and supervising volunteers. *If there is no allocation for these costs—if staff are expected somehow to fit these activities into their workload— they are more likely to resent than appreciate the contributions of volunteers.* Volunteers coming on a situation such as this may be puzzled by how the paid staff respond to them. But these staff attitudes have little to do with the enthusiasm, skills, or competence of the volunteers. The morale problem reflects an organizational issue—that working with volunteers is now part of their jobs but is not really "counted in" (see also Brudney, 1990b). A report on volunteer programs for older persons in the Boston area found considerable variability in how well volunteers are integrated into programs. The authors commented that some organizations, such as hospitals, have well-developed volunteer programs with full-time directors of volunteers.

> In contrast, many other organizations are both generally short of resources and poorly organized to make use of volunteers. Lacking personnel skilled in making use of volunteers, they do not know how to recruit volunteers. When potential volunteers offer their services, the organizations do not know how to set up suitable roles, do not know how to integrate the efforts of volunteers with that of their paid staff, and do not know how to train, supervise, and recognize their efforts. Some organizations do make effective use of some volunteers but do not know how to accommodate the unique needs and interests of older volunteers. Other organizations do know how to draw on the talents and energy of older people, but they simply lack the resources to do so. (Caro & Bass, 1991, pp. 5-6)

Volunteer Programs Require Adequate Funding

A related problem is that volunteers are not used effectively when programs are undersupported. In effect, opportunities to recruit volunteers and make use of their time and talents are lost because of a lack of resources. We found a number of examples of such problems in our case studies. One volunteer director complained: "If I didn't always have to be looking for funding, there would be a lot of other things I could be doing." Another commented: "I know that, as the director, I should interview new recruits, but my time doesn't stretch far enough to do that, and we know that we lose people if we don't follow up."

We heard several stories about new programs that were aborted due to lack of funds. The director of a Jewish agency described a tutoring program that was tried and failed for lack of funds:

One program we tried to launch was an intergenerational service program where we had older volunteers helping students in Hebrew school. . . . It was very successful, and everybody was very excited about it, and we expected to get some foundations to support it, but we didn't—so there was no funding. And it was very painful for the volunteers to have to end this program.

In one of our case studies a small group of retired engineers and other professionals formed an organization to study water pollution. After several months of work, the group produced a report for the state government, and their findings, we were told, now are being used in treating water problems in their area. Even so, the group was short lived. The frustration that this group encountered is a particularly striking example of a lost opportunity.

We had a core group of people who wanted to continue the project. We contacted the city council and then the mayor to say here we have trained and knowledgeable people who have something to offer. Well, they said we really ought to talk to the county health department. . . . In October of 1990, the director of the health department wrote us a letter and said, "Let's get together and talk." . . . Well, finally he said, "What you propose is very good, but I can't use volunteers because the state has mandated that governmental agencies cannot use volunteers unless we have a volunteer coordinator. We don't have the money for a volunteer coordinator."

In the end, it seems that the project unraveled because no public funds were available to support the work of these talented, retired professionals.

A number of federally sponsored programs have experienced cutbacks in funding in the last several years. As a consequence, these programs provide less service. The director of a Senior Companion Project in a small town in the Midwest commented: "We don't have problems getting enough recruits, but we have had some substantial budget cuts and have lost volunteer positions. . . . We've had a 25% cut in our Senior Companion Project. We lost 10 volunteers. Each volunteer serves 4 clients, so that is about 40 clients not getting help." The director of another Senior Companion Project reported a similar problem. When asked whether she was trying to raise funds, she said: "No, we just don't have the staff to begin to think about doing something like that."

For a few programs included in our case studies, their very survival is at stake. In one of our interviews, the coordinator of a new program in which older volunteers work with homeless children made an offhand comment that "the whole program is to end in December unless we get other funding." This program ostensibly has been very successful and has received considerable publicity. But without funding, it simply will end. Two other exemplary volunteer programs in our case studies also were dependent on short-term grants, and at the time of the interviews, it was not clear whether these programs would continue when the grants terminated.

Summary of Key Themes

- For virtually all volunteer programs, the quality of the work that volunteers do is important. Programs vary widely, however, in how they supervise and monitor volunteers as workers.
- There is a potential tension between quality control and compassion. It is common for volunteer organizations to describe their volunteers as a family. An implication is that volunteers are treated with caring and kindness. Firing a volunteer is extremely difficult, and most volunteer coordinators try to avoid it.
- Volunteers are motivated to do good work by intrinsic rewards, especially by having jobs that are challenging, interesting, and important.
- Structuring a volunteer job as a job, with formal guidelines and expectations, appears to be an effective way to ensure high-quality work performance.
- It appears that the most successful volunteer programs are those that ask the most of their volunteers (e.g., require training and time commitments) and invest the most in their volunteers (e.g., offer training and regular supervision).
- Volunteers are not free. They require investments in training and supervision. Inefficient management can raise costs to the point that volunteers cost more than they give.

- If paid staff are not allocated time to train and supervise volunteers and if they are expected somehow to fit these activities into their workload, they are more likely to resent than appreciate the contributions of volunteers.
- A lack of adequate resources substantially limits the effectiveness and scope of many programs for older volunteers.

Part III

Special Topics

EIGHT

Ethics and Other Thorny Issues

Drinking on the volunteer job is absolutely forbidden. We have had
a few volunteers who have shown up at the school drunk, and that
is a cause for dismissal. But the biggest problem is the violation of
confidentiality. Sometimes volunteers will talk about clients with
their friends. We counsel them not to do this because everybody
knows each other in this town.

▼

From the *Consultants' Guide:* "We ask that you refrain from accepting Board membership or paid employment while you are serving
as an assigned volunteer."

▼

A certain museum got a new director of volunteers, and this person
fired everybody who was 70 and over. So we [RSVP] sent somebody
over to this museum director and suggested that maybe this was
discriminatory and that they ought to be dealing with people on an
individual basis. If they had problems with particular volunteers,
that was one thing, but it is not right to fire everyone just because
of their age. Many of the volunteers were devastated by this experience. Some of them had been working there a long time.

Volunteer programs confront diverse ethical dilemmas. There are
concerns about the behavior of volunteers. There are problems of
discrimination—antivolunteerism, ageism, racism, and/or sexism.
There are questions about when (or whether) it is appropriate to
replace paid workers with volunteers. There are general issues

about what constitutes "exploitation" of volunteers. And, then, there are legal/ethical concerns about liability and the potential risks to volunteers, clients, and volunteer organizations.

There is no dividing line between ethical questions and practical questions. Ethical questions are practical. And practical questions of all sorts very often touch on matters of ethics. Ethical dilemmas by definition do not have clear or easy answers. In the pages that follow, we will examine a number of value issues confronted by volunteer organizations. We will see that sometimes there are "correct" ways to "solve" or at least deal with ethically difficult situations. But that is not always the case. What is imperative, however, is that matters of ethics be recognized and considered.

The Ethic of Community Responsibility

Volunteerism has, intrinsically, an ethical component. For an individual, to volunteer is to confirm the value of giving to others in the community and to express a spirit of generosity. Whatever the personal motivations or the benefits to the volunteer, the act itself almost always includes some form of giving to others. For a community, to encourage its citizens to volunteer also reflects a moral perspective—the ethic of community responsibility. This ethic is based on the premise that responsibility for the "general good" goes along with enjoying the benefits of being a member of society.

Robert Wuthnow, in *Acts of Compassion* (1991), said that volunteer work is important because it symbolizes our bond to society. Volunteering is an act of faith and of hope.

Volunteer work . . . gives us a sense of efficacy, of being able to make a difference. It inspires confidence in the human condition, in the goodness of those who are truly needy and deserve our help. To participate in voluntary organizations means we are making a choice for the better, siding with the good, doing something, rather than sitting idly by while the specter of chaos and corruption advances. (Wuthnow, 1991, p. 233)

Ethical Issues for Individual Volunteers

There are inherent paradoxes in the ethic of community responsibility. From the perspective of individuals come the following caveats.

- Volunteering, by definition, is based on choice. Thus, although we "should" fulfill our social obligations, as individuals we choose if, when, how, or how much to volunteer. An individual can choose to be a "free rider"—that is, to benefit from the voluntary work of others without making his or her own contributions (see Crenson, 1987). In fact, all people at some times are free riders.
- The social responsibility of individuals has limits. These limits are not clearly specified, but when helping becomes self-sacrifice, there is a sense that we have given "too much." Although we sometimes admire self-sacrifice (we give posthumous medals for heroes), we do not expect individuals to neglect their own interests for the sake either of other individuals or of the common good.[11] The expectation, perhaps especially in American society, is that helping others should be mutually beneficial rather than harmful to the giver (see Bellah, Madsen, Sullivan, Swidler, & Tipton, 1985; Wuthnow, 1991).
- Foregoing a livelihood for the sake of volunteering is a form of self-sacrifice. With a few exceptions, if a person expends all of his or her time and energy on voluntary service, has no other source of a livelihood, and receives no compensation for this service, this would be eschewed as inappropriate (and possibly a neglect of family duties).
- Removing someone else's livelihood also may be ethically problematic. Thus for an individual to accept a volunteer position that replaces a paid position may be comparable to being a "scab" worker.

Ethical Issues for Volunteer Organizations

All of the above constitute ethical issues for individuals as potential volunteers. From the perspective of volunteer organizations come these ethical caveats.

- Despite the fact that citizens should take responsibility for various social problems, social agencies in the private, nonprofit sector can in no way demand that they do so. Volunteer organizations have no claims on individuals; at best, they can induce or persuade persons to donate their time and other resources.

- Even so, it is possible that, under certain conditions, agencies may be in the position of "exploiting" volunteers. Such conditions would apply if there is any coercion. For example, when prisoners, soldiers, employees, or students "volunteer" for their institutions, there is an implicit structure of coercion, in the sense that those requesting volunteers have power over potential recruits, who may find it difficult to refuse to participate.

- Volunteers also are exploited if they are subject to discrimination. For example, if they are treated as "just" volunteers and are given menial jobs, the implication is that their labor and contribution are devalued (see Barber & Scheier, 1979; Rakocy, 1981).

- Potentially a converse form of exploitation exists if no distinction is made between a paid worker and a volunteer. For example, if two people have the same responsibilities, workload, and expectations and if one is a paid worker and the other is a volunteer, a problem of equity exists. The equity issue is particularly troublesome if the decision to pay one person and not the other is based on status characteristics (e.g., gender, age).

- This final caveat concerns the broad issue of replacing paid workers with volunteers. It is ethically troublesome for an organization to fire a paid worker and "hire" volunteers to replace the lost worker. This tactic constitutes a devaluing of labor and ultimately an exploitation of all workers, in the sense that they are treated as expendable because their services are available for "free."

Older Volunteers, Public Policies, and Ethical Dilemmas

Several potential ethical dilemmas come from the perspective of public policy planning.

- It is problematic for governments to expect volunteers to provide vital services. A reliance on the voluntary sector increases the risk that those in need will not receive services.

- It is ethically problematic, but not uncommon, for governments to replace funded programs with voluntary efforts, especially in the provision of critical services. Studies have suggested, in fact, that when the government reduces spending on social welfare, increases in volunteer programs occur (see Brudney, 1990a; Cnaan & Nuikel, n. d.; Lackner & Koeck, 1980; Menchik & Weisbrod, 1987).

- When governments rely on volunteers as part of a program of services, it is problematic to provide inadequate support for volunteer programs.

                          *   *   *

From a policy perspective there are also the following ethical caveats specifically concerning older volunteers.

- It is problematic to limit productive opportunities for older persons to volunteering. When the overwhelming focus of program development is on volunteering, no affordable opportunities are provided for poor elderly who are seeking productive activities. Substantial numbers of elderly are poor or near-poor, particularly nonmarried older women and minority elderly (see Harris & Associates, 1981; Minkler & Stone, 1985). Even for middle and upper income retirees, the expectation that the elderly should volunteer their time rather than work for pay can be undesirable. Many retirees believe that giving away their time devalues their work.
- The potential for replacing younger, paid workers with older volunteers is a broad issue that has ramifications for policy planning. A volunteer force of retirees may be especially threatening to paid workers in the sense that retirees are supported by Social Security and other pensions and can "afford" to offer their services on a volunteer basis. The implication is that retirees can select desirable roles for themselves and can take over some of the "best" jobs in the labor pool, while younger workers who need to be paid for their services are at a competitive disadvantage. Even if retired volunteers work part-time, as a group they are able to contribute considerable numbers of hours in labor. Do five retired volunteers, each working 8 hours a week, essentially "replace" one 40-hour paid worker?

Why Volunteers?

Given all the ethically problematic issues we have raised, we need to ask, Why should any organization recruit volunteers, including older volunteers? Of course, cost is a factor. We began this book by noting that older volunteers can "make miracles" and that their accomplishments are sometimes extraordinary. We also pointed out (see Chapter 7) that volunteers are not "free" and that, in fact, running volunteer programs involves considerable costs. Even so, volunteers, when managed properly, can be an efficient use of resources. Undoubtedly one reason for recruiting volunteers rather than paid workers is that the cost is generally less. Older volunteers, in particular, are an available resource with many talents. That is part of the rationale for recruiting older volunteers.

But another factor also comes into play. In many contexts *a volunteer has a distinctive position as a concerned citizen who is part of an organization and yet is also independent.* Two examples of volunteer roles will illustrate this point: a board member for a nonprofit organization and a volunteer advocate for vulnerable clients.

The *board member* of a nonprofit organization is in a different position from a paid staff person. Typically the volunteer officers and members of a board represent the constituency (funders and recipients of services), oversee activities of the organization, and provide guidelines for allocation of resources. Many organizations have parallel hierarchies for volunteers and paid staff. Why are volunteers needed, since these parallel structures would seem to be inefficient? In part the reason is fund-raising. Board members of well-established nonprofits are typically wealthy citizens who not only donate large sums of money themselves but also help convince their peers to make large contributions. But there also is an expectation of service—that persons who serve on boards contribute their time and efforts, not just their funds. In this role they act as citizens. They do not owe their livelihoods to the organization and in this sense are "independent." When they make decisions about the allocation of resources, presumably they are not influenced by their own direct financial benefit.[12]

The independence of a *volunteer advocate* is also a significant factor. A volunteer advocate, for example, might represent nursing home patients who are vulnerable and unable to represent their own interests. Volunteers in this position have certain advantages over paid workers: They are part of the community, they have no official status (no obligations to the nursing home or to the government), and they can be flexible and independent. Although volunteers may not have the same kinds of skills as social workers or health care providers, they can serve a useful role as intermediaries. Vosburg (1982) pointed out that volunteer advocates may have the best overview of client needs and the quality of services. He observed: "Violations of dignity are among the easiest difficulties for other lay persons to discover" (pp. 88-89; see also Conner & Winkelpleck, 1986; Hembree, 1991; Schiman & Lordeman, 1989; van Iwagen, 1986).

Volunteers in a great variety of other roles also function as concerned citizens, whether they are tutoring children or serving as companions for frail elderly, are delivering Meals on Wheels or helping on fund-raising committees, are working as docents in a museum or serving as buddies for AIDS patients, and so forth. Volunteers often have the following qualities.

- *They serve as intermediaries.* Volunteers often help link clients (individuals or groups) with formal institutions. In their role as volunteers, whatever their professional background or training, they are lay persons who work within, but are not completely part of, organizations and agencies. Because they are not employees, they are relatively free to place the needs of clients before the needs of the organization (Brudney, 1990b).
- *Their activities are flexible.* Often their responsibilities are defined as doing what paid workers do not do. In hospitals, nursing homes, or other facilities, for example, it is common to recruit volunteers primarily to spend time with patients/residents. They may have assigned tasks, but part of the rationale for hiring volunteers is that they are not bound by hourly wages. Conversely, staff typically do not have "extra" time just to be with clients beyond performing their required tasks.
- *They represent the community.* Volunteers are participants by choice, in the sense that their activities are not driven directly by their work or family obligations. Their very participation as volunteers is a confirmation of the importance of citizenship. Through their service, they give a message that they care and are committed to a person (a client), an organization, an ideology, and/or a community.

We should not idealize the volunteer role, of course. There are many forms of volunteering and a range of motivations. Even when volunteers are supposed to serve as independent citizens, they may not do this—for a variety of reasons. For example, volunteers, in their efforts at being "intermediaries," may find themselves with split loyalties (see, for example, Conner & Winkelpleck, 1986). Moreover, the flexibility of volunteer roles undoubtedly varies, depending not only on the guidelines and rules of volunteer organizations but also on their openness. Some organizations want volunteers to operate as independently as possible and encourage them to use their own creativity; many do not.

A serious challenge to the independent citizen role of volunteers relates to the problem of funding. The activities of both individual volunteers and especially of volunteer organizations may be restricted by the values, guidelines, or biases of their funding source—whether government or private foundation. This restriction seriously limits the "citizenship" role of volunteers. In a discussion of nonprofit organizations, Manser and Higgins-Cass (1976) reported:

> One of us was surprised to hear a voluntary agency executive, with great concern for people and a long record as an activist in their behalf, say that neither he nor his organization could publicly take a stand on a regressive public welfare policy adopted by the county authorities, which directly affected persons served by his agency, because 80 percent of his budget came via the same county authorities! (p. 167)

One further point: If volunteer roles have special advantages, they also have limitations. The volunteer director of a successful, well-established health care program commented:

> There are certain things you can ask paid staff to do but that you can't ask volunteers. Also there is better continuity with paid staff. For example, volunteers are not in the office as much, and we don't give clients their home phone numbers. So if there are health problems that come up, the volunteers are less accessible. They are not there every day. Also they take more vacations.

In the real world, as these observations suggest, volunteers are different from paid staff. They may be intelligent, talented, and well skilled, but they are "less accessible." Their responsibilities are limited by the fact that they are volunteers. If volunteer roles are independent and flexible, then *tasks may not be appropriate for volunteers* when the work requires staff that are full-time, closely tied to the institution, and explicitly bound by professional standards. Specifically how volunteer roles are limited, however, and what the distinctions are between volunteers and paid staff are open issues. We can offer some guidelines about what is not ethically appropriate, but, as we will see in the discussion that follows, it is much more difficult to articulate positive guidelines for determining when a position is appropriate for a volunteer or when it is unethical to hire a volunteer instead of a paid employee.

Antivolunteerism and Other "Isms"

In our case study interviews, we heard stories about antivolunteerism and other biases. One of the most striking examples of ageism is found in the introduction to this chapter—the story about the museum director who summarily fired all the volunteers who were age 70 or older. There ought to be no question that such blatant discrimination is unethical.

More commonly, the evidence for bias is rather subtle. In an article on senior volunteers, the author (an RSVP director) described the following scene: "An older volunteer sat down to a staff meeting. The team leader began by saying, 'It is nice that the five of you could make it,' not counting the sixth person, a volunteer" (Rakocy, 1981, p. 37).

In some of our case studies, we inferred that a systematic discounting of volunteer efforts occurs because they are "just" volunteers (or older volunteers or older women volunteers). The volunteer leader of a police auxiliary program, which is comprised almost entirely of older women volunteers, observed: "The community doesn't appreciate what they are getting. . . . There's no money that's allocated to spend on volunteers, so anything we've done we've had to spend ourselves."

One volunteer organization in our study decided to counter ageism and antivolunteerism by placing a monetary value on the work of volunteers. This organization offers retired professionals as consultants to foundations, social service agencies, and other nonprofit organizations. The director commented:

Sometimes volunteers are not taken seriously. They [those receiving services] don't return phone calls; they don't keep appointments; they don't follow through. But when they pay a fee, they always take it seriously and they are always committed. So, for that reason alone, it is worth charging fees. These fees go to our organization, of course, not to the volunteers.

The retirees who contribute their time to this organization almost all had high-status positions during their working years; they were successful business executives, lawyers, and so forth. Interestingly, although the volunteer consultants receive no monetary compensation, the fee for service supports not only the program but also the status of the volunteers.

Conversely an implicit form of antivolunteerism occurs when volunteers are denied any status or authority. Several studies have suggested that volunteers in some organizations are placed in subordinate positions and are given only menial tasks, that jobs often are structured so that all decisions are made by paid staff, and that paid employees resent volunteers who try to boss them. The subordination of volunteers may happen particularly with older volunteers (see Chambre, 1987; Goldberg-Glen & Cnaan, 1989; Manser & Higgins-Cass, 1976; Sachs, 1983).

In our case studies, we heard several accounts that were suggestive of power struggles, with volunteers given the message that they were not supposed to make decisions for their organizations. The (paid) volunteer director of one organization, for example, commented: "Sometimes volunteers get carried away, and they want to determine how things should be done. But we hire professionals who know what to do and how to do it, and volunteers don't always accept this." A volunteer director of a large cultural organization described an incident in which volunteers tried to initiate their own special event. She reported that the volunteers "didn't understand why the Director of Promotions had to approve their publications." She insisted that volunteers sometimes have a hard time understanding the "big picture."

Of course, these are large organizations, and it is not surprising to find a hierarchy for decision making. Nonetheless, when volunteers are told to "know their place" and they are implicitly accused of being "uppity" if they try to assert authority, antivolunteerism is a real possibility.

But we also need to consider the potential reasons for antivolunteerism. Is this just a matter of prejudice and discrimination? In Chapter 7 we discussed the morale problem that occurs when paid staff are expected to train and supervise volunteers but are given no support for these activities. It is not surprising to find staff feeling burdened when they are given an add-on responsibility. From their perspective, especially initially, volunteers are likely to be viewed as extra work while their value is unknown.

Professional staff also may distrust the reliability of volunteers. Because they are not paid, there is no way to ensure that volunteers come when they are supposed to, that they are available when needed, or that they do not quit after having received expensive training. Furthermore, like other workers, professionals, such as social workers and health care providers, may worry about volunteers intruding on their own positions. Professional staff are often protective of their professional turf and are wary of nonexperts (volunteers or others) taking over some of their specialized activities (see Fischer et al., 1989, 1991; Kieffer, 1986; Romero, 1986).

There is also the fear factor. Paid workers and labor unions have ample reason to be suspicious of volunteer programs (see Kieffer, 1986). Both unskilled and professional staff might view volunteers as competition. In nonprofit organizations the line between work done by unskilled staff and volunteers often may be unclear. The number of paid jobs available may very well reflect the availability of unpaid workers. It is likely, moreover, that the number of volunteers will vary with rates of unemployment; that is, when paid jobs are scarce, there are more volunteers (and vice versa). In a recession, therefore, workers might very well view volunteers as potentially taking away their much-needed jobs.

What all of this suggests is that antivolunteerism is not a simple issue. Obviously discrimination against a class of persons—older people, women, blacks, or volunteers—is unpalatable. But volunteers and paid workers sometimes have conflicting interests. We have no prescriptions for combatting antivolunteerism and other isms. Rather, we offer the following consciousness-raising suggestions.

- *Be alert to the possibility of discrimination*—against volunteers or against certain groups. Bias can appear in subtle forms—for example, through discounting the value of certain persons' work.
- *Be sensitive to the differing needs of volunteers and paid staff.* Any organization has a hierarchy of positions and is not simply a happy family.
- *Carefully evaluate the time costs involved in training and supervising volunteers.* The allocation of responsibilities for volunteers by paid staff should be thought of as matters of equity and ethics, not simply as a cost-benefit problem.

When Volunteers Replace Paid Staff

Volunteerism contains a fundamental ethical dilemma: On the one hand, volunteers, at least under some circumstances, compete with workers in need of paid jobs. On the other hand, to restrict the use of volunteers is also to deny services to those in need. Many human service organizations and other nonprofits have explicit rules against replacing paid staff positions with volunteers. Guidelines on working with volunteers, developed for the National Association of Social Workers (1978), for example, stipulate: "Volunteers should not supplant or decrease the need for suitably qualified regularly employed staff" (p. 5). Similarly the handbook of an organization for retired professionals who serve as volunteer consultants advises: "You are to supplement, *but not to supplant,* the staff."

But the issue is not so simple. All volunteers replace potential paid workers, because any job could be either paid or unpaid. The objective of nonprofit organizations is to provide services that meet critical needs and that cannot be met in any other way (Brudney, 1990b). Restricting the use of voluntary labor, therefore, places limits on the services that volunteers can provide.

Even so, it is understandable why stipulations about not replacing paid workers are important. By defining volunteer roles as offering "extra" services, organizations are assuring their paid staff that they will not be penalized for cooperating with volunteers. Conversely, without this assurance, paid workers can see their labor devalued and are at risk of losing their livelihood.

In our case study interviews, when we asked volunteer directors about "replacing paid staff with volunteers," they usually answered that this is against their policy. For example, RSVP directors, who create positions for senior volunteers by developing contacts with agencies in their area, insist that they are "absolutely forbidden to replace paid staff with volunteers." But in practice, what does this prohibition mean? One RSVP director, when pressed on this issue, acknowledged: "Well, basically the cuts have to come first. So if they have already lost a position and they are having trouble making ends meet, then they maybe could get a volunteer. But volunteers are supposed to enhance a program, not substitute for paid personnel." Another RSVP director observed:

> In the job climate as it exists today, people are afraid of losing jobs, so they don't want volunteers to take their place. It is our policy that we don't replace paid workers. . . . One time somebody called up and said, "Our secretary just quit and we want to get a volunteer." I told her, "We can't replace a paid staff job. However, if you have a secretary and you want a volunteer that is going to enhance what you already have, that is what we can do." . . . If they want a few hours of light typing or 2 days a week to answer phones, that's one thing. But if they expect a 5-day-a-week job, they are talking about a paid job. . . . Here's another example: This is for positions in a physical therapy office. We place people who help by giving extra workouts. They're not physical therapists who are professionals and who are providing physical therapy and therefore replacing a paid position, but they're allowing patients to have more time in workout.

There are many gray areas. Volunteers ostensibly are supposed to enhance programs. But according to the first RSVP director quoted above, a program that has suffered from budget cutbacks might be able to employ volunteers to take the place of workers who have been lost. The second director quoted here makes some important distinctions: Volunteers are not to replace staff, they should not be placed in full-time positions, and they should not replace professional roles. But even these distinctions are not really clear-cut. For example, if this volunteer director were asked to find a placement for a retiree who is a professional, licensed physical therapist, would such a person be prohibited from providing physical therapy? This seems unlikely, because we have come across numerous examples of retirees who contribute their time as skilled professionals.

The issue of volunteers replacing paid workers is complicated by one other factor—the low wages paid to professionals in volunteer organizations and social service agencies. The director of a social service program in a small college town, for example, reported that when her agency advertised a position for a volunteer coordinator with a salary of only $5.75 an hour, more than 70 people applied, including a number of people with advanced degrees. One might argue that the distinction between paid and volunteer positions is muted when the wages are so low. The social service professional who has invested many years in education and whose peers in other fields command much higher salaries is, in some ways, a semivolunteer.

Volunteer organizations and programs vary widely in how they are structured and in how they define their missions (see Chapter 3). In some organizations no one may question the appropriateness of volunteer roles because volunteers fill a niche that has no paid workers. Conversely, in some programs volunteers have replaced paid workers (we discussed one such program in Chapter 7). In many agencies, volunteers work side by side with paid employees, and their responsibilities often overlap. In such situations, as we have observed in our case studies, the volunteer labor issue often seems to be an underlying factor when morale problems develop and when volunteers find their efforts stonewalled.

In this issue, as in much of our discussion of ethics and volunteerism, we can offer no simple solutions for managing volunteer programs. As we keep pointing out, there are many gray areas. We offer the following suggestions.

- *Volunteer programs need to be sensitive to the volunteer labor issue.* If conflicts of interest are possible, volunteer organizations should include policies about replacing paid workers in their policy statements and guidebooks.
- *Individual volunteer managers need opportunities for discussing the ethics of volunteer placements.* Professional organizations and peer groups should include such topics on their agendas.

"Exploitation" as an Issue for Older Volunteers

For many reasons, volunteerism may be seen as a positive force in the lives of older persons. Volunteering represents one type of opportunity for "productive aging" and can provide meaningful activities in postretirement years. Moreover, given the plethora of social needs and the fact that older persons often have time and talent to contribute, it would seem a shame not to recognize the older population as a valuable resource. So, what could be wrong with encouraging older persons to volunteer?

Just as certain feminist leaders began to argue that volunteerism is a form of exploitation of women, some leaders among older persons see parallel issues for the elderly (see Cnaan & Nuikel, n. d.). A director of the National Council of Senior Citizens (Hutton, 1981) pointed out that many elderly cannot afford to volunteer and argued that for the elderly poor, the "best answer" to the need for income is "not an opportunity for volunteer service. The best answer is jobs" (p. 13). He seemed to view the whole concept of volunteerism for retirees, in fact, as ethically troublesome.

We are unalterably opposed to any programs that exploit older people by asking them to perform, on a voluntary basis, community service work for which younger people would receive a nominal wage. If an older person has the skills to perform such work satisfactorily, and the service being provided is one needed by the community, then the community should be willing to pay for it. (Hutton, 1981, p. 13)

Any form of volunteerism is problematic if it entails direct or implied coercion (Smith, D. H., 1975). If retirees were "drafted" into voluntary service as a requirement for receiving benefits such as Social Security and Medicare, such activities would no longer be based on choice. Although unlikely, such arrangements have been proposed from time to time (Manser, 1982). The perception of older volunteers as "cheap labor" also touches on exploitation. The labor of older volunteers is devalued if older persons are given only menial tasks and/or are treated as if their time is expendable and therefore can be wasted in trivial activities (see Lackner & Koeck, 1980; Manser & Higgins-Cass, 1976). Organizations and programs that work with older volunteers need to be sensitive to the potential for exploitation. The following questions need to be addressed routinely.

- Are we treating older volunteers differently from working-age volunteers; specifically, are we treating them with respect and not condescension?
- Are we making the most of the skills and talents of older volunteers and not devaluing their time and labor?
- Are we making unwarranted assumptions about the income needs of retirees, tracking them into volunteer jobs and preventing them from pursuing paid work?

Ethics for Volunteers

In much of this chapter, we have addressed ethical issues from the perspective of how organizations and agencies need to approach and work with volunteers. But there are also ethical concerns about the behaviors of volunteers. What standards or guidelines are appropriate for volunteers? How strict do volunteer organizations need to be in imposing and enforcing rules for volunteer behavior?

Of course, as we have pointed out many times in this book, there is tremendous variety in volunteer organizations. Clearly standards for volunteer behavior need to vary across organizations, at least somewhat. For example, in social service agencies confidentiality is often an important issue because volunteers may be privy to sensitive information. But this concern might be irrelevant in cultural organizations that have no direct client contacts.

Despite the diversity, there is a general reason for concern about ethical standards for volunteers because *volunteers are more independent than paid workers.* Their independence has several implications.

- Volunteers are, in some ways, harder for an organization to control because they are not dependent on the organization for their livelihood and also because typically they spend much less time in this role than paid workers.
- Compared to professional workers, volunteers are lay persons who are not obliged to follow professional standards. Even if they are professionally trained, their role as volunteers is more flexible.
- It is difficult to supervise the behavior of volunteers because if they are offended and become unhappy, they will leave. Because no money is available to replace them, the tendency may be to turn a blind eye to ethical compromises.
- It also is difficult to impose restrictions on the behavior of volunteers because the obligation is to treat them with kindness (see Chapter 7). This is another reason that volunteer programs may tend to ignore infractions of their rules.

To some degree, ethical obligations for volunteers are the same as ethics in everyday life: to treat others with respect, to be honest, to refrain from doing harm, and so forth. But volunteers have some special standards that are different from the rules of everyday behavior. Findings from our case studies suggest that the ethical guidelines for volunteer behavior often mirror standards for professional workers.

The first vignette in the introduction to this chapter referred to volunteers in a small town where the "biggest problem is the violation of confidentiality" (see also Brudney, 1990b). Volunteers working in hospitals, police departments, or schools sometimes have to sign contracts stipulating that information will not be shared with others outside the organization. Particularly striking about the ethic of confidentiality is that it follows a professional or quasi-professional standard. Many professions—doctors, social workers, lawyers, therapists, and so forth—have confidentiality rules (and sometimes laws) governing client relations.

However, the confidentiality ethic is not necessarily a precept for everyday behavior. The small town volunteers who have a tendency to tell their neighbors about their clients and thereby break the rules of their organization are behaving in a way that is otherwise acceptable in daily interactions. It is common for friends and neighbors to share "news" about one another. Although in some situations friends are supposed to keep confidences, sharing information (gossip) is often useful. When someone is ill or has a personal problem, his or her neighbors and friends let others know about the situation and mobilize a network of helpers.

Another example of a quasi-professional standard concerns prohibitions against receiving gifts of any sort. The director of a Senior Companion Program reported:

> Something that we are constantly trying to get people to under-stand is that they can't accept any kind of gratuity, even to the point of Christmas cookies. This has really been an issue because lots of times the person who is receiving the services is so thankful for the things they've had done for them and they want to show their appreciation. But we tell the Senior Companions they must be very careful in not accepting anything because that is really one of the big taboos. In October we were talking to each of the volunteers, explaining to them that they can't do this. And someone asked, "What about the cookies that they baked?" and we said, "Well, as long as you eat them at the person's house or their apartment [it is okay], but you cannot take them with you."

Similarly the director of a hospital volunteer program said:

> Recently I heard a complaint from some staff in the hospital that a certain volunteer was accepting gifts from residents. Well, hospital staff are not supposed to accept gifts, and so they said that this vol-unteer isn't supposed to either. So I talked to the volunteer—that no one is supposed to accept gifts. . . . [The volunteer] wasn't very happy about this and didn't think she was being treated fairly. . . . Ac-tually I felt like this volunteer was being dumped on. What she was accepting was some clothing, and it wasn't a big deal. . . . She is coming here 4 days a week, and she is doing a lot of good work.

As the volunteer directors reported such incidents, they often seemed to have a note of uncertainty. On the one hand, they were confirming the existence of ethical standards for volunteer behavior. These ethics are virtually identical to professional standards. There is logic to these rules. The gift taboo is important, for example, because clients or patients should not be obliged to "bribe" their service providers. On the other hand, the volunteer directors were aware that the particular circumstances seemed trivial —being prohibited from accepting used clothing or taking home a box of cookies. Something does not seem quite right here, not only because these gifts are small but also because there is a counter-logic for allowing volunteers the freedom to accept such token gifts. To the extent that volunteers are like friends (or like neighbors) rather than quasi-professionals, such prohibitions impede their work. In friendship, people want to balance their exchanges. An elderly person receiving visits from a Senior Companion would naturally want to offer something to reciprocate for the help and to express his or her appreciation. It becomes awkward for everyone—the agency, the client, and the volunteer—that such token exchanges are "one of the big taboos."

We do not propose that volunteer organizations should ignore ethical standards for their volunteers. To the contrary, we believe that much more, not less, attention needs to be placed on all matters of ethics. Part of the dilemma, however, seems to arise from the definition of volunteers as quasi-workers and the insistence that the standards be essentially the same for volunteers and paid workers. We have argued that volunteers play a role different from that of paid employees. Volunteers can be more flexible and independent. Their role is often as intermediary between the client and the institution. *The standards for the behavior of volunteers should be based on diverse models—not just as quasi-professionals, but also as like-friends, like-neighbors, and sometimes even like-family.*

Volunteers as a Liability

The liability potential in working with volunteers is another thorny issue. Risks to volunteer organizations, to their clients, and to volunteers come in a number of forms. For example, a volunteer could have an automobile accident and injure or kill someone while on an assigned task. Both the volunteer and the agency might be sued. Or a frail, elderly person might fall and break a hip while being helped by a volunteer. Again it is possible that legal action could be taken against both the agency and the individual volunteer.

A survey of volunteer administrators attending a national conference on volunteerism found that the liability issue is their "foremost concern" (Kahn, 1985-1986). Out of about 400 volunteer administrators in the survey, 50 said their agency had been involved in some kind of legal action or lawsuit. In some ways the liability issue is a practical and utilitarian problem. Legal action can drain staff time and funds and, at worst, can destroy an organization if it is not properly insured.

But the liability problem is also an ethical concern in at least two ways. First, the fear of legal action provides a major rationale for limiting the activities of volunteers and may be a factor in antivolunteerist attitudes. Second, and in some ways even more important, *it is unconscionable for a supposedly humanistic organization to fail to protect its volunteers and / or its clients.* This appears to be a common failure, however. According to some reports, most volunteer organizations do not adequately protect either themselves or their volunteers (see Kieffer, 1986).

Our case studies also suggest that liability problems are commonplace, even in high-quality volunteer programs. These problems affect volunteering in both overt and subtle ways. We heard anecdotes about people who refused to work for a volunteer program because of liability risks. In one program, we were told, "occasionally a volunteer might say they don't want to take somebody to the doctor because of the liability insurance problems." In another program, a woman refused to take a position as a volunteer coordinator because "her husband was a prominent lawyer and because of their many assets they were afraid that somebody could go after their money. So she declined to take the position."

We found a number of examples of limiting what volunteers could and could not do, based on legal issues and/or insurance coverage. For example, volunteers working in a rehabilitation hospital program are "not allowed to lift residents, because they are not covered by our employee insurance." Or a paid staff is required to monitor carefully the work of volunteers because of the liability issue. In many of these situations, the responses of the agencies appear to be appropriately cautious. It seems reasonable, in providing health care services, for instance, to insist that volunteers are supervised by professional staff and also to place restrictions on what they can do, based on their skill level (see Barber & Scheier, 1979; Schiman & Lordeman. 1989). Occasionally the limitations of agencies or programs seem unreasonable, especially when government or other large bureaucracies place blanket restrictions on the use of volunteers (Kieffer, 1986, p. 68).

A far more serious issue is the lack of liability coverage for many volunteer programs. The stories we heard were worrisome.

> We worry a little about liability. We take kids out to a farm or to other outings, and we don't really have appropriate insurance. I don't know what would happen if there were an accident. . . I really don't know who is liable.

> We had one volunteer who wanted to put three children in a pickup truck with no seat belts, and I said, "You can't do that." I said it over and over, and I told it to the children as well. [But it was apparent that she could not enforce this.]

> People are not allowed to transport anyone officially for the program because of the high insurance rates. We simply can't afford to pay those rates. [Does this mean that people unofficially, without insurance, sometimes provide transportation?]

> In the beginning we did not do police checks on our volunteers, but now we're more careful, and we check records. . . . There was one incident of a problem of sexual molestation—concerning one person that was hired to work with the developmentally disabled. He was later dismissed from our program. But after that, something happened where this child came to his house and there was some incident of sexual molestation. The man was found guilty. But the program was not sued.

We are very concerned about liability issues. Could we be liable for abuse, neglect, or for a traffic accident? Who would be responsible? How can we protect ourselves? Our whole association is really struggling with this. Should we have background checks? Right now we get written letters of reference, but we don't do background checks. Even if we found out that somebody had previously been jailed and served time, we couldn't discriminate [because they get federal funds].

It seemed to us, as we reviewed our case studies, that a frightening number of near misses occur in programs for volunteers: accidents that might happen while children or adults are riding without belts and uninsured in the vehicles of volunteers, possibilities for matching vulnerable clients with volunteers who have serious emotional problems or criminal backgrounds, and a woeful lack of accountability concerning insurance coverage for either the organization or the volunteers. We are not saying, of course, that accidents or other problems are inevitable, but each year millions of hours are contributed in volunteer time. All this beneficence has a dark side: Given so many hours and the substantial gaps in liability protection, the odds are that problems will occur. And both volunteers and volunteer programs are seriously at risk.

Volunteer organizations often are run on shoestring budgets. Some federally funded programs have regulations and, to some extent, provisions for insurance. But for small, locally supported volunteer programs, it is not surprising that the cost for any kind of insurance seems prohibitive. Even so, for volunteer programs to disclaim their lack of adequate insurance coverage by saying that they "simply can't afford to pay those rates" is rather like the shoplifter who says he has to steal because of inflation. The lack of adequate liability coverage is an alarming ethical problem in volunteerism.

Summary of Key Themes

- Volunteerism is based on the ethic of community responsibility— that responsibility for the general good goes along with enjoying the benefits of being a member of society. The expectation is, however, that individual citizens choose if, when, how, or how much to help and volunteer.

- A volunteer has a distinctive position as a concerned citizen who is part of an organization and yet is also independent. Volunteers serve as intermediaries between clients (individuals or groups) and formal institutions. Their activities are flexible; often their responsibilities are defined as doing what paid workers do not do. They represent the community.

- Antivolunteerism includes systematically discounting the work of volunteers, resisting volunteer efforts, and/or denying decision-making authority to volunteers. Antivolunteerism also may be associated with ageism, sexism, and/or racism—that is, when certain volunteers experience a double discrimination based on their status characteristics, as well as their being "just" volunteers.

- Negative attitudes toward volunteers may occur for the following reasons: (a) Paid staff distrust the reliability of volunteers; (b) professional staff resent nonprofessionals, including volunteers, intruding onto their professional turf; and (c) paid workers fear that volunteers will take over their positions.

- Even when volunteer organizations have policies against the replacement of paid workers with volunteers, there are many gray areas. It is important for volunteer managers to have opportunities for discussing the ethics of volunteer placements, both within their agencies and at the meetings of professional associations.

- Volunteer work for retirees could be defined as "exploitation" (a) if any form of direct or implied coercion is used; (b) if older volunteers are treated as "cheap labor" (are given only menial tasks and/or are treated as if their time is expendable); and (c) when paying jobs are withheld from older persons, with the expectation that they should volunteer their time.

- Ethical standards for the behavior of volunteers need to be based on diverse models because volunteers function not only as quasi-professionals but also like friends or even family members.

- It appears to be commonplace for volunteer programs to have inadequate liability protection. With a lack of appropriate insurance coverage, volunteers, clients, and volunteer programs are all at risk. This situation is ethically troublesome.

NINE

Minority Elders as Volunteers

Shirley P. is a 68 year old Indian woman. She lives near a small town in northern Minnesota. There is a Community Center there and they have programs for seniors. She wishes she could join. But the people in the town won't accept Indians. (Fischer et al., 1989, p. 2)

▼

One of our senior volunteers called us about her mother, who was becoming so dependent, critical, and dogmatic. Basically the mother was depressed. She didn't have lots of skills, spoke very little English, and had little self-confidence. The daughter wanted us to find something for her to do. We were her only hope. So we asked the mother to be part of our telephone reassurance program. Here she could speak Spanish, and no one would think less of her. Now she has a sense of responsibility and good contacts.

Although in many ways older volunteers from racial and ethnic minority communities are similar to other older volunteers, there are also special factors and concerns. In this chapter we discuss the implications of cultural variations for volunteer programs. Because of the numerous ethnic groups, we cannot provide a prescription for any particular one. Instead we raise issues to consider when recruiting and working with an ethnically and culturally diverse volunteer pool.

In our case studies, we noticed that many volunteer organizations whose missions are humanitarian and ecumenical have virtually no minority volunteers, even though they are in cities with large minority populations. Conversely most of the minority volunteer organizations in our sample have very few, if any, nonminority volunteers. This discrepancy suggests that volunteer organizations are largely segregated. The opening story in this chapter offers one possible reason for segregation: Minority persons may feel excluded from programs available in the general community. A recent survey concerning the United Way of Minneapolis revealed that minority persons tend to perceive this organization as a "downtown, traditional, white-only fund raiser and fund distributor that does not involve communities affected by its decisions" (Franklin, 1992, p. A1). This prevalent feeling of mistrust is interesting because, in fact, 20% of the board of directors is minority, and 39% of the funds go to people of color.

Discrimination can be subtle. A study of a volunteer organization in England, for example, found that White applicants tend to be given a favorable response when they inquire about volunteer positions and to be offered interesting assignments, whereas Black volunteers are more likely to be discouraged either by being told no positions are available or by being given less interesting volunteer opportunities (Davis, 1984; Howitt & Owusi-Bempah, 1990). It seems that volunteer organizations need to examine not only their written policies but also their informal practices and unspoken, unintended messages.

Defining Minority Status

Minority group does not necessarily refer to numerical status. The term usually is used for groups or subgroups whose members have less control or power over their own lives than the members of a dominant group. *Lacking power* means lacking access to resources: money, material goods, political influence, education, health care, and so forth. Both the individuals and their communities feel the effects and develop adaptive behaviors. For people who have struggled at low-paying jobs with little or no pension plan, retirement may not be an option (Zsembik & Singer, 1990). Thus finding activities to fill the "extra time" provided by retirement is not always relevant. Moreover, minority communities often find that their needs are poorly met by the institutions of the general society and have developed parallel institutions. An *ethnic group* is a minority group that is distinctive because of either its national origin or its cultural patterns. The ethnic groups discussed here are those that have experienced very limited access to resources. A *racial group* is a group in which obvious physical characteristics set the people apart from others. Sorting out definitions of minorities, ethnicity, and race is no easy task and can fill volumes. Here *race* and *ethnicity* are used to describe minority groups.

One common experience of minority populations is discrimination. Beyond that, however, there is great diversity both among and within minority groups in their values, histories, and experiences. It is wrong to assume that African Americans or Native Americans or any other group speaks with a monolithic voice. There are, for instance, at least 266 Indian nations, tribes, bands, villages, pueblos, and groups in the United States. Also Mexican Americans consist of people who can trace their heritage to the Spanish conquistadors, while others have just recently arrived in the country. Diversity also is based on different regional backgrounds, differences in social class, and individual philosophical differences.

The Meaning of Volunteering
in Minority Communities

In Chapter 2 we discussed the different meanings of *volunteering*. Some definitions are broad and include both formal volunteering for organizations and informal help to family, friends, and neighbors. In many studies, however, the definition is narrow and includes only volunteering in formal organizations. This distinction is particularly important for estimating the amount of volunteering in minority communities. *Most minority populations in the U.S. have strong volunteer systems based on informal helping;* that is, the helping tradition is strong in these communities, but the helping arrangement is often informal. Dorothy Height, president of the National Council of Negro Women, asserts that the major type of volunteer activity in the Black community is informal (Height, Toya, Kamikawa, & Maldonado, 1981). A similar pattern is found in the Native American community. Pueblo villages, for instance, foster a philosophy of giving, sharing, and interdependence. Serving members of the community is the norm. Structured volunteer programs, such as Senior Companion and Foster Grandparent, that also serve the community are relatively new, but volunteering is not. All of the 18 Pacific Asian groups in the United States have some volunteer system based on family ties. In the Chinese community, for example, family associations or benevolent societies provide help to the needy of their community. A director of a Hispanic volunteer program in a Southwestern state commented: "Informal volunteering is how we are making it. That is how we survive as a community." *Any survey that does not count informal service will seriously undercount the volunteer activities among minority groups.*

Another aspect of the term *volunteering* involves the notion of responsibility. Some define *volunteering* as going beyond one's "basic obligation" (see Ellis & Noyes, 1990). Height pointed out that Black seniors do not necessarily categorize their helping activity as volunteer work, not only because the helping often is provided without agency or organizational links but also because they view their informal helping behavior as nothing special, as something that they do as members of their community. Helping is a responsibility or obligation of group membership (Height et al., 1981). It is likely, therefore, that people who define helping others as part of their basic responsibility would not count those activities as "volunteering" when responding to a survey.

An additional issue in definition concerns activities done through the church. Recent studies have identified the strong link between the church and volunteer work. In the 1960s and 1970s, religious volunteering was not counted in national volunteer surveys (see Smith, 1984). This exclusion resulted in a substantial undercounting of volunteerism, especially in minority populations. Moreover, even when church work is included in surveys on volunteerism, members of minority communities—who may view church work as a service to God and as part of their religious obligation—may not count their work as volunteering. The director

of a church volunteer program in the South said, during our interview, "Volunteerism here is really outreach ministry."

How Many Volunteers?

Very little research has been conducted on minority volunteering, and even less has been conducted on minority senior volunteerism. Most research that examines minority participation
focuses on the broader field of voluntary participation in work
and social groups, as well as voting activities, and may not even
measure formal volunteer activities. Some studies have examined the differences between White and Black volunteering, but
only a few have looked beyond that dichotomy to include Hispanic
Americans, Native Americans, and Asian Americans. There is little
consistency in the research to date. Table 9.1 shows the wide variation in survey findings.

Some studies, while finding that minorities are less likely to volunteer, also have reported that, among volunteers, certain minority
populations spend more time volunteering. The Independent Sector
survey of 1990, for example, found that, for those reporting both
giving and volunteering, Blacks give more hours per week than
Whites, and Hispanics spend even more time volunteering than
Blacks. Similar findings were reported in a study comparing volunteering among White and minority elderly in Minnesota (Chase,
1990).

In Chapter 2 we reported that people with higher incomes, more
education, and professional types of occupations are more likely
to volunteer for organizations than persons with lower socioeconomic status characteristics. Employed people are more likely to
volunteer than those who are unemployed. People in poor health
are less likely to volunteer than people in good health.

If social class is significant in the rate of volunteering, we already can see a possible reason for a lower rate of volunteering
among minority persons. Median household income for whites is
much higher than for Blacks or Hispanics. Mean school years is
lower for most minorities. For Whites the median schooling includes "some college." For Hispanics and Blacks it is less than

TABLE 9.1 Rates of Volunteering by Race/Ethnicity

Reference	White	Non-White	Black	Non-Black	Hispanic	Native American	Asian American
	Surveys based on general populations						
Hayghe, 1991	22%	—	12%	—	9%	—	—
Independent Sector, 1990[a]	57%	—	38%	—	36%	—	—
Independent Sector, 1988[a]	48%	—	28%	—	27%	—	—
Independent Sector, 1985[a]	49%	38%	—	—	—	—	—
Independent Sector, 1981[a]	54%	41%	—	—	—	—	—

Reference	White	Non-White	Black	Non-Black	Hispanic	Native American	Asian American
	Surveys based on older populations						
Marriott Seniors Volunteerism Study, 1991	42%	38%	—	—	—	—	—
Herzog & Morgan, in press	—	—	31%	36%	—	—	—
Chase, 1990[b]	60%	—	58%	—	36%	49%	15%
Chambre, 1987	26%	16%[c]	17%	—	13%	—	—

NOTE: a. Includes both formal and informal volunteering.
b. Based on Minnesota population 60 years and older.
c. Includes all other racial groups.

sophomore year of high school (*Statistical Abstract of the United States,* 1991).

In studies of voluntary participation, when social class is controlled for, Blacks actually are more likely to participate than whites (Antunes & Gaitz, 1975; Olsen, 1970; Williams, Babchuk, & Johnson, 1973). A study of minority elders in Minnesota found that more education is associated with higher rates of volunteering, regardless of race or ethnicity (Schaffer, 1992).

It is also possible, however, that cultural factors influence volunteering. Chambre (1987) found that socioeconomic status explains differences between Black and White rates of volunteering but does not entirely explain the differences in volunteering between Hispanics and other groups. In Minnesota, Native American elderly with very low incomes and very little education appear to have unexpectedly high rates of volunteering (Schaffer, 1992).

Poorer health also may help explain a lower rate of volunteering among minority elders. Many surveys have linked volunteering and good health. For minority persons a lifetime of reduced access to medical treatment and inadequate nutrition often undermines health in old age. Over 60% of the general population lives to age 65 or over, while only 33% of Native Americans can expect to reach age 65 (Block, 1979). According to a recent study of minority elders in Minnesota, the 60-year-old minority population, especially Native Americans and Southeast Asians, are more like the 85-year-olds and older in the general population in terms of their functional health (Chase, 1990).

If the rate of volunteering is actually lower among minority elders, it may be explained by differences in social class and levels of health. Of course, minority communities also have a middle class, so not all minority individuals are poor, sick, or old before their time.

In sum, our review suggests the following.

- Although minority elderly volunteers may report a somewhat lower level of formal volunteering, the amount of help given may be much greater than is indicated now in national surveys.
- Social class and health status may explain, to a considerable extent, differences in rates of volunteering between white and minority elderly.
- Volunteer directors should not throw up their hands when reading survey reports on lower volunteer participation among minorities but should look beyond the surface statistics.
- The communities of minority elderly potentially are an important pool from which to draw.

Voluntary Ethnic Organizations and Churches

Two types of volunteer programs stand out in minority communities: voluntary ethnic organizations, sometimes called self-help groups,[13] and churches. Voluntary ethnic organizations provide services to members of the communities in myriad ways. They feed and clothe the poor, tend the sick, care for both young and old, and even bury the dead (Height, 1989). Their services range from education to social welfare and can include employment referral services, parenting-skills development, education centers, clothing distribution centers, and food shelves. Ethnic organizations frequently have had to contend with governmental bureaucracies in their efforts to bring about changes. The Wyoming Indian Education Association, for example, fought various levels of government to finally establish the Wyoming Indian High School (O'Connell & O'Connell, 1989). Various forms of mutual aid societies, voluntary associations, community self-help organizations, and *mutualistas* also have been an integral part of Latino life in the United States for more than 100 years and have provided health insurance, death benefits, and other services for new immigrants and displaced persons (Cortes, 1989; Pardo, 1990).

Earlier in the book (see Chapter 4) we discussed the importance of religion in volunteering, especially for the older population. Churches and temples serve as the center for charity in most of the ethnic populations. In the Black community, the church is truly the mother of philanthropy. Because it is independent and autonomously controlled by the Black community, the church has been able to support critical programs and has helped develop an environment in which other Black voluntary ethnic groups are able to develop. The Black church offers not only spiritual guidance but also social service and political direction. Church volunteers provide help to senior citizens, troubled families, children, the sick, and so forth. These services can include distributing food and clothing, giving music lessons, operating free medical clinics, or staffing a legal clinic. Services from ethnic community churches, however, are neither exclusively for congregation members nor performed in isolation. Often the churches are part of a broad network, including local, state, and federal government services. Governmental agencies often refer people to the churches for services that other agencies do not provide. Sometimes the churches operate programs supported through government grants or contracts (see Carson, 1990b).

For other ethnic minorities, the church or temple also plays an important, although somewhat different, role. In the Hispanic communities the Roman Catholic Church, as well as other religious organizations such as the Presbyterian and Methodist churches and the Church of Latter Day Saints, serve not only as a place to volunteer but also as a place to learn of other volunteer activities (Independent Sector, 1990; Maldonado, n. d.). Japanese American elderly often meet other elderly in their temples and religious organizations, where they perform work for the temple and the worshippers. Traditionally, elderly Buddhists in Cambodia had similar ties to their temples, and leaders of Cambodian refugee communities hope to reestablish the temple involvement for their elders in the United States (Kalab, 1990).

Voluntary ethnic organizations and ethnic churches are major participants in the volunteer sector, both providing needed services and acting as a center for volunteers. When other nonminority volunteer organizations seek to attract volunteers from minority communities, they may find themselves competing with these community programs. Carson (1990b) reported that the majority of Blacks at all socioeconomic levels give most of their time to organizations either run by Blacks or primarily serving Blacks. Similarly in Hispanic communities, lower income persons tend to be involved heavily with voluntary ethnic service agencies (Hutcheson & Dominquez, 1986).

The Case Studies

Our case studies included 10 volunteer organizations whose mission or goals are directed at serving primarily, if not exclusively, minority populations and in which a majority of the volunteers are minority group members. Five organizations are classified as Black organizations, two are Asian American, two are Hispanic, and one is Native American. Two organizations are church programs; the other eight are community based. Two are rural; eight are urban.

These organizations often serve many subgroups in their communities: youth and elderly, and also poor people who are nonminority. The director of one church organization in the South said that the most common job was working person-to-person with seniors or youth, but, he added, they also serve the homeless and provide access to food shelves regardless of people's color.

It appears that minority communities have many pressing needs that are not dealt with effectively by outside organizations. Sometimes outside agencies have no one to speak the language; sometimes the general organizations simply do not provide critical services. Whatever the reason, minority organizations recognize that their mission is to meet needs that no one else would or could. The director of one organization stated the issue well when she said:

> We are the only Hispanic program in the whole city. We are bilingual. People can call us when they are overwhelmed by the other agencies who are supposed to help them. A lot of our seniors do not understand computers and calculators and other technology. More and more agencies are going to the phone system that asks the caller to push a certain number to get the information. This is a real problem. First of all, Hispanics may not understand what to do because of the language. Second, many of them are living in places that don't have a touch tone phone, and so they get so overwhelmed that they call us in tears. They want someone who is sensitive and warm and friendly and who understands them.

> Mainly what we do is to provide transportation to elderly. We get them to the doctor, or to the drugstore, or to the grocery store for food—that kind of thing. And that is what is distinctive about us. We are filling a great need! Transportation is critical for these people, and we are one of the few places that is doing that.

Compared to the nonminority organizations in our case studies, the minority organizations in our case studies are much more likely to have volunteers with very low incomes and with little formal education (many have not even completed eighth grade). The vast majority of volunteers for these organizations are women. If the status of an organization is determined in large part by the status of its volunteers, these minority organizations probably should be considered "low status" groups.

In almost all of these minority organizations, a large number of clients are served by a relatively small number of volunteers. For example, one nationally affiliated organization in a Midwestern city has only 3 volunteers serving 800 clients; another has 15 volunteers serving 2,500 people. The minority volunteer programs are twice as likely as the nonminority programs to have fewer than 50 volunteers. And the minority organizations are twice as likely to serve more than 400 clients. Most minority organizations in our case studies have a very small paid staff. The organizations in our case studies were established 15 to 55 years ago. Thus these groups have been operating for some time. The small number of staff and volunteers is not due to their just getting started.

One organization in the Southwest was looking frantically for an executive director with previous volunteer experience, who was bilingual, and who had grant writing experience. Yet this had to be a volunteer position because no money was available for a salary.

All of the minority organizations listed money as one of their greatest problems. One director of a program in the Southwest illustrates the point well:

> We deliver meals to people and take them all over the area. We put over 120 miles on the van per day, and it's old. Constantly I worry about the van breaking down in the middle of the summer in the desert. Remember, these are seniors driving that van, as well as seniors who we serve. The van has already broken down on an isolated road, but we were lucky that time—it was winter, and someone came by soon. We have two solutions. Either someone wins the lottery or I fight and lobby for more funds for a new van.

The funding problems are not likely to be solved easily. Minority programs in our case studies are twice as likely as the nonminority organizations to receive government funding, yet they are still overstretched. Moreover, these organizations tend to receive less corporate and private support. To increase funding, volunteer organizations must have staff who can apply for grants and devote time to other forms of fund-raising (see Galaskiewicz, 1990). These organizations already appear to have staff and volunteers stretched very thin.

The picture that emerges is one in which *the needs are very great and the organizations are very small.* It appears that the staff and volunteers in these programs all are working very hard to bring assistance to as many people as they can.

Over and over again, directors and leaders of these groups said they prefer to keep their organizations informal and flexible. It seems that service is more important than administration, so anything that is seen as complicating the process appears to be left out. None of the volunteer organizations in our case studies require a minimum time commitment. These organizations do not have volunteer contracts, job descriptions, or formal reviews. Flexibility and creativity are highly valued. All of the directors we interviewed indicated that formal procedures seem to discourage participation.

Ironically these organizations were developed to meet the needs of populations that were underserved by other programs. But they continue to operate only if they comply with regulations established by the nonminority community. Public money requires compliance with regulations. Although voluntary ethnic organizations value flexibility and informality, they are bound by the restrictions of their funding source. One director spoke of her organization's dilemma:

> We provide essential transportation to older people in our community. Our funds come from the government and are restricted to transportation for medical purposes. Transportation of any kind around here is a real serious problem. Sometimes one of our clients needs a ride to a shopping center for vitamins or nonmedical things. Occasionally we stretch to take them because the trip helps their mental outlook. We can't do this very often, but sometimes we just can't be so narrow.

In brief, the findings about minority organizations suggest the following.

- Minority volunteer organizations are meeting needs that other organizations are unable to address.
- Strong helping networks exist in minority communities, but the demand for services is greater than the available resources.
- Many organizations are performing "miracles" with few personnel and even less money.

- Volunteer record keeping and policies such as job descriptions are kept informal.
- Flexibility is highly valued but often is compromised due to funding regulations.

Understanding Older Minority Volunteers

When volunteers of any background join a program, they come to it rich with life experiences. Successful volunteer directors tap into these experiences and adapt their programs to use fully the talents and skills of individual volunteers. It is not uncommon, however, for volunteer directors to be unfamiliar with the backgrounds and experiences of minority volunteers. In recruiting and working with minority elderly as volunteers, volunteer professionals need to be sensitive to the following issues:

The history and experience of various cultural groups
Culture and language that affect communications
The resources of subpopulations of minority elderly

Although the following discussion focuses on issues and concerns of racial/ethnic groups, it is not meant as a description of how all people of a certain ethnicity behave or think. All White Anglo-Saxons do not act in the same way, nor do all Hispanics, Native Americans, Asian Americans, or African Americans. Even when certain behaviors are part of the Hispanic culture, for example, not all individual Hispanics follow those patterns. Nor, for that matter, are such cultural traits found only in the Hispanic culture.

History. Each minority group has unique histories and experiences that continue to influence its economic resources, health, social status, attitudes, and values. In attempting to build a broad, ethnically and culturally inclusive volunteer cadre, volunteer directors need to understand the various backgrounds of the people they wish to enlist.

The diversity of the American population represents great contrasts in where people came from and how they came here. Some of our people were here long before European explorers came. Others were brought here in bondage. Several groups came seeking new opportunities. Many fled from their homelands because of persecution or political upheaval.

For example, today's Black elders were born prior to the Depression and at the peak of the migration from the South to the North. They are the great-grandchildren of former slaves and have experienced discrimination and racism throughout their lives (Harel, McKinney, & Williams, 1990). They grew up and came of age before the end of legal segregation and the start of equal employment and educational opportunities. Consequently older Blacks, compared to older Whites, have lower Social Security benefits, less access to and lower private pension plans, and greater incidence of illness and disability (Atchley, 1988). Thus they may have fewer resources.

Native American elderly face a somewhat different situation from Blacks, due largely to their isolation on reservations for more than 100 years. Today not all Native Americans are on reservations. Four distinct Indian populations are in the United States: reservations Indians, rural Indians, migrant Indians, and urban Indians (Block, 1979). Yet they all have experienced fluctuating government policies that ranged from neglect to near total control of Indian lives, from separatism to expected conformity. Their life histories often included removal from their families and forced assimilation in boarding schools. When these young people came back to their families, they suffered from lack of identities—being neither really White nor completely Native American. Recruiting older American Indians requires sensitivity to such historical issues.

The Asian Americans are extremely diverse, ranging from the Chinese to the Pacific Islanders to Southeast Asians, as well as Indians and Pakistanis. We would need to be very cautious in making any general statements about such historically and culturally diverse groups. Those people who immigrated prior to 1924, during a period of restrictions against Asians, tend to have occupational, educational, and family backgrounds different from those who came later. Many of the elderly still speak their native languages. These individuals usually came by themselves, often with the intent of returning to their homelands. The recent immigrants from Southeast Asia are notably different in that they often fled with their families or tried to bring their families over soon after they arrived. Among the new immigrants are many war refugees who are still grieving the loss of loved ones and homeland.

Elderly Korean immigrants have strong ties with other Koreans but also tend to have positive attitudes toward Whites generally. In contrast, second-generation Japanese elderly often view White Americans much less favorably (Kurzeja, Koh, Koh, & Liu, 1986). The histories of these two populations are rather different both in their reasons for leaving their homelands and their treatment by the American government. Many Koreans fled political upheaval in their country and have enjoyed relative freedom in the United States. Japanese Americans are likely to be more sensitive to anti-Asian sentiment. Many Japanese who are currently elderly were forced to live in internment camps during World War II.

Many diverse groups compose what is called the "Hispanic" population. Primarily, but not exclusively, these are Cubans, Puerto Ricans, and Mexican Americans. Even among the Mexican Americans there is great diversity. Some trace their heritage to the Spanish conquistadors in California; others are recent arrivals from Mexico. Each of the groups came for different reasons and became part of the American population by different means. These differences shape their attitudes, values, and experiences.

Culture and Language. A major consideration in recruiting minority older volunteers is understanding their languages and cultures. Unless the atmosphere is comfortable and the language appropriate, the best recruitment campaign will fail. One director from a Hispanic senior volunteer program in the Southwest said:

> We need to feel comfortable where we volunteer. Our people need to have someone of their own they can really talk to—not only speaking their language, but who can speak their culture and their life. The atmosphere must be very welcoming. Even when I go to the

senior center in the next town, one run by Anglos, I feel unwelcome. There is just a physical feeling that I get that sets me apart.

Often cultural factors can be subtle. For example, there are cultural differences in how much spatial closeness is appropriate. Many Hispanic people tend to feel comfortable when physically close to people with whom they are interacting. It is important to understand the differences because these may affect the emotional reaction of individuals in a given situation. Sometimes a Hispanic may find non-Hispanics to be cold and distant because of their preference for more physical distance. Another Hispanic cultural ideal is *simpatia*—an emphasis on behaviors that promote smooth and pleasant social relationships. Avoidance of confrontation is part of this pattern (Marin & Van Oss-Marin, 1991). In social interactions, then, some Hispanics may go to great lengths to avoid conflict by agreeing to do something they do not want to do or by not voicing complaints. A volunteer director seeking feedback may not get an honest appraisal but, instead, get a culturally acceptable response.

Some anthropologists suggest that to understand the values of people from China, Japan, Korea, and Vietnam, it is necessary to look at Confucian values (Berling, 1988; Ching, 1986; Lee, 1989). A central theme of Confucianism is the quest for *sagehood,* which involves service to others and/or commitment to public service. Confucian values stress responsibility in social relationships, equity among people, and a regard for the inherent goodness of human nature.

It is difficult to generalize cultural values across the great diversity of Native American people, but some basic concepts are shared by most tribal groups. Extended family relationships and kinship obligations are among the most important factors in Native American lives. Moreover, a key to social relationships is *reciprocity*—that is, an exchange of goods and services according to carefully prescribed norms (Kidwell, 1989). Anthropologists have reported that on the Plains, the tribal chief was generally the poorest man in the village because he assumed the responsibility of providing for the needs of all members of the community who could not provide for themselves, especially widows and orphans who had no male relatives to hunt for them (Weitzner, 1979).

Another relevant American Indian custom is the *give-away*, which is best illustrated by the potlatch of the Northwest Coast. In potlatch ceremonies the host—an individual or group—gained status by giving away material possessions (Rosman & Rubel, 1971). In these communities, then, status depended on accumulating property not to hold, but to give away.

A further consideration in recruiting and working with older minority volunteers is to understand the position of the elder in the community. Many of the communities hold the elderly in high esteem. Age has certain privileges and statuses. For example, the director of a Native American organization commented on the great value placed on elders in her community:

> Yes, we have many senior volunteers here. Their job is just to be here, to be available for young people to see and sometimes to talk to. They show the importance of survival. Our most distinctive part of the program is the value we have for the knowledge of the seniors. It is very important to have them here.

To this organization, seniors are "volunteers" if they are there because their very presence is a valued act. We should be cautious, however, about romanticizing the status of elders in Native American or other ethnic communities. Studies have found, for example, that Native American elders often seem to be concerned about a lack of community support or traditional respect (see Manson & Pambrum, 1979).

Language is also an important consideration. Many of the older ethnic group members still speak primarily in their native languages. For example, only 1% of the foreign-born Chinese and Japanese elderly speak English (Kii, 1982). A very important feature of the Hispanics is that they have retained their native language, especially the elderly. Preserving language helps preserve a cultural identity, but it also sometimes prevents access to services (Torres-Gil, 1982).

Resources. Volunteering incurs costs. The likelihood of volunteering may depend in part on how individuals can spend their resources and how great the costs are to them. The costs of volunteering may not matter much to middle-class volunteers, whether they are minority or nonminority persons. But large percentages of minority elderly have been poor for most of their lives (see Farley, 1988). Transportation is also a problem for many minority elderly. Minority elderly are far more likely than other older persons to be unable to go places because they lack transportation. They cannot afford their own cars, and/or they do not drive. A lack of transportation often means being isolated from social activities. Older people who do not drive are much less likely to volunteer (Chase, 1990; Fischer et al., 1989, 1991).

Recruiting and Retaining Older Volunteers

In asking minority volunteers to help, volunteer directors must let them know that their work is needed and valued and will contribute to the goals and mission of the organization (Tomeh, 1981). It appears that too often minority volunteers feel as if they are being asked for window dressing rather than wanted for themselves. A volunteer director voiced the issue this way: "People really need to think over the question of why you want minority volunteers, because unless that can be specifically answered and in a positive way, with commitment to the minority volunteer, then they will have no success in recruiting Hispanics to Anglo organizations."

Churches are an important organization in soliciting volunteer help. More than two thirds of all requests to volunteer for Hispanics and Blacks come through organizational ties, including churches, schools, work, and other organizations (Carson, 1990a; Independent Sector, 1990). Successful recruitment appears, then, to require tapping into these organizational ties.

Recruiting volunteers from racial/ethnic communities demands that we pay attention to issues that shaped the people we are trying to involve (see Morrow-Howell, Lott, & Ozawa, 1990). Because of past experiences, minority persons often are wary of mainstream organizations. Volunteer programs need to do more than establish policies of inclusion. To involve a group of people who speak little or no English, for example, requires going beyond having bilingual job descriptions and training manuals. It also may require having bilingual staff and clients who can converse on more than just a surface level. Staff at one organization we interviewed wanted to include more Hispanics. They had gone as far as to translate all written material into Spanish and actually had recruited a few Spanish-speaking volunteers. However, the new recruits were placed in positions with only English-speaking staff, clients, and other volunteers. The recruits did not stay with the organization long. They did not have anyone with whom to socialize and to exchange friendly conversation. Socializing is an important benefit often associated with volunteering, and the Spanish-speaking volunteers were unable to achieve this. Some research suggests a strong relationship between minority staffing in an organization and the levels of minority participation (Cunningham, 1991).

Volunteer directors also may need to consider possible ways to attract elderly individuals who do not find retirement an economic option. Perhaps more material incentives need to be offered that actually help the volunteers' personal situations. One hospital volunteer program whose volunteers were quite poor provided a hot meal for them each day that they came in. The director felt that this benefit was a key to both recruiting new volunteers, as well as retaining them. She added that the meal was never considered to be a handout, which would have offended the volunteers, but rather an earned reward for help given.

Summary of Key Themes

- Minority volunteers contribute large amounts of time and energy to solve problems in their communities but often may not call their efforts "volunteering."
- Who volunteers may depend in part on social class rather than on race and ethnicity alone. However, cultural variations are also important.

- Churches and ethnic volunteer organizations are key service providers in minority communities.

- Minority volunteer organizations are stretched very thin both in personnel and in dollars and tend to operate fairly informally.

- In recruiting and working with older minority volunteers, the following factors must be considered: history and life experiences, culture and language, and access to resources.

TEN

The Benefits to Older Volunteers

A new program in a small, Southern town matches older volunteers with children from poor and troubled families. A volunteer from this program says: "I get out more. I have lost weight. I have played games and rode a bicycle since I started visiting Wesley, and I had not done much outside for a long time until me and Wesley started visiting each other. We take walks, play ball, ride bicycles, swim and go fishing. We also go out to eat a lot. Wesley is a wonderful friend. . . . think [this program] is what every child and old person needs. It gets your time clock started again. I think it gives new meaning to my life, also to Wesley." (Landmann, 1991, p. 14)

What do people "get" from their commitment to helping others and volunteering? Are volunteers healthier and more likely to live longer than people who do not volunteer? Are they happier with their lives? Do older volunteers have more friends? Are tangible or intangible rewards more important for older volunteers?

The Benefits of Productive Aging

The potential benefits from volunteering may be especially important for older persons. Old age brings a number of hazards: an accumulation of chronic conditions (ranging from heart disease to impaired vision and hearing), a special vulnerability to acute illnesses, a steeply rising risk of dying, and inevitable experiences of loss as spouses, siblings, friends, and other peers die. Some research suggests that people are healthier and happier in old age if they remain socially involved and participate in "productive" and meaningful activities. Orenstein and Sobel (1987), for example, in *The Healing Brain,* tried to show that social contacts help maintain health. Similarly Butler and Gleason (1985), in their book *Productive Aging,* argued that the unproductive person is at a higher risk for illness and dependency (see also Baldassare, Rosenfeld, & Rook, 1984; Berkman & Symes, 1979; Chambre, 1987; Hooker & Ventis, 1984; House, Landis, & Umberson, 1988; Okun, Stock, Haring, & Witter, 1984).

Volunteer work brings opportunities for both social involvement and productive activities. These are essential parts of volunteerism. We should expect, then, that the benefits of volunteering might be especially important in the later years of life.

The Problem of Cause and Effect

Do volunteers become or stay healthier because they volunteer, or are healthy people more likely to volunteer? Does life satisfaction increase because people volunteer, or are those with higher life satisfaction just more inclined to volunteer? Although some research indicates associations between volunteering and good health, greater life satisfaction, better friendships, and so forth, *causality is extremely difficult to prove.* Disentangling whether volunteering actually causes these conditions or whether volunteers start out with these "benefits" is like trying to pull apart a Gordian knot (see Chambre, 1987; Okun, Stock, Haring, & Witter, 1984; Rushton, 1984).

It is difficult to prove that volunteering enhances health and happiness, in part, because *the possible benefits are largely indirect.* If volunteering were to make people less prone to diseases such as heart disease and cancer, *the potential benefit would not occur until years after the volunteer experience.* Moveover, there are many mediating factors, such as personality, other health-related activities, genetic disposition, exposure to health risks, general long-term health, and so forth.

Volunteer professionals often seem eager to prove that volunteering makes people happier and healthier. To demonstrate such effects, we would need carefully designed research. However, *it may be risky to link volunteer work to such indirect and extrinsic benefits and rewards.* If we had research confirming an association between volunteering and good health, it is nonetheless likely that exercise and diet would have more directly beneficial effects on health. Potential older volunteers might logically conclude that exercising and watching their diets would be more effective in sustaining their health than doing volunteer work. Conversely, if valid research were to show conclusively that volunteering does not make people healthier and/or happier, what inferences should be drawn—that people should not volunteer?

What Are the Benefits?

As Table 10.1 shows, a number of studies have linked volunteering with better health, improved life satisfaction, and increased social ties. Other studies, however, have failed to demonstrate such effects from volunteering. Taken together, *the research on the benefits to volunteers is inconclusive.*

Health Benefits. As Table 10.1 shows, a number of studies have suggested that volunteering is associated with better health. For example, an evaluation of a Foster Grandparent Program compared Foster Grandparent volunteers with potential volunteers—that is, older persons on a waiting list to participate in the program—and found that after 3 years, the volunteers indicated better health than those on the waiting list and were less likely to have died (Litigation Support Services, 1984). Allan Luks with Peggy Payne (1991), in *The Healing Power of Doing Good,* reported that volunteers who experience a "helper's high" perceive their health as far better than the health of other people their age (Luks with Payne, 1991, pp. 81-82; see also Fogelman, 1981; Hulbert & Chase, 1991; Lackner & Koeck, 1980; Newman, Vasudev, & Baum, 1983).

However, not all studies agree. A carefully designed longitudinal study of Foster Grandparent volunteers compared with control groups found no correlation between better health and volunteer activity (Tobis et al., 1991). Similarly Lee and Markides (1990) also reported no correlation between mortality and an active lifestyle (see also Kornblum, 1981). Some research even indicates that

TABLE 10.1 How Do Volunteers Benefit From Volunteering?

Type of benefit	*Finding*	*References*
Health benefits		
Physical health	Volunteers are better off physically than non-volunteers.	Litigation Support Services, 1984 Fogelman, 1981 Lackner & Koeck, 1980 Luks with Payne, 1991 Newman, Vasudev, & Baum, 1983
	No correlation was found between health and volunteering in a well-controlled longitudinal study.	Tobis et al., 1991
	Volunteers were healthier than nonvolunteers to begin with. There is no effect on health from volunteering.	Kornblum, 1981
Functional health	Volunteers either maintained or improved physical functioning during their time as volunteers.	Litigation Support Services, 1984
Mortality	The study found lower mortality for volunteers.	Litigation Support Services, 1984
	Increased activity does not decrease mortality.	Lee & Markides, 1990
Psychological benefits		
Life satisfaction	Volunteers have higher life satisfaction.	Litigation Support Services, 1984 Gray & Kastler, 1970 Hulbert & Chase, 1991 Hunter & Linn, 1980-1981 Lackner & Koeck, 1980
	No difference in life satisfaction was found between volunteers and nonvolunteers.	Newman, Vasudev, & Baum, 1983 Kornblum, 1981
	Volunteers had lower morale than participants in recreational groups.	Mellinger & Holt, 1982
Self-esteem	Volunteers have higher self-esteem.	Luks with Payne, 1991
Social benefits		
Friendship	Volunteers are less lonely, and they increase friendship through volunteering Volunteers anticipate meeting new friends	Litigation Support Services, 1984 Hulbert & Chase, 1991 Fogelman, 1981 Gidron, 1978

TABLE 10.1 Continued

Type of benefit	Finding	References
	through the volunteer experience.	
	Volunteers and non-volunteers were no different in loneliness or friendship.	Kornblum, 1981 Mellinger & Holt, 1982
Social resources	Volunteers gain more social skills, new roles, and better social resources.	Litigation Support Services, 1984 Payne, 1977 Newman, Vasudev, & Baum, 1983 Seville, 1985

Implications of research findings
- Some studies suggest that volunteering has beneficial effects on physical and emotional health. However, the research evidence is inconclusive.
- If volunteers perceive a change in their physical health or mental outlook, perhaps these perceptions are important in themselves.
- Recruiting volunteers based on the physical, psychological, or social benefits they will receive can be a problem because such benefits are difficult to document.

helping others might be detrimental to health. In one study patients with AIDS responded to a survey about their impulses to help others. Those who said they would do a favor for a friend "even though they didn't feel like it" actually died sooner than other patients (Solomon, Temoshok, O'Leary, & Zick, 1987, cited in Wuthnow, 1991).

Psychological Benefits. Some research, especially studies focusing on older adults, suggests that volunteers are more satisfied with their lives than nonvolunteers. Gray and Kasteler (1970), for example, found that after 1 year of work as Foster Grandparents, older volunteers were better adjusted and more satisfied with their lives than a comparable group of older persons who were not involved in the program. Another study compared volunteers and nonvolunteers who were age 65 and over and reported that volunteers had a significantly higher degree of life satisfaction, a stronger will to live, and fewer symptoms of depression, anxiety, and somatization (Hunter & Lin, 1980-1981; see also Hulbert & Chase, 1991; Lackner & Koeck, 1980; Litigation Support Services, 1984). Luks (with Payne, 1991), on the basis of his survey of volunteers, reported that the helper's high brings a heightened sense of emotional well-being, optimism, and self-worth.

But this research is also contradictory. Some research has noted no differences in life satisfaction between volunteers and nonvolunteers (Kornblum, 1981; Newman et al., 1983). One study found that older volunteers have somewhat lower morale than older participants in recreational groups (Mellinger & Holt, 1982). More commonly, much research supports the concept of continuity in personality. A longitudinal study that followed people over several decades concluded that people who are optimistic and satisfied with their lives are more likely to be active at all stages of their lives (Mussen, Honzik, & Eichorn, 1982). If volunteers are found to be happier than nonvolunteers, then the most reasonable explanation seems to be that happier and more optimistic people are more active in general and therefore are more likely to volunteer (see Chambre, 1987; Edwards & Klemmack, 1973; Lawton, 1977; McClelland, 1982; Midlarsky, 1990; Newman et al., 1983; Wuthnow, 1991).

Social Benefits. A number of studies on older volunteers have documented the social benefits from volunteering—that volunteers (compared to nonvolunteers) are less lonely, are more satisfied with their friendships, develop better social resources, and have more "structure" in their postretirement lives (Fogelman, 1981; Gidron, 1978; Hulbert & Chase, 1991; Litigation Support Services, 1984; Newman et al., 1983; Payne, 1977; Seville, 1985; Smith, 1985).

Even so, the importance of these social benefits for older volunteers is not entirely clear. A study of RSVP volunteers found that volunteering did not necessarily lead to more friendships (Kornblum, 1981). Most older volunteers, according to many studies, are interested primarily in providing "useful services" rather than in making friends through their volunteer work (Mellinger & Holt, 1982; see also Chapter 4). Furthermore, to expect that lonely elderly will be the ones to volunteer may be unrealistic. It would seem far more likely for an older person with a wealth of other social opportunities to volunteer than someone who is isolated and really needs the social contacts (see Chapters 4, 5, and 6).

Tangible Versus Intangible Rewards

Some kinds of volunteering have tangible benefits that have a material and/or monetary value. Volunteers can receive perks such as free meals, special parking passes, free admission for places or events, or even free trips. The director of one nationally affiliated volunteer program commented: "There's going to be a training session coming up in Hawaii. We'll send one of our very best people out as a reward for all of the good work this person has done."

Symbolic perks also are offered by volunteer programs, including recognition dinners, ceremonies, and plaques. Catalogues are available that offer nonprofits a variety of items with which to honor their volunteers. How important are recognition events and symbolic perks? Some studies have found that *volunteers rate banquets, letters of appreciation, pins, or other awards as much less important than the intrinsic rewards of volunteering* (Brown, 1991; Gidron, 1978).

In our case studies, we observed that having substantial, tangible rewards can sometimes create problems. When certain individuals are selected for special attention and material benefits (such as the White House Thousand Points of Light Awards), other people in these organizations are often jealous. Morale may plummet, at least temporarily. Thus there appears to be some danger in giving prominence to awards and prizes—that these material compensations may diminish the importance and value of the intangible benefits from volunteering (see Organ, 1988).

Much of the research in volunteerism, perhaps especially on older volunteers, suggests that the most critical benefits are intangible. Earlier in this book we noted that most volunteers describe their motives in terms of a desire to help and to be useful (see Chapter 4). Such motivations suggest intangible, or "spiritual," benefits from helping and volunteering, including a feeling of fulfillment because someone else is benefiting, a sense of connectedness to others, and a sense of meaning and purpose.

In our case studies of 57 volunteer programs, we asked volunteer coordinators and directors what they thought were the benefits to volunteers from participation in their programs. Only three of the volunteer directors mentioned good health as a benefit. Conversely *the vast majority of these directors, when asked about benefits, spoke about volunteers being rewarded by having an impact, making a contribution, and feeling useful.*

The main thing [benefit] was this very good feeling, this sense that we had done a job very successfully, had done it in record time, and done it quite well. It's a feeling of accomplishment.

All of the volunteers say that one of the biggest benefits for them is a very strong sense of civic responsibility and satisfaction. They are really doing something vital for the community and are really contributing.

They have activities that are meaningful for them. As one senior put it, "It's not just stringing beads at a senior center."

A lot of people, when they retire, feel lost, and this [volunteer work] is really important—to be able to make a contribution. There is a lot of satisfaction from visitors [to the museum]—a kind of immediate feedback, sharing information; eyes light up when people discover something; being able to reach out to visitors. A lot of the volunteers just say "I'll go where I am most needed."

The term *generativity*, borrowed from Erik Erikson's theory of life span development, seems to express the essence of these statements about the benefits from volunteering. *Generativity* refers to the human need to be productive and creative, to have meaning in one's life, and to be connected to others across generations. If an individual does not have meaning and a sense of connection with others, his or her life may seem empty and purposeless. Without this sense of purpose, Erikson said, adults will have a "pervading sense of stagnation and personal impoverishment" (Erikson, 1963, p. 267).

The need for generativity becomes increasingly important as we grow older. Erikson noted that in later stages of life we become aware of our own mortality. The great fact of our lives is that we die. When we are young, we deny, ignore, and disbelieve our own mortality. When we are old, we struggle to find meaning in our lives as we confront the fact of death (Erikson, Erikson, & Kivnick, 1986).

Summary of Key Themes

- The potential benefits from volunteering—that is, opportunities for productive and meaningful activities—may be especially important in adapting to the changing physical, mental, and social conditions of later life.

- Although some research indicates associations between volunteering and good health, greater life satisfaction, more friendships, and so forth, it is very difficult to prove whether volunteering actually causes these benefits or whether people who volunteer are more likely to have these characteristics.

- It appears that an important, direct benefit from volunteering is generativity: a feeling of fulfillment because someone else is benefitting, a sense of connectedness to others, and a sense of meaning and purpose. According to Erik Erikson's theory of human development, generativity becomes increasingly important in later life.

Part IV

Conclusions and Implications

ELEVEN

Thinking Strategically About Older Volunteers

Imagine a force—like an army. It is made up of millions of people, but many are in the reserves, not on active duty. And millions of others have not been recruited yet for this all-volunteer force. It is a force that already has won battles—small, personal, important battles. But what are the limits of its powers? If this force were truly mobilized, what could or would it do? No one really knows yet.

Sometimes politicians seem to view older Americans as a powerful force because their rate of voting is much higher than for younger people. Older Americans also are part of a volunteer force. In increasing numbers they offer their time and talents to help others in their communities for a myriad of causes. They are not the only volunteers, by any means. Even so, in a number of ways, older people constitute a special force for volunteerism.

The large and growing population of older persons is in a key position to volunteer. The older population is the most rapidly growing segment of our society. Moreover, older people today have more resources than previous generations: They are healthier into older ages, more educated, and less likely to be very poor. Older people have time for activities like volunteering; they have an accumulation of abilities, skills, and experiences to offer; and many have a driving need for meaningful and productive endeavors.

In fact, large numbers of retirees already are volunteering; they constitute a sizable volunteer "force" that contributes billions of hours in services every year. They do all sorts of work—helping children at risk, caring for frail elderly, serving on boards, working as docents, building homes for poor families, and so forth. In American society the needs for the services of volunteers seem more critical than ever. Burgeoning numbers of youth are at risk—

young people whose schools and neighborhoods are dominated by crime, drugs, lethal weapons, and armed gangs and who, in large numbers, have babies for whom they are not mature enough to care. The gap between rich and poor has widened. Increasing numbers of children are living in poverty. The numbers of homeless people, including homeless families with young children, are rising. Also more and more elderly are at risk; they become increasingly frail and poor and outlive their spouses, their friends, and even their children. At the same time, there are economic pressures on younger persons, who, living in two-earner or single-parent families, may have little discretionary time for such activities as volunteering.

In recent years many successful volunteer programs have recruited older volunteers and have provided vital services of all sorts. Even so, most of these organizations operate on small budgets, and many of the most successful programs are found in only a few areas. A recent report on innovative programs that match older volunteers with teenagers at risk noted that "intergenerational programming for at-risk youth now consists of only a handful of initiatives, most of them relatively new and small in size" (Freedman, 1988, p. 1). Moreover, although a small percentage of older volunteers consistently contribute a day or more per week, the vast majority spend much less time in volunteering.

Is there an untapped potential among older volunteers? That is, is it possible to mobilize a much larger and more effective volunteer force among the older population? The purpose of this chapter is to examine how volunteer programs might be improved to more effectively match the time and talents of retired persons with the many needs for services. We summarize and synthesize conclusions from previous chapters and propose strategies for recruiting, retaining, and working with older volunteers. We also discuss how volunteer organizations can improve their programs through systematic evaluation. We offer guidelines for assessing volunteer programs, based on findings from this book. Finally we briefly address a broader issue: How should we reshape social policies to include meaningful and productive opportunities for the last third of life?

An Untapped Potential?

Many older people who do not currently volunteer say they would like to. Many current volunteers say they would be willing to spend more time volunteering. Is this evidence for a volunteer potential—that is, that many more older persons would or could volunteer? Unfortunately it is not easy to make extrapolations based on what people say they might or should do. As we have noted in earlier chapters, motivations for volunteering are complex. When people say they "might" or they "should" volunteer, it is hard to know what this means.

If there is an untapped potential for recruiting older persons as volunteers, it is limited in several ways. First, millions of older persons are volunteering now. It is not as if the older population is really untapped. Second, many effective programs for older volunteers are well established. It makes no sense to ignore what has been accomplished already. Third, it is unrealistic to expect that all older people will volunteer. Many elderly either are not interested in volunteering or have health and physical limitations that seriously limit what they can do. When older nonvolunteers are asked why they are not volunteering, by far the most common reasons they give are health problems and their age (Independent Sector, 1990).

It is also clear that an older volunteer force does not offer a "cure" for shortages in public funding for human services. Even if it were possible to recruit millions more older persons as volunteers, their work would largely complement rather than supplant other health and social services. An older volunteer force, by itself, cannot be expected to solve serious social problems confronting American society today, such as poverty, drug abuse, crime, and teenage pregnancy (see Cnaan & Nuikel, n. d.).

We suggest, nonetheless, that much more could be done. Our case studies and other research show that many volunteer programs—especially service-oriented programs—are small because their funds are very limited. When public and/or private monies are available to support volunteer programs, these programs thrive and grow. The implication is as follows.

- *To the extent that more opportunities are developed and more funds are invested in programs for older volunteers, the "payoff" should be more older volunteers and increased services provided by older volunteers.*

In Chapter 5 we reported that volunteer organizations rely heavily on word-of-mouth recruitment in part because this is an effective method of recruitment but also because they do not have the funds to develop larger programs. We also noted that volunteers tend to be recruited from closed networks and that many people who are different from the people in these networks simply never are asked to volunteer. But research indicates that recruitment campaigns, including the use of mass media, can be effective in broadening the scope of volunteer programs. Moreover, the most effective helping relationships are between people with similar backgrounds. But it is often difficult to recruit volunteers from the populations most in need of services (such as people living in poverty and certain minority groups). Again the implication is intriguing.

- *With systematic recruitment efforts, many more older persons from diverse backgrounds and experiences could be recruited as volunteers.*

Both theory and research support the importance of "productive aging"—that older persons are interested in and can benefit from opportunities for productive activities, including volunteerism. According to theorists like Erik Erikson, the human need to be productive and to have meaning in our lives becomes increasingly poignant as we age (Erikson et al., 1986). Most older people believe strongly that "life is not worth living if you can't contribute to the well-being of others" (Herzog & House, 1991). Even so, older people spend much of the "extra" time they have gained through retirement in passive activities, such as watching television (Chambre, 1987). Thus the implication is as follows.

- *Many older people might be attracted to enhanced opportunities for productive activities through volunteerism.*

We began this chapter with the image of a force, like an army. To stretch this metaphor, we can envision this force of older volunteers as built on their knowledge, skills, experiences, abilities, and talents, all developed and accumulated over a lifetime. Much of this knowledge is practical: how to soothe a child, how to drive nails into a corner beam, how to make chicken soup, how to adjust a pair of eyeglasses, how to teach someone else to read. What structures or opportunities are readily available for older persons to make use of the full range of their accumulated talents and skills? As we have just shown, investment in volunteerism has been very limited. We have noted also that retired individuals spend considerable time in passive activities but might be interested in spending more time in productive efforts. From this we conclude the following.

- *It is unlikely that the accumulated life experiences and skills of older persons are being as well used as they might be.*

For all of these reasons, we suggest that there is a substantial untapped potential for recruiting older volunteers. To maximize this potential, volunteer programs need to develop effective strategies for recruiting and working with older volunteers. We also need to reshape public policies to both encourage and support volunteerism in the older population.

Five Principles of Volunteer Recruitment

We have identified five principles of recruitment, based on our research review.

1. Some people are more likely to volunteer than others and, therefore, are easier to recruit.
2. People are most likely to volunteer their help under conditions of a strong helping situation—that is, if there is a pressing need, no alternative source of help, and a likelihood that their help will have a direct and positive impact.

3. The decision to volunteer is based on a calculus of the costs and the benefits.
4. People are attracted to particular opportunities and causes, not to volunteering in the abstract.
5. People are more willing to volunteer for high-status than low-status organizations.

These principles are not prescriptions. We are not offering a step-by-step recipe for recruiting older volunteers. Nonetheless each of these principles has implications for how to recruit, as we amplify below.

1. *Some people are more likely to volunteer than others and, therefore, are easier to recruit.* Both demographic and personality factors influence recruitment. People who have resources (high income, high level of education, good health, and so forth) are more likely to volunteer than their counterparts. People who volunteer tend to be relatively active, socially involved, empathic, and self-confident. People are more likely to volunteer if they have an "altruistic identity." To a large degree this identity is based on previous helping experiences. This does not mean that persons without resources, with different personality types, or with no previous experience in volunteering do not volunteer at all. It is important to recognize, however, that different strategies may be needed for people who are more difficult to recruit. (Examples of differing strategies are discussed in the next section.)
2. *People are most likely to volunteer their help under conditions of a strong helping situation—that is, if there is a pressing need, no alternative source of help, and a likelihood that their help will have a direct and positive impact.* Volunteer organizations can emphasize one or more of these conditions, for example, by showing that particular volunteers are in a unique position to help. A critical social factor is the volunteer's assessment of how much "good" will be accomplished. Older volunteers, like all volunteers, do not want to waste their efforts and time. Evaluations of volunteer programs can be useful for providing feedback to volunteers on the impact of their work.

3. *The decision to volunteer is based on a calculus of the costs and the benefits.* The costs include such factors as the time expended (especially the time lost from other potential activities) and the inconvenience. The benefits are the gains both to self and to others. The cost-benefit calculus in the decision to volunteer is different for older and younger persons, at least in some ways. For example, retired persons typically do not forego salaried hours when they volunteer. Even so, other costs are associated with age. For instance, many older persons have difficulty with night driving, and the cost of participating in a volunteer program during evening hours may seem insurmountable. The potential benefits from volunteering also differ somewhat with age. Older volunteers are attracted to volunteering as an opportunity for learning, personal growth, and socialization but tend to have little interest in volunteering for the sake of enhancing or developing their careers. Volunteer programs that wish to attract older persons rather than younger persons need to reduce the costs or barriers for older persons and to emphasize personal enrichment and meaningful experience rather than utilitarian ends for the volunteer.

4. *People are attracted to particular opportunities and causes, not to volunteering in the abstract.* Both personal ties and ideology are important in the decision to volunteer. The process of recruitment, therefore, is a process of matching volunteers with appropriate programs and positions. When volunteers are recruited carefully and selectively, they are more likely to be involved, active, and committed to their voluntary organizations.

5. *People are more willing to volunteer for high-status than low-status organizations.* High-status volunteer organizations have the following characteristics: The organization is very visible in the community and is considered to be prestigious; the members are well educated, upper class, and/or male; and the organization is well funded. These features are interrelated. A circular effect is associated with status: High-status individuals are attracted by high-status organizations, and vice versa. High-status organizations typically have no problems in recruiting volunteers. A volunteer organization can improve its status in the following ways: by making its program more visible in the

community, by joining coalitions with higher status organizations, by developing community leadership roles both for the
organization and for individual members, by suggesting that its
membership is "selective" so that not just anyone can join, and
by developing symbols of membership, such as special insignia
and ceremonies.

Creative Strategies
for Recruiting Older Volunteers

Throughout this book we have stressed that volunteerism is
complex and multifaceted. There are many kinds of volunteer programs and organizations and enormous variability in volunteer
jobs and services. There are also many differences among people
who volunteer. It is not surprising, then, that research does not
show one "right" way to recruit volunteers.

The five principles of recruitment, outlined above, offer a way
to understand the diverse conditions of recruitment. In developing a recruitment strategy for a particular volunteer program, we
would need to assess how each principle applies to the program.
For example, is this a low-status or high-status volunteer organization? The director of a low-budget program whose volunteers are
all working class may want to find ways to compensate for the
program's lack of status appeal. Possibly someone with high prestige and visibility in the community might be persuaded to
sponsor the program or to serve as the president of the organization. This approach potentially would elevate the program's status,
enlarge its funding source, and improve its ability to recruit a
wider spectrum of volunteers.

*The effective recruitment of older volunteers requires varied and
creative strategies.* In the next few pages we illustrate the process
of generating recruitment ideas, based especially on the first
principle: Some people are more likely to volunteer than others
and, therefore, are easier to recruit. The first principle suggests
that potential volunteers can be divided into two types: those who
are easy to recruit and those who are difficult. Even though this
dichotomy oversimplifies a complex set of distinctions, it is useful

to imagine the different strategies needed for "easy" versus "difficult" targets for recruitment of volunteers.

As we noted above, demographic, personality, and experience factors are associated with volunteering. This association suggests certain "natural" target markets for recruitment. We know, for example, that college-educated retirees are much more likely to volunteer than their less-educated peers. People who are active and who are "joiners" are also likely to volunteer for various causes. It is relatively easy to recruit such people, both because they are accessible through other organizations and because they are likely to be receptive to recruitment messages. To recruit older volunteers from these natural markets, we would want to work through the organizations to which they belong, such as churches, senior centers, unions, corporations, and civic societies. We probably would be most successful if we could engage the leaders of these organizations either to participate as volunteers or, at least, to help with recruitment. The major problem we would confront in our recruitment effort would be competition from other activities. Potential older volunteers in these natural markets already are busy: They are active in organizations, are involved in friendship networks, and have to make choices about the use of their time. To recruit such people, we do not need to worry so much about barriers (or the costs of volunteering) because we are addressing a target market that is, in general, receptive to the volunteer message. But we do need to emphasize the potential benefits of this particular volunteer opportunity—that this volunteering will provide enriching and meaningful experiences, will make use of their unique skills, and will provide major benefits for those served.

Recruiting older persons who are not members of community groups presents different challenges. With "difficult" target markets, the focus needs to be on overcoming the barriers or on diminishing the costs of volunteering. Media campaigns and other indirect approaches may be the only way to reach older people who are not active in senior centers, churches, or other organizations and who are relatively isolated from other networks of their peers. But there is a problem: Nonjoining older people are likely to ignore volunteer job postings. To reach relatively isolated older persons for volunteering, it is necessary to develop active, even aggressive, outreach strategies that include:

directive messages that appeal to diverse motives for volunteering, concrete information on types of volunteer opportunities,

detailed information on how to become a volunteer: how to apply, how to select a volunteer position, how to decide how much time to volunteer, and what organizations can provide information, with their phone numbers, and

advice on how to overcome barriers (for example, how to arrange for transportation).

This information can be presented through the general media—advertisements, articles in local papers, television specials, and so forth. In addition, these messages can be delivered indirectly to older persons, for example, through schools or businesses where children or working-age adults serve as messengers to bring information on volunteer opportunities to their elderly relatives and neighbors.

But advertising or providing information is not enough. Recruiting people who are outside of natural markets also requires special efforts to overcome specific barriers to volunteering. A few examples follow.

- Older people who lack transportation might be recruited either if arrangements for transportation could be made (a van or a car pool) or if the volunteer work could be brought to the volunteers.
- Minority elderly might be attracted to mainstream volunteer organizations if more efforts at outreach were made into minority communities—to develop neighborhood-based programs and to involve local community leaders in recruitment.
- The recruiting of older men (who have been difficult target markets for some volunteer organizations) would be more successful if activities were developed that specifically appealed to their interests and tastes.

These are just a few illustrations to suggest how to expand the recruitment of older volunteers. Strategies for recruiting from easy and difficult markets are both important. Recruitment in natural markets can have a multiplicative effect, as older volunteers subsequently help recruit their friends from these networks. This scenario is less likely to occur when recruiting persons who are nonjoiners. Even so, outreach beyond the usual networks can both increase the numbers of volunteers and expand the scope of a volunteer program by bringing in people with diverse interests and experiences.

Five Principles of Volunteer Retention

We also have identified five principles, or factors, based on our research review, that affect the retention of volunteers:

1. Selective recruitment, or matching volunteers with appropriate assignments and screening out people who are likely to be uncommitted volunteers, is a central factor in the retention of volunteers.
2. Careful monitoring of new volunteers can help avert the post-honeymoon blues effect during the first few months of volunteering.
3. To maintain the commitment of volunteers, it is important to offer intrinsic rewards—that is, jobs that are challenging, interesting, and important.
4. A critical factor in sustaining the commitment of volunteers is to provide for successful experiences.
5. Friendship is an important factor in volunteer commitment.

These principles have a number of implications for keeping older volunteers:

1. *Selective recruitment is a central factor in the retention of volunteers.* Several selection factors appear to be associated with retention.
   - People who have volunteered before seem to be more likely to remain committed.
   - People who volunteer for altruistic reasons are more likely to remain committed than those who are motivated by nonaltruistic or extraneous reasons (not associated with the volunteer work itself).
   - Ideology is an important factor in volunteer commitment; that is, people are willing to commit their time when they believe that the cause and the goals are worthy.

If selective recruitment has a major impact on retention, this has two rather different implications for keeping older volunteers. First, the selection of volunteers with a high-commitment potential can maximize a program's efficiency and effectiveness, particularly for organizations that require volunteers with long-term commitments.[14] But second, when volunteers with a low-commitment potential are recruited, it is important to anticipate and compensate for possible problems with retention. Thus, for example, inexperienced older volunteers are likely to require substantial supervision and training, not only to ensure specific skills but also to enhance their commitment. In a later section of this chapter, we discuss crea-tive strategies for working with high-commitment versus low-commitment potential volunteers.

2. *Careful monitoring of new volunteers can help avert the post-honeymoon blues effect during the first few months of volunteering.* Some research suggests a critical time for volunteers—within the first few months of service—when there appears to be a strong likelihood of dropping out. We have speculated that a gap may exist between the idealistic expectations of new volunteers and the actual experience of volunteering, so after a honeymoon stage (when volunteers may have a sense of euphoria about being a volunteer) there is likely to be a letdown. Possibly the post-honeymoon blues problem is especially likely for inexperienced, or low-commitment potential, volunteers, who may begin with misunderstandings about what realistically can be accomplished. With older volunteers the post-honeymoon blues problem also might reflect certain age-related barriers to volunteering. For example, an older volunteer who signs up for an intergenerational volunteer program but who has difficulty with night vision might feel stymied in his or her efforts if participation in the program requires some night driving. (This problem can easily happen in winter, even for after-school programs.) Volunteer coordinators need

to be alert to possible age-related problems in designing programs for older volunteers,

to be sufficiently involved with new volunteers to monitor problems as they arise, and to offer volunteers opportunities to develop their own strategies and solutions for countering difficulties.

3. *To maintain the commitment of volunteers, it is important to offer intrinsic rewards—that is, jobs that are challenging, interesting and important.* It is no surprise to find that intrinsic rewards affect volunteer satisfaction and commitment, because these factors are also important in the retention of paid workers. Yet, according to some surveys, it is common for older volunteers to be given busywork. Perhaps it is assumed that just keeping busy is good for older people (the "inoculation" perspective). Of course, volunteers differ from one another in terms of what they find interesting. Even so, busywork is unlikely to be conducive to volunteer commitment. A major challenge in working with older volunteers in particular is to make use of their accumulated skills while also presenting opportunities for doing something different—work that does not simply repeat the jobs from which they retired.

4. *A critical factor in sustaining the commitment of volunteers is to provide for successful experiences.* This theme has been reported in a number of studies: Volunteers who believe that they are capable of helping and that their investment is worth their efforts are much more likely to continue their work than those who feel frustrated, rejected, and incompetent. There may be a somewhat delicate issue in efforts to retain volunteers. On the one hand, if success and feelings of competence are related to commitment, then challenging assignments are risky because of the possibility of failure. On the other hand, volunteer jobs that are too easy are likely to offer few rewards for success.

5. *Friendship is an important factor in volunteer commitment.* To an important degree, volunteers sustain their commitment to particular volunteer organizations because of their personal relationships with their fellow volunteers, paid staff, and/or their clients. It is personal ties and obligations that keep people coming back, not simply interest in volunteering in general or even interest in a particular cause. Many retirees have few structured opportunities for socializing with their peers. One of the hazards of old age is the death of peers. Thus the social relationships developed through volunteering may be especially important for older volunteers.

Two Principles for Working
With Older Volunteers

Research on volunteers, especially older volunteers, has been quite limited; only a few empirical studies have been conducted on the specific issue of working with older volunteers. Nonetheless the research we have reviewed and the findings from our case studies, taken together, are suggestive that effective management of volunteer programs, especially programs for older volunteers, is based on two apparently contradictory principles:

1. A volunteer program should be managed as a serious business, with clear expectations for volunteer workers, adequate investment in volunteer training and supervision, standards of quality, and careful accounting of program costs.
2. A volunteer program should be managed as a "gentle" society that cares about volunteers more as people than as workers, that is flexible and allows individuals to use their own creativity, and that follows high ethical standards.

Can both principles be applied at the same time? In this section we try to reconcile the paradox.

1. *Volunteer management is serious business.* It appears that the most successful volunteer programs both invest the most and ask the most of their volunteers. When volunteers are required to commit a specified amount of time to their jobs, when they are given training, and when their work performance is monitored, a message is conveyed: that their volunteering is serious business. It is likely that this is a circular process. When volunteers are given this message about the seriousness of their work, they are motivated both to remain committed, at least for a specified period of time, and to maintain a high level of work quality. The converse is also likely to be true. If older volunteers are treated as if their work does not matter at all, there is no reason to maintain a reliable standard of work performance. An important component of volunteer management as a business is an appropriate assessment of the costs incurred in working with volunteers. Volunteer programs require investments in training and super-

vision. Inefficient management can raise costs to the point that volunteers cost more than they give.

2. *Volunteer management is gentle—more like a family than a business.* Volunteers are valued for who they are rather than what they can do. With volunteers, there is no stick (no punishment) with which to stimulate good work—only positive encouragement. This is, however, an effective way to maintain commitment and to sustain a high quality of work. Volunteers are different from paid workers in that their activities are flexible and often their responsibilities are defined as doing what paid workers do not do. Within this gentle world of volunteerism, people should be treated ethically. Discrimination (based on ageism, sexism, or antivolunteerism), in particular, violates this principle.

*   *   *

We noted in earlier discussions, especially in Chapter 7, that sometimes difficulties arise in treating volunteers both as like-a-family and as workers. Firing a volunteer whose work is inadequate can be a traumatic experience, when expectations for quality and compassion turn out to be incompatible. Even so, these principles are not entirely contradictory. As one authority on volunteerism commented, it is possible to be "business-like" but not entirely "like a business" (Van Til, 1988, p. 213). Effective management of volunteers, perhaps especially with older volunteers, requires a delicate balance: having serious expectations and standards but also never forgetting kindness, humanness, patience, and compassion.

Creative Strategies for Keeping and Working With Older Volunteers

How can we apply the five principles of retention and the two principles for working with older volunteers? What kinds of creative strategies might be effective? Here are a few examples based in part on the experiences of successful volunteer programs.

It is clear, according to the first retention principle, that an important strategy for maximizing retention is to recruit persons with a high-commitment potential and to effectively match potential volunteers with appropriate positions. Therefore, screening out people who are likely to drop out is cost effective. One implication from the first principle is that communication is important. Potential volunteers need to know what is expected of them. Most volunteer programs have some form of interview. Some have formal contracts. What else might be done for the screening and selection process? There are a number of possibilities. For example, potential volunteers might be introduced to current volunteers. They could spend some time observing current volunteers. Or they might have an apprenticeship or internship, a brief time in which an experienced volunteer functions as their mentor. An apprenticeship could function as both training and screening because the volunteer mentor could assess the abilities and commitment of the volunteer-in-training.

But let us suppose that staff at a volunteer program decide to broaden the scope and recruit older people who have had virtually no previous experience as volunteers. What kinds of training and supervision might be effective with low-commitment potential volunteers? It is possible that these volunteers have relevant skills; they just have not been volunteers before. A mentorship system might be helpful with low-commitment potential volunteers. However, if the volunteer mentor and new recruit come from very different worlds, it might be difficult to establish a bond between them. If a program wanted to recruit older volunteers from a black community, for example, it might be important to establish peer support for the new volunteers. This support could be accomplished (a) by recruiting groups rather than individuals (e.g., recruiting through a community church as a church project) and (b) by facilitating a support group for this group so that new volunteers could share both their skills and their feelings.

Probably of all the principles that we have outlined in this chapter, the third retention principle—it is important to offer jobs that are challenging, interesting, and important—is the most crucial and calls for the most creativity. This principle relates to the types of jobs that are developed for older volunteers, the process of matching jobs with persons, and the involvement of volunteers in their own job creation. At the beginning of Chapter 1, we described several volunteer experiences from our case studies: a band of retirees playing for elderly patients at a medical center, a group of retired engineers designing prosthetic devices for disabled people, a 100-year-old woman doing telephone outreach, and a retired executive serving as a mentor for a high school girl and arranging a scholarship for her at an art institute. What is particularly striking in these examples is the creativity of the volunteer placements. The older volunteers described in these stories are all able to provide services that make use of their particular abilities and skills.

The two principles for working with volunteers—that volunteerism is serious business and that volunteers are like a family —seem to be mutually inconsistent. What strategies for working with older volunteers might reconcile this apparent paradox? The issue is particularly relevant to the problem of "retiring" older volunteers whose ability to do their jobs is compromised by disabilities, frailty, or health problems. The following examples were suggested by volunteer professionals.[15]

- Having a time-limited contract is one way to solve the "retirement" problem. When volunteers are committed to working for a specified period of time, this conveys the message that the work is serious business but also makes it easy to terminate a volunteer role without embarrassing the volunteer.

- It is also useful to offer multiple alternative roles to older volunteers. This proposal could involve developing volunteer career paths that progressively build on skills gained through volunteering. Offering multiple alternatives entails a dynamic, rather than a stable, perception of volunteer roles—an expectation that volunteers move around: They may stay in a job for a period of time, then drop out for a while, and later move to other kinds of volunteer positions. To encourage dynamic volunteering requires regular reviews that explicitly give volunteers an opportunity to "move on."

- Old age may bring diminishing functional abilities, so it is especially important to have volunteer positions available for persons who are not completely able-bodied. In one of our case studies, for example, we were told about an older woman who had become blind. A volunteer organization gave her the task of placing tickets in envelops, by touch. This job apparently was very meaningful for her ("We saw her crying and we asked, 'What's wrong?' She said, 'I'm so happy. I'm helping someone else—and I'm doing it right.' "). A type of job that is available to people who are homebound, including frail elderly, is telephone reassurance. Older persons who cannot drive or even who have rather serious health or functional problems might be able to use the telephone for volunteer work. They can call other homebound elderly, or they can talk on the phone with latchkey children and provide grandparently support, as well as practical advice. Creating positions that people can fall back on for reversed volunteer careers has a double benefit: More services are available because persons who are frail or disabled can remain in the volunteer pool, and enhanced opportunities are provided for individual elderly who can continue to have meaningful volunteer activities.

Guidelines for Assessing Volunteer Programs

For several reasons, volunteer programs should have regular assessments or evaluations. First, evaluation can identify both strengths and weaknesses and can help improve a program. Second, an evaluation can provide useful feedback about the effectiveness of the services that the volunteers provide. A survey of clients, for example, might give information on how clients are helped. This information, on the impact of services, can motivate both current volunteers and potential volunteers. Third, information from assessments can be important in securing further funding for a volunteer program. Volunteer programs can use data to demonstrate why funding is needed, how it will be used, and what effect the investment will have on service recipients.

Despite some cogent reasons, our case studies and research review suggest that *most volunteer organizations have only minimal efforts at evaluating their programs.* In this section we offer a list of questions to address in assessing the effectiveness of volunteer programs. These questions are based on our research synthesis and are intended as guidelines, or a checklist, so that volunteer organizations can identify the strengths of their programs, possible problems, and approaches for improving their work with volunteers. To some degree, of course, these questions may need to be modified for particular programs.

The checklist is presented as sets of open-ended questions. At the end of each set of questions we refer to the chapters in which these issues are discussed. The checklist is intended to help volunteer managers reflect on the effectiveness of their organizations in working with older volunteers. The checklist also can serve as an outline for an annual assessment, so that the content of the report would consist of "answers" to the sets of questions listed below.

- What efforts do we make for generating diverse volunteer opportunities for older volunteers? How do we let potential and current volunteers know about these opportunities?

    Chapters 1, 5, 6, 7
- What efforts do we make for overcoming barriers for older volunteers?

    Chapters 5, 9
- What systems or procedures do we use for word-of-mouth recruitment? How many older volunteers did we recruit this year by word of mouth? Has our approach been adequate for recruiting a sufficient number of volunteers to maintain our program, and if not, how do we plan to change?

    Chapter 5
- What efforts do we make to reach out to potential volunteers who are unlikely to hear about our program through word of mouth? How many older volunteers did we recruit this year by media-based recruitment methods? Is our volunteer pool sufficiently diverse, and if not, how do we plan to change our recruitment procedures?

    Chapters 5, 9
- What specific efforts do we make to reach out to minority elders as volunteers? How do we take into account diverse cultural factors in designing volunteer activities?

    Chapter 9
- What arrangements do we have for matching volunteers with appropriate assignments? How do we monitor the effectiveness of these placements? Under what circumstances and in what ways do we help volunteers develop or tailor their own volunteer positions to fulfill their special skills, interests, or needs?

    Chapter 6
- What commitments do we expect from volunteers? Are we expecting too much or too little?

    Chapters 5, 6, 7, 8

- What methods do we use for communicating expectations to both new and continuing volunteers? Are these methods adequate?
  Chapters 5, 6, 7
- How effective is our training and supervision so that we fulfill our commitment to our volunteers?
  Chapters 6, 7
- What special arrangements do we have for monitoring new volunteers, especially during their first few months? What feedback do we receive from and about volunteers during this time? In what ways are we prepared to change or modify new assignments, if necessary?
  Chapter 6
- What are the intrinsic rewards for our volunteers? What efforts do we make to maximize these rewards?
  Chapters 6, 7
- How do we ensure that volunteers have successful experiences?
  Chapters 4, 6, 7
- How do we assess the impact of volunteer services on service recipients? What methods do we use for giving feedback to volunteers about the impact of their services?
  Chapters 4, 5, 6, 7
- How do we recognize and deal with burnout problems? Do we have adequate support systems for volunteers? Do we offer effective guidelines that set boundaries around what volunteers are and are not supposed to do?
  Chapter 6
- What costs are incurred from working with volunteers in our program—in dollars and/or in staff time? Do we have adequate funds to support our volunteer program, and if not, what plans do we have to secure further funding?
  Chapter 7
- How are paid staff compensated for working with volunteers? How do we ensure that the job descriptions of paid workers include their responsibilities for training or supervising volunteers? What efforts do we make to prevent the positions of paid workers being jeopardized by the placements of volunteers?
  Chapters 7, 8
- What forms of liability insurance do we have for our volunteers, clients, and paid staff? In what ways is our program at risk because of liability problems, and how will we rectify this situation?
  Chapter 8

- What strategies do we use for discouraging antivolunteerism, ageism, or other biases? In what ways have we included antidiscrimination materials in our education and training programs?
  Chapters 7, 8

The Future of Old Age

He is 79, in reasonably good health, thin, and muscular. He lives with his wife in a cottagelike Florida home, surrounded by fruit trees—orange, banana, grapefruit, mango, and avocado. He likes to work in his garden, and he gives boxes of fruit as presents to his friends and neighbors. When asked about how he likes retirement, he smiles and says, "There is no future to old age. That's what I always say. There's no future to old age."

It is a cliche—that childhood and youth look to the future but the only future for old age is death. But it is not really true, especially today. When Social Security first was enacted in the United States in the 1930s, average life expectancy was about age 47. For those who survived to retire, Social Security was intended to provide a small stipend for the few remaining years. Now, in the 1990s, many people live a third of their lives postretirement. So living, not dying, is the future of old age.

Our current social policies and most of our public expenditures on aging focus on old age as a terminal stage. The problems of old age—frailty and sickness—cost hundreds of billions of dollars. The lion's share of the aging budget, both federal and state, is for health and long-term care. Although some publicly supported programs provide activities for senior citizens, the budget for these projects is almost negligible.

It is time to refocus. We need to develop social definitions and public policies that are future focused—that offer meaningful futures to older citizens and that use their capacities to help shape a better future world for everyone. We need to re-envision our aging policies on the basis of the following premises:

1. The productive potential of the older population constitutes an important social and economic resource.

2. It is a social and public responsibility to create opportunities for productive aging through volunteerism, paid employment, and entrepreneurship.

3. Although an older volunteer force cannot solve social problems, it can have a substantial and meaningful impact on social welfare.

4. It is the responsibility of a public-private partnership to invest in and support an older volunteer force.

These premises are interrelated, as we discuss below.

1. *The older population constitutes an important resource.* In part, this is a matter of perspective—how older people are seen. Much discussion has taken place, on all levels of government, about how to reduce governmental expenditures on caring for the elderly. It may be important simply to review our thinking—not just how much it costs to provide services, but how much and in what ways the older population does and can contribute. According to a recent report, "Persons at or beyond the retirement age may have more to give and more reason to benefit from national service than any other age group" (Danzig & Szanton, 1986, cited in Freedman, 1988, p. 68). Perhaps we should consider establishing a National Senior Volunteer Corps to parallel the Peace Corps, which was largely a youth volunteer movement, and to galvanize and energize a volunteer movement of older persons. Current programs for older volunteers (such as RSVP and Foster Grandparent) would provide a good starting point, but much more substantial support is needed to create a national older volunteers movement.

2. *It is a public responsibility to create opportunities for productive aging.* Productive aging is not merely a private or individual matter. Individual older persons can choose to continue working, to begin a new career, or to volunteer. But efforts to engage in such productive activities often encounter barriers, including disincentives to remain in the labor force, age discrimination, negative attitudes about the capacities of older persons, and disparaging remarks about the appropriateness of working beyond "normal" retirement age. Public programs and policies can use incentives and opportunities to address the whole system of

aging. It is important, for the sake of individual older persons and also for society, that opportunities for productive aging include both paid and unpaid work. What is needed are choices—varieties of opportunities and prospects for maximizing the productive contributions of older persons.

3. *An older volunteer force can have a meaningful impact on social welfare.* Even if older volunteers cannot be expected to "solve" problems of drugs, crime, teen pregnancy, and so forth, older persons have time to give and skills and life experiences to offer. Their contributions can make a difference, both for individuals and for their communities. An older volunteer working with teenagers at risk commented: "Me, I don't have an education, but I have an education what I went through in life, in real life, and that's what I teach them" (Freedman, 1988, p. 23).

4. *Investing in an older volunteer force is both a public and a private responsibility.* As our research review and case study findings show, lack of resources often is an obstacle to the development of volunteer programs. We noted also that few programs cover liability insurance for either volunteers or clients because small organizations cannot afford the costs. To maximize the productive potential of our older population will require additional funding from both the public and private sectors.

*   *   *

Volunteerism is a major social phenomenon in this country. Older volunteers in particular constitute a powerful force that already contributes substantially to the welfare of our society. But we need to do much more for the future of old age. We believe that there is an untapped potential for developing an older volunteers' movement. But to realize this potential will require efforts that go well beyond business as usual. We need creative strategies for recruiting and working with older volunteers. We also need to expand public-private investments in programs for older volunteers and to develop a new social vision of the last third of life.

The Older Volunteers Project

The Older Volunteers Project brings together two sources of knowledge on volunteerism: (a) a synthesis of research literature, both published and unpublished, and (b) case studies of exemplary programs as identified by a network of experts.

The Research Review

The research review entailed a broad-based and systematic search for research literature relevant to the topic of older volunteers.[16] We identified research literature in the following ways: through computer-based literature searches, bibliographic searches (selected sources cited in key articles), published bibliographies on aging and volunteerism, and interviews with experts on volunteerism, including researchers, directors of national programs, and other volunteer professionals.

We reviewed approximately 350 articles and monographs related to the topic of volunteering. This list includes some literature on related topics (e.g., prosocial behavior, the impact of activity on life satisfaction, recruitment and retention of paid workers, and informal help networks among minority elderly). The list also contains some literature that presents theory but no empirical research. Of all the literature identified, 125 are specifically on older volunteers.

We did not review work done before 1975, with very few exceptions (if the articles were by prominent researchers or seemed to be key works). We also did not review how-to manuals—that is, literature not based on theoretical or empirical research.

The computer-based literature search covered a broad field and included the following files: Lumina, AGELINE, ERIC, MOVS (Minnesota Office of Volunteer Services), PsychLit, Sociofile, and EconLit. A computer-based literature search is based on a key word strategy. For example, we searched for *volunteer* (or any version of that word), along with *elder* (or any version of that word), as descriptors in the abstract or title. The files vary somewhat, however, in the meaning of particular words. For example, in PsychLit the word *volunteer* caused problems because it included numerous articles in which subjects "volunteered" for a study. The abstracts had to be screened carefully.

We developed research review coding forms so that we could analyze systematically large amounts of information. The coding sheets looked at the design characteristics, the variables, the hypotheses, the characteristics of the participants, the definitions, and the outcomes. We also included a discussion of the strengths, weaknesses, and implications of the study. A summary of the bibliographic information was placed on a Microsoft Excel file so that we were able to identify, sort, and retrieve literature sources by author, title, year, and topic.

Although we attempted to identify systematically current research literature on volunteering and especially on older volunteers, we believe it is virtually impossible to have a truly comprehensive review, for two reasons. First, many "hidden pockets" of research are not found on computer data files. We often were surprised, in our interviews with "experts" on volunteerism, to come across interesting, unpublished reports—especially evaluations of volunteer programs. We just stumbled across several such reports and have no way of knowing how many other "hidden" research reports we have missed. Second, research is an ongoing process, and we had a publication deadline. We knew of some large studies that currently were being done, the results of which would be available too late to include in our book.

A more serious problem is the quality of research on the topic of volunteers, particularly the narrower topic of older volunteers. We reviewed a rather large number of articles, but we are quite critical of much of this research. Some of the research reports were so poor that we did not use their findings.

Case Studies

In-depth case data on "exemplary" programs provide an additional source of information on the "best practices" for recruiting, retaining, and working with older volunteers. We conducted 57 case studies of exemplary volunteer programs.[17] All of these programs work with older volunteers.

They were identified by national experts in volunteerism as having exceptionally high quality and/or innovative programs.

Although the sample is not random, we have endeavored to include a diverse sample of programs. The 57 programs represent the following types of volunteer organizations:

Type of Volunteer Organization	Number of Cases
Advocacy	2
Religious	6
Civic	1
Consulting	4
Corporate	3
Counseling	2
Crime prevention	2
Cultural	3
Education	4
Eldercare	4
Environment	1
Exchange	2
Fund-raising	2
Health	3
Intergenerational	3
Minority[18]	8
Referral	6
Senior center	1
TOTAL	57

We attempted to generate a national sample, with case studies in all regions of the United States. The regional distribution of organizations is as follows:

Location of Volunteer Organization	Number of Cases
Eastern states	14
Southern states	11
Midwestern states	18
Western states	11
National organizations	3
TOTAL	57

The interviews with volunteer coordinators were conducted over the telephone. Each interview lasted 45 to 90 minutes, and notes from the interviews were dictated and transcribed. In addition, we collected written information (such as brochures, newsletters, and evaluation reports) from most of the participating organizations.

The case study data were analyzed in two ways. First, almost all of the questions were coded and computer analyzed so that we could examine correlates of different types of volunteer organizations. We need to be cautious about drawing inferences from such analyses, however, because the sample is nonrandom. Second, the interview transcripts were analyzed contextually, as qualitative data. We have included and discussed quotes from the case studies throughout the book. The analysis of the case study data is intended both to illustrate themes from the research review and to provide additional insights on practical issues in working with older volunteers.

Sources of Information on Volunteerism

For readers who are interested in obtaining information about particular types of volunteer opportunities, here is a list of organizations that serve as resource centers on volunteering.[19] Most of these organizations are national, but many have local affiliates that are listed in telephone directories. Because of the many different types of volunteer programs, this list is not comprehensive, but rather is intended as a representative sample of places to contact.

For information about programs for older volunteers in a particular community, a good central source of information is the local office of the Retired Senior Volunteer Program (RSVP), whose mission is to find placements for older volunteers in many different agencies. Churches, synagogues, and other religious organizations also usually offer programs for volunteers. A number of large corporations also have volunteer programs for their retirees.

ACTION
1110 Vermont Avenue, NW
Washington, DC 20525
202/634-9108

ACTION is the federal agency for volunteer service. Its purpose is to stimulate volunteerism in general and, in particular, to demonstrate the effectiveness of volunteers in problem solving. Its major programs include Foster Grandparent Program (FGP), Retired Senior Volunteers Program (RSVP), Senior Companions Program (SCP) for elders, Volunteers in Service to America (VISTA), and a variety of programs for youths.

Periodical: *Action Update*

American Association for Museum Volunteers
1225 I Street, NW, Suite 200
Washington, DC 20005
202/289-6575

Formerly the United States Association of Museum Volunteers, this membership organization holds its annual training conference in conjunction with the American Association of Museums.

Periodicals: *Museum News, AVISO*

American Association of Retired Persons (AARP)
Office of Volunteer Coordination
601 E Street, NW
Washington, DC 20049
202/434-3200

This nonprofit, nonpartisan organization's members are all 50 years of age and over. AARP offers a wide range of membership benefits and services and education and advocacy materials. The AARP Volunteer Talent Bank matches volunteers age 50 or older with suitable volunteer positions nationwide in both AARP programs and other organizations.

Periodicals: *Prime Time, Modern Maturity, AARP News Bulletin* (monthly), *Legislative Report*

American Red Cross
National Headquarters
17th and D Streets, NW
Washington, DC 20006

The American Red Cross brings together trained volunteers and paid staff to help prevent, prepare for, and cope with emergencies. The ARC is chartered by Congress to provide disaster relief at home and abroad. It collects, processes, and distributes voluntarily donated blood and involves 1.4 million volunteers.

Habitat for Humanity International, Inc.
Habitat and Church Streets
Americus, GA 31709-3498
912/924-6935

Habitat for Humanity is an ecumenical Christian housing ministry whose objective is to eliminate poverty housing from the world and to make decent shelter a matter of conscience. More than 40,000 volunteers have helped build or rehabilitate more than 2,000 homes for low-income families in the United States and in developing countries.

Independent Sector (IS)
1828 L Street, NW
Washington, DC 20036
202/223-8100

IS is a national membership organization formed through the merger of the Coalition of National Voluntary Organizations (CONVO) and the National Council of Philanthropy (NCOP). It works to preserve and enhance the national traditions of giving, volunteering, and not-for-profit initiative.

Periodical: *Update*

International Association for Volunteer Effort (IAVE)
c/o Ruth March
P.O. Box 27095
Los Angeles, CA 90027
213/467-6443

Membership in IAVE is open to volunteers everywhere who share the desire to encourage and promote worldwide volunteer action dedicated to improving the quality of life. Membership fee is $30 for individuals and $60 for organizations.

Periodical: *LIVE Newsletter*

Minnesota Office on Volunteer Services (MOVS)
500 Rice Street
St. Paul, MN 55155
612/296-4731

The Minnesota Office of Volunteer Services, Department of Administration, strives to improve the quality of life in Minnesota through voluntary action. It works with both public and private organizations. MOVS is involved in the following activities: advocacy for volunteers and volunteer service, publishing a bimonthly newsletter, operation of a resource library, technical assistance and information, research on special volunteer issues and projects, convening meetings of volunteer groups and leaders, and providing training opportunities. Membership is not required for MOVS services.

Periodical: *Volunteers Move Minnesota*

National Assembly of National Voluntary Health
and Social Welfare Organizations
1319 F Street, NW, Suite 601
Washington, DC 20004
202/347-2080

The National Assembly is an organizational membership association formed to facilitate cooperation and communication among voluntary organizations and to pursue mutual goals and convictions. It also acts as a clearinghouse and resource center.

National Association of Partners in Education (NAPE)
601 Wythe Street, Suite 200
Alexandria, VA 22314
703/836-4880

NAPE (formerly National School Volunteer Program [NSVP]) is a membership organization comprised of those involved in or interested in school volunteer programs. It functions as a resource for its members and as an advocate activity within the educational field.

Periodicals: *School Volunteering, Partners in Education*

National Council on Corporate Volunteerism (NCCV)
c/o The National VOLUNTEER Center
1111 North 19th Street, Suite 500
Arlington, VA 22209
703/276-0542

NCCV, a corporate membership organization, promotes volunteerism by serving as a national resource for the development and expansion of corporate employee volunteer programs. The council also serves as a clearinghouse for the exchange of information on corporate volunteerism and produces a quarterly newsletter as part of VOLUNTEER's Volunteers from the Workplace service.

Periodical: *Corporate Newsletter*

National CASA Association (CASA)
2722 Eastlake Avenue East, Suite 220
Seattle, WA 98102
206/328-8588

This membership organization for court-appointed special advocates was formed in 1982 to provide coordination, technical training, and assistance to CASA/guardian programs nationwide. CASA is a nationwide movement of community volunteers who speak for abused or neglected children in court. The National CASA Association represents more than 377 CASA programs and 13,000 CASA volunteers in 47 states.

Periodical: *The CASA Connection*

National Council on Aging, Inc. (NCOA)
P.O. Box 7227
Ben Franklin Station
Washington, DC 20044
202/479-1200

The NCOA is a resource for information, training, technical assistance, advocacy, publications, and research on every aspect of aging. The membership organization offers various networking opportunities and sponsors an annual conference.

National Executive Service Corps (NESC)
257 Park Avenue South
New York, NY 10010
212/867-5010

NESC uses senior, unpaid business executive retirees to counsel national nonprofits in the fields of education, health, religion, social services, and the arts for periods of 3 to 6 months. They also coordinate the efforts of a network of local Executive Service Corps, which work with local nonprofit organizations.

National Retiree Volunteer Center (NRVC)
905 Fourth Avenue South
Minneapolis, MN 55404
612/341-2689

The NRVC is the catalyst that empowers retirees to be a contributing force in their communities through the investment of their skills and expertise. It initiates, develops, and expands retiree volunteer programs for community benefit, in cooperation with corporations, government, educational institutions, and professional associations.

Points of Light Foundation
736 Jackson Place
Washington, DC 20503
202/408-5162

The mission of the recently created P.O.L. Foundation is to make community service aimed at serious social problems central to the life of every American. The foundation will work to stimulate new initiatives and will build on and enhance the efforts of existing organizations in addressing its goals. These goals include enlisting the media in making people aware of the benefits of engaging in service; persuading businesses, unions, schools, civic groups, religious institutions, and other organizations to mobilize all of their members for community service; and identifying and disseminating community service ideas that work.

Service Corps of Retired Executives (SCORE)
1825 Connecticut Avenue, NW
Washington, DC 20009
202/653-6279

SCORE is sponsored by the Small Business Administration, but it is an independent, nonprofit organization. SCORE's primary purpose is to render a community service by providing, without charge, the expert assistance of its volunteer counselors in solving the problems encountered by small businesses.

United Way of America (UWA)
701 North Fairfax
Alexandria, VA 22314
703/836-7100

UWA provides leadership and service to more than 2,200 local United Ways in fund-raising, fiscal, and program management. It also is engaged in research and liaison activities with other national organizations and the government.

Periodical: *Community*

National Volunteer Center
1111 North 19th Street, Suite 500
Arlington, VA 22209
703/276-0542

VOLUNTEER was created in 1979 through the merger of the National
Center for Voluntary Action and the National Information Center on
Volunteerism. It serves as the only national voluntary organization whose
sole purpose is to encourage the more effective use of volunteers in community problem solving. VOLUNTEER helps improve the effectiveness of volunteer management skills by providing information sharing, training,
and technical assistance services. It operates special projects to demonstrate new, unique, and innovative ways to get people involved, and it
serves as a national advocate for volunteering and citizen involvement.

Periodicals: *Voluntary Action Leadership, Volunteering, Volunteer Readership
Catalog*

Volunteers in Prevention and Probation, Inc. (VIP)
527 North Main
Royal Oak, MI 48067
313/398-8550

VIP is an organization to support and promote citizen involvement in court
and correction programs.

Periodical: *VIP Examiner*

Notes

1. A description of the methods used for collecting and analyzing information for this book can be found in Appendix A.

2. The federal minimum wage is $4.25 per hour as of April 1, 1991.

3. To add even further to the confusion in definition, some terms are similar and overlapping but not quite the same: *volunteering, voluntary action, voluntary associations,* and *voluntarism. Voluntary action* often refers to political or community action and therefore appears to be a subset of *volunteering.* The word *voluntarism* is used to mean either contributing time through charitable organizations or participating in voluntary associations or both. Sometimes voluntary associations are charitable or civic organizations (e.g., Kiwanis, Shriners). But many voluntary associations, such as athletic or social clubs, entail no service to others. We will report some research on voluntary associations because these findings can be relevant to volunteering. We are concerned, however, about the muddling of terms.

4. Voluntary action includes a variety of activities, including volunteering.

5. In surveys, "learning and personal growth" motivations for volunteering tend to refer to both personal (or spiritual) development and learning that is associated with career development (see, for example, Independent Sector, 1990). It appears that older volunteers are less motivated by career-related learning but are nonetheless interested in learning as a form of personal enrichment.

6. All of the voluntary organizations in this sample were located in cities and towns of Massachusetts. However, we need to be somewhat cautious in drawing inferences about volunteering from this study. This was a sample of voluntary organizations (or associations); some, not all, entailed volunteer work. Nonetheless this study is unusual in its comparative framework and offers some interesting insights into what makes voluntary organizations exceptionally effective.

7. There is, however, one catch in interpreting findings from this study. We cannot determine from these findings which came first: the ideology or the involvement; that is, it is possible that people who are active in an organization are socialized into ideological commitment.

8. This was not a controlled evaluation; that is, no one approached volunteers who were *not* at critical points to see whether they would like changes.

9. This program had been recommended to us but was not one of our 57 case studies. The volunteers in this program are almost all young or middle-aged adults.

10. For a discussion of the principles of bureaucracy, see Gerth & Mills 1946.

11. Simmons (1991), from her research on kidney transplants, reported that organ donors often find other people censuring them for making this kind of sacrifice. See Chapter 4.

12. Many organizations have rules about conflicts of interest for board members. In practice, these rules are sometimes violated. Certain individuals with questionable ethics have profited from their "citizenship" activities. (See Galaskiewicz, 1985; Galaskiewicz & Schaffer, 1990).

13. Self-help groups should not be confused with groups such as Alcoholics Anonymous or Parents Without Partners, whose purposes focus on a common need or overcoming a common problem.

14. As we noted in Chapter 6, volunteer organizations vary widely in their expectations of volunteer retention. Rapid turnover of volunteers is a problem only under certain conditions: if extensive investment in volunteer training and supervision is needed, if jobs require long-term commitments, if clients can be harmed when volunteers leave, and/or if there is a shortage of qualified volunteers.

15. The ideas for this section were generated by the case studies and also by discussions with volunteer professionals at the meetings of the American Society on Aging (San Diego, March 1992) and at a special focus group of volunteer directors in Minnesota (St. Paul, March 1992).

16. For a discussion of how to conduct a systematic literature review, see Harris M. Cooper, 1989, *Integrating Research: A Guide for Literature Reviews.*

17. One organization refused to participate (the director said that she was just "too busy"), and another organization was dropped when the interview had been postponed, the director could not be reached subsequently after multiple attempts, and it became too late to include the data.

18. These eight volunteer programs identified their mission either as serving minority persons and/or as recruiting volunteers from minority communities. Two other organizations reported that a majority of their volunteers were black but did not identify the mission of their organizations specifically as tied to an ethnic community.

19. Adapted from a list prepared by the Minnesota Office of Volunteer Services.

References

Allen, K. K. (1981). The challenges facing senior volunteering. *Generations, 5,* 8-9.
Antunes, G., & Gaitz, C. (1975). Ethnicity and participation: A study of Mexican-Americans, blacks and whites. *American Journal of Sociology, 80,* 1192-1211.
Arella, L. R. (1984). The Green County RSVP: A case study. *Journal of Voluntary Action Research, 13*(3), 53-64.
Atchley, R. C. (1988). *Social forces and aging.* Belmont, CA: Wadsworth.
Baker, B. J., & Murowski, K. (1986). A method for measuring paid staff support for volunteer involvement. *Journal of Voluntary Action Research, 15,* 60-64.
Baldassare, M., Rosenfeld, S., & Rook, K. (1984). The types of social relations predicting elderly well-being. *Research on Aging, 6,* 549-559.
Barber, P., & Scheier, I. (1979, Winter). NICOV takes a look at ethics in volunteerism. *Voluntary Action Leadership,* pp. 35-39.
Batson, C. D., Bolen, M., Cross, J. A., & Neuringer-Benefiel, H. E. (1986). Where is the altruism in the altruistic personality? *Journal of Personality and Social Psychology, 50,* 212-220.
Batson, C. D., Dyck, J., Brandt, J. R., Batson, J., Powell, A., McMaster, M. R., & Griffitt, C. (1988). Five studies testing two new egoistic alternatives to the empathy-altruism hypothesis. *Journal of Personality and Social Psychology, 55,* 52-77.
Batson, C. D., Fultz, J., Schoenrade, P. A., & Paduano, A. (1987). Critical self-reflection and self-perceived altruism: When self-reward fails. *Journal of Personality and Social Psychology, 53,* 594-602.
Bellah, R. N., Madsen, R., Sullivan, W. M., Swidler, A., & Tipton, S. (1985). *Habits of the heart: Individualism and commitment in American life.* New York: Harper & Row.
Berkman, L. F., & Syme, S. L. (1979). Social networks, host resistance, and morality: A 9-year follow-up study of Alameda County residents. *American Journal of Epidemiology, 109,* 186-204.

Berling, J. (1988). Theological education in a global context: Reflections on Confucian-Christian dialogue. In *China notes* (pp. 482-488). New York: National Council of Churches.

Block, M. R. (1979). Exiled Americans: The plight of Indian aged in the United States. In D. E. Gelfand & A. J. Kutzik (Eds.), *Ethnicity and aging: Theory, research and policy* (pp. 184-192). New York: Springer.

Bosse, R., & Ekerdt, D. J. (1981). Change in self-perception of leisure activities with retirement. *The Gerontologist, 21*, 650-655.

Bould, S., Sanborn, B., & Reif, L. (1989). *Eighty-five plus: The oldest old.* Belmont, CA: Wadsworth.

Brown, N. S. (1991). *Jewish Family and Children's Service of Minneapolis volunteer focus group report.* Minneapolis: Jewish Family and Children's Service of Minneapolis.

Brudney, J. L. (1990a). The availability of volunteers: Implications for local governments. *Administration and Society, 21*, 413-424.

Brudney, J. L. (1990b). *Fostering volunteer programs in the public sector: Planning, initiating, and managing voluntary activities.* San Francisco: Jossey-Bass.

Brummel, S. W. (1984). Senior companions: An unrecognized resource for long term care. *Pride Institute Journal of Long Term Health Care, 3*, 3-12.

Burke, R. S., & Lindsay, L. (1985). Motivation and goal setting. In L. F. Moore (Ed.), *Motivating volunteers* (pp. 93-127). Vancouver, BC: Vancouver Volunteer Center.

Butler, R. N., & Gleason, H. P. (1985). *Productive aging: Enhancing vitality in later life.* New York: Springer.

Cahn, E. S. (1988). Service credits: A market strategy for redefining elders as producers. In R. Morris & S. Bass (Eds.), *Retirement reconsidered: Economic and social roles for older people* (pp. 232-249). New York: Springer.

Caro, F. G., & Bass, S. A. (1991, November). *Effective structuring of volunteer roles for the elderly.* Paper presented at the Annual Meeting of the Gerontological Society of America, San Francisco, CA.

Carson, E. D. (1990a). Black volunteers as givers and fundraisers. *Working papers: Center for the Study of Philanthropy.* Washington, DC: Independent Sector.

Carson, E. D. (1990b). Patterns of giving in black churches. In R. Wuthnow & V. Hodgkinson (Eds.), *Faith and philanthropy in America: Exploring the role of religion in America's voluntary sector* (pp. 232-252). San Francisco: Jossey-Bass.

Chambre, S. M. (1984). Is volunteering a substitute for role loss in old age? An empirical test of activity theory. *The Gerontologist, 24*, 292-298.

Chambre, S. M. (1987). *Good deeds in old age: Volunteering by the new leisure class.* Lexington, MA: Lexington.

Chambre, S. M. (1989). Kindling points of light: Volunteering as public policy. *Nonprofit and Voluntary Sector Quarterly, 18*, 249-268.

Chambre, S. M. (n. d.) *Volunteerism in an aging society.* Unpublished manuscript.

Chapman, T. H. (1985). Motivation in university student volunteering. In L. F. Moore (Ed.), *Motivating volunteers* (pp. 231-242). Vancouver, BC: Vancouver Volunteer Center.

Charner, I., Fox, S. R., & Trachtman, L. N. (1988). *Union retirees: Enriching their lives, enhancing their contribution.* Washington, DC: National Institute for Work and Learning.

Chase, R. A. (1990). *Minority elders in Minnesota.* St. Paul, MN: Amherst H. Wilder Foundation.

Chin, J. C. (1989). Participation in a voluntary organization: A case study. *Free Inquiry in Creative Sociology, 17,* 29-32.

Ching, J. (1986). What is Confucian spirituality? In *Confucianism: The dynamics of tradition* (pp. 74-83). New York: Macmillan.

Cialdini, R. B., Schaller, M., Houlihan, D., Arps, K., Fultz, J., & Beaman, A. L. (1987). Empathy-based helping: Is it selflessly or selfishly motivated? *Journal of Personality and Social Psychology, 52,* 749-758.

Clary, E. G., & Miller, J. (1986). Socialization and situational influences on sustained altruism. *Child Development, 57,* 1358-1369.

Clary, E. G., & Orenstein, L. (in press). The amount and effectiveness of help: The relationship of motives and abilities to helping behavior. *Personality and Social Psychology Bulletin.*

Clary, E. G., & Snyder, M. (1991a). A functional analysis of altruism and prosocial behavior: The case of volunteerism. *Review of Personality and Social Psychology, 12,* 119-147.

Clary, E. G., & Snyder, M. (1991b). *The recruitment of volunteers: Persuasive communications.* Working draft prepared for the Spring Research Forum on Leadership and Management, Cleveland, OH.

Cnaan, R., & Nuikel, J. G. (n. d.). *Elderly volunteers: assessing the availability of the untapped resource.* Unpublished manuscript.

Cohen-Mansfield, J. (1989). Employment and volunteering roles for the elderly: Characteristics, attributions, and strategies. *Journal of Leisure Research, 21,* 214-227.

Conner, K. A., & Winkelpleck, J. (1986, April). *Training the volunteer advocate: Training needs and concerns.* Paper presented at the annual meetings of the Midwest Sociological Society, Des Moines, IA.

Cook, A. F. (1991). *The Foster Grandparent Program: An analysis of changing trends.* Missoula, MT: Missoula Aging Services.

Cook, A. F. (n. d.). *Listening, learning, supporting and caring: A case study which examines the role of senior companions and the support they offer to their home-bound clients.* Missoula, MT: Missoula Aging Services.

Cooper, H. M. (1989). *Integrating research: A guide for literature reviews.* Newbury Park, CA: Sage.

Cortes. M. (1989). *Latino philanthropy: Some unanswered questions* (Report prepared for Pluralism in Philanthropy Project). Washington, DC: Council on Foundations.

Coughlin, T. A., & Meiners, M. (1990). Service credit banking: Issues in program development. *Journal of Aging and Social Policy, 2,* 25-41.

Crenson, M. A. (1987). The private stake in public goods: Overcoming the illogic of collective action. *Policy Sciences, 20,* 259-276.

Cunningham, C. V. (1991). Reaching minority communities: Factors impacting success. *Journal of Gerontological Social Work, 17,* 125-135.

Dailey, R. C. (1986). Understanding organizational commitment for volunteers: Empirical and managerial implications. *Journal of Voluntary Action Research, 15,* 19-31.

Daniels, A. K. (1985). Good times and good works: The place of sociability in the work of women volunteers. *Social Problems, 32,* 363-374.

Danzig, R., & Szanton, P. (1986). *National service: What would it mean?* Lexington, MA: Lexington.

Davis, K. E. (1984). An alternative theoretical perspective on race and voluntary participation. In F. Schwartz (Ed.), *Volunteerism and social work practice: A growing collaboration* (pp. 147-163). Lanham, MD: University Press of America.

Dynes, R. R., & Quarantelli, E. L. (1980). Helping behavior in large-scale disasters. In D. H. Smith & J. Macauley (Eds.), *Participation in social and political activities* (pp. 339-354). San Francisco: Jossey-Bass.

Edwards, J. M., & Klemmack, D. L. (1973). Correlates of life satisfaction: A re-examination. *Journal of Gerontology, 28,* 497-502.

Edwards, J. N., White, R. P., & Owens, A. (1977). Age and social involvement. *Journal of Voluntary Action Research, 6,* 127-138.

Eisenberg, N. (1986). *Altruistic emotion, cognition, and behavior: The development of self-perceptions: Empathy and sympathy.* Hillsdale, NJ: Lawrence Erlbaum.

Eisenberg, N., Miller, P. A., Schaller, M., Fabes, R. A., Fultz, J., Shell, R., & Shea, C. L. (1989). The role of sympathy and altruistic personality traits in helping: A reexamination. *Journal of Personality, 57,* 41-67.

Ekerdt, D. J. (1986). The busy ethic: Moral continuity between work and retirement. *The Gerontologist, 26,* 239-244.

Ellis, S. J., & Noyes, K. H. (1990). *By the people.* San Francisco: Jossey-Bass.

Erikson, E. (1963). *Childhood and society.* New York: Norton.

Erikson, E., Erikson, J., & Kivnick, H. (1986). *Vital involvement in old age.* New York: Norton.

Farkas, K. J., & Milligan, S. E. (1991). *The Family Friends evaluation project: Final report.* Washington, DC: National Council on Aging.

Farley, J. E. (1988). *Majority-minority relations.* Englewood Cliffs, NJ: Prentice-Hall.

Faulkner, A. (1975). The black aged as good neighbors: An experiment in volunteer service. *The Gerontologist, 15,* 554-559.

Fischer, L. R., Mueller, D. P., & Cooper, P. W. (1991). Older volunteers: A discussion of the Minnesota Senior Study. *The Gerontologist, 31,* 183-194.

Fischer, L. R., Mueller, D. P., Cooper, P. W., & Chase, R. A. (1989). *Older Minnesotans: What do they need? How do they contribute?* St. Paul, MN: Amherst H. Wilder Foundation.

Florin, P., Jones, E., & Wandersman, A. (1986). Black participation in voluntary associations. *Journal of Voluntary Action Research, 15,* 65-86.

Fogelman, C. J. (1981, Summer). Being a volunteer: Some effects on older people. *Generations,* pp. 24-25, 49.

Francies, G. R. (1983). The Volunteer Needs Profile: A tool for reducing turnover. *Journal of Volunteer Administration, 2,* 17-33.

Franklin, R. (1992, March 12). Study: Minorities feel Minneapolis United Way shuns grass-roots input. *Minneapolis Star Tribune*, p. A1.

Freedman, M. (1988). *Partners in growth: Elder mentors and at-risk youth.* Philadelphia: Public/Private Ventures.

Galaskiewicz, J. (1985). *The social organization of an urban grants economy: A study of business philanthropy and nonprofit organizations.* New York: Academic Press.

Galaskiewicz, J. (1990). *Corporate-nonprofit linkages in Minneapolis-St. Paul: Findings from a longitudinal study 1980-1988.* Minneapolis: University of Minnesota.

Galaskiewicz, J., & Schaffer, K. (1989, March). Contributions and volunteering of a community elite: A test of four theories of donative behavior. Paper presented at the Annual Meetings of the Midwest Sociological Society, St. Louis, MO.

Gallagher, S. K. (1991). *Family and community caregiving by the elderly: The new volunteers?* Unpublished doctoral dissertation, University of Massachusetts, Amherst.

Gerth, H. H., & Mills, C. W. (1946). *From Max Weber: Essays in sociology.* New York: Oxford University Press.

Gidron, B. (1978). Volunteer work and its rewards. *Volunteer Administration, 11,* 18-32.

Gidron, B. (1983). Sources of job satisfaction among service volunteers. *Journal of Volunteer Action Research, 12,* 20-35.

Gidron, B. (1985). Predictors of retention and turnover among service volunteer workers. *Journal of Social Service Research, 8,* 1-16.

Gillespie, D. F., & King, A. E. O. (1985). Demographic understanding of volunteerism. *Journal of Sociology and Social Welfare, 12,* 798-816.

Goldberg-Glen, R. S., & Cnaan, R. A. (1989, November). *Testing theories of adaptation to old age through volunteer traits, management, activities and satisfaction.* Paper presented at the annual meetings of the Gerontological Society of America, Minneapolis, MN.

Gray, R. M., & Kasteler, J. M. (1970). An evaluation of the effectiveness of a Foster Grandparent Project. *Sociology and Research, 54,* 181-189.

Grieshop, J. I. (1985). How art thou motivated? Let me count the ways! In L. F. Moore (Ed.), *Motivating volunteers* (pp. 215-228). Vancouver, BC: Vancouver Volunteer Center.

Grusec, J. E. (1991). The socialization of altruism. In M. Clark (Ed.), *Prosocial behavior* (pp. 9-33). Newbury Park, CA: Sage.

Hamilton, Frederick, & Schneiders Company. (1981). *AARP survey of volunteers.* Washington, DC: AARP.

Hamilton, Frederick, & Schneiders Company. (1988). *Attitudes of Americans over 45 years of age on volunteerism.* Washington, DC: AARP.

Harel, Z., McKinney, E. A., & Williams, M. (1990). *Black aged: Understanding diversity and service needs.* Newbury Park, CA: Sage.

Harris, L., & Associates. (1975). *Myth and reality of aging in America.* Washington, DC: National Council on Aging.

Harris, L., & Associates. (1981). *Aging in the 80s: America in transition.* Washington, DC: National Council on Aging.

Hayghe, H. V. (1991). Volunteers in the U.S.: Who donates the time? *Monthly Labor Review, 114,* 17-23.

Height, D. (1989, July). Self-help—A black tradition. *The Nation,* pp. 136-138.

Height, D. I., Toya, J., Kamikawa, L., & Maldonado, D. (1981). Senior volunteering in minority communities. *Generations, 5,* 14-17, 46.

Hellebrandt, F. A. (1980). Aging among the advantaged: A new look at the stereotype of the elderly. *The Gerontologist, 20,* 404-417.

Hembree, D. (1991, September). The new volunteers. *Parenting,* pp. 114-122.

Henderson, K. (1984). Volunteerism as leisure. *Journal of Voluntary Action Research, 13,* 1, 55-63.

Herzog, A. R., & House, J. S. (1991). Productive activities and aging well. *Generations, 15,* 49-54.

Herzog, A. R., Kahn, R. L., Morgan, J. N., Jackson, J. S., & Antonucci, T. C. (1989). Age differences in productive activities. *Journal of Gerontology: Social Sciences, 44,* S129-138.

Herzog, A. R., & Morgan, J. N. (in press). Formal volunteer work among older Americans. In S. Bass, F. Caro, & Y. P. Chen (Eds.), *Achieving a productive aging society.*

Hodgkinson, V. A., & Weitzman, M. S. (1989, March). *From commitment to action: Religious belief, congregational activities, and philanthropy.* Paper presented at the Independent Sector Spring Research Forum, Chicago, IL.

Hodgkinson, V. A., Weitzman, M. S., & Kirsch, A. D. (1990). From commitment to action: How religious involvement affects giving and volunteering. In V. Hodgkinson, R. Wuthnow, & Associates (Eds.), *Faith and philanthropy in America: Exploring the role of religion in America's voluntary sector* (pp. 93-114). San Francisco: Jossey-Bass.

Hooker, K., & Ventis, D. G. (1984). Work ethic, daily activities, and retirement satisfaction. *Journal of Gerontology, 39,* 478-484.

Hougland, J. G., & Shepard, J. M. (1985). Voluntarism and the manager: The impacts of structural pressure and personal interest on community participation. *Journal of Voluntary Action Research, 14,* 65-78.

Hougland, J. G., Turner, H. B., & Hendricks, J. (1988). Rewards and impacts of participation in a gerontology extension program. *Journal of Voluntary Action Research, 17,* 19-35.

House, J., Landis, K. R., & Umberson, D. (1988). Social relationships and health. *Science, 241,* 540-545.

Howitt, D., & Owuau-Bempah, J. (1990). The pragmatics of institutional racism: Beyond words. *Human Relations, 43,* 885-899.

Hulbert, J. R., & Chase, R. A. (1991). *Retiree volunteers and the agencies they serve: A national survey.* Report prepared for the National Retiree Volunteer Center, Amherst H. Wilder Foundation, St. Paul, MN.

Hunter, K. I., & Linn, M. W. (1980-1981). Psychosocial differences between elderly volunteers and non-volunteers. *International Journal of Aging and Human Development, 12,* 205-213.

Hutcheson, J. D., & Dominquez, L. H. (1986). Ethnic self-help organization in non-barrio settings: Community identity and voluntary action. *Journal of Voluntary Action Research, 5,* 13-22.

Hutton, W. R. (1981). Volunteering: Unaffordable luxury for the elderly. *Generations, 5,* 12-13, 47.

Independent Sector. (1981). *Americans volunteer.* Findings from a national survey conducted by the Gallup Organization, Washington, DC.

Independent Sector. (1985). *The charitable behavior of Americans.* Findings from a national survey conducted by Yankelovich, Skelly, and White, Inc., Washington, DC.

Independent Sector. (1986). *Americans volunteer.* Findings from a national survey conducted by the Gallup Organization, Washington, DC.

Independent Sector. (1988). *Giving and volunteering in the United States.* Findings from a national survey conducted by the Gallup Organization, Washington, DC.

Independent Sector. (1990). *Giving and volunteering in the United States.* Findings from a national survey conducted by the Gallup Organization, Washington, DC.

Isley, P. J. (1990). *Enhancing the volunteer experience.* San Francisco: Jossey-Bass.

J. C. Penney Company. (1988). *Study on volunteerism.* Washington, DC: VOLUNTEER The National Center.

Jenner, J. R. (1982). Participation, leadership, and the role of volunteerism among selected women volunteers. *Journal of Voluntary Action Research, 11,* 27-37.

Johnson, K. G., & Schiaffino, V. (1990). *A follow-up in 1990 of projects in the Robert Wood Johnson Foundation's Interfaith Caregivers Program (1984-87).* Kingston, NY: National Federation of Interfaith Caregivers.

Kahn, J. D. (1985-1986). Legal issues survey results. *Journal of Volunteer Administration, 4,* 28-32.

Kalab, M. (1990). Buddhism and emotional support for elderly people. *Journal of Cross-Cultural Gerontology, 5,* 7-19.

Katz, A. H. (1981). Self-help and mutual aid: An emerging social movement? *Annual Review of Sociology, 7,* 29-155.

Kelley, J. (1981). Seniors talk about why they volunteer. *Generations, 5,* 18-19.

Kelly, J. R., Steinkamp, M. W., & Kelly, J. R. (1986). Later life leisure: How they plan in Peoria. *The Gerontologist, 26,* 531-537.

Kidwell, C. S. (1989). *Indian giving* (Report prepared for Pluralism in Philanthropy Project). Washington, DC: Council on Foundations.

Kieffer, J. A. (1986). The older volunteer resource. In Committee on an Aging Society (Ed.), *Productive roles in an older society* (pp. 51-72). Washington, DC: National Academy Press.

Kii, T. (1982). Japanese American elderly. In N. J. Osgood (Ed.), *Life after work: Retirement, leisure, recreation and the elderly* (pp. 201-218). New York: Praeger.

Koeck, C., Gagnier, D., Shreve, D., Lackner, R., & Jensen, V. (1981). *Minnesota's elderly in the 1990s.* Minneapolis: State Planning Agency.

Kornblum, S. F. (1981). *Impact of a volunteer service role upon aged people.* Unpublished doctoral dissertation, Bryn Mawr College, Bryn Mawr, PA.

Kurzeja, P., Koh, S. D., Koh, T.-H., & Liu, W. T. (1986). Ethnic attitudes of Asian American elderly. *Research on Aging, 8,* 110-127.

Lackner, R., & Koeck, C. (1980). *The elderly as a resource.* St. Paul: Minnesota State Planning Agency, Human Resources Planning.

Landmann, R. (1991). *West Virginia Rural Family Friends Project: Evaluation report.* Washington, DC: National Council on Aging.

Lawton, P. (1977). Morale: What are we measuring? In C. N. Nydegger (Ed.), *Measuring morale: A guide to effective assessment* (pp. 6-14). Washington, DC: Gerontological Society.

Lazarus, M., & Lauer, H. (1985). Working past retirement: Practical and motivational issues. In R. Butler & H. P. Gleason (Eds.), *Productive aging: Enhancing vitality in later life* (pp. 47-76). New York: Springer.

Lee, D. J., & Markides, K. S. (1990). Activity and mortality among aged persons over an eight-year period. *Journal of Gerontology: Social Sciences, 45,* S39-42.

Lee, R. (1989). *Misconceptions about giving by Chinese Americans: Confucian social ethics and the spirit of philanthropy* (Report prepared for Pluralism in Philanthropy Project). Washington, DC: Council on Foundations.

Leigh, G., Gerrish, R., & Gillespie, E. (1986). *Why volunteer?* Toronto: Addiction Research Foundation.

Lemke, S., & Moos, R. (1989). Personal and environmental determinants of activity involvement among elderly residents of congregate facilities. Age differences in productive activities. *Journal of Gerontology, 44,* S139-148.

Litigation Support Services. (1984). Impact evaluation of the Foster Grandparent Program on the foster grandparents: Final report. Washington, DC: ACTION.

Luks, A., with Payne, P. (1991). *The healing power of doing good.* New York: Fawcett Columbine.

Mahoney, J., & Pechura, C. M. (1980). Values and volunteers: Axiology of altruism in a crisis center. *Psychological Reports, 47,* 1007-1012.

Maldonado, D., Jr., (n. d.). *African American and Hispanic older persons: A preliminary report on their religiosity, religious participation, and attitudes toward the church and clergy.* Unpublished manuscript.

Manser, G. (1982). *Volunteer action and contributive roles for elders.* Washington, DC: National Council on Aging.

Manser, G., & Higgins-Cass, R. (1976). *Voluntarism at the crossroads.* New York: Family Service Association of America.

Manson, S. M., & Pambrun, A. M. (1979). Social and psychological status of the American Indian elderly: Past research, current advocacy, and future inquiry. *White Cloud Journal, 1,* 18-25.

Marin, G., & Van Oss-Marin, B. (1991). *Research with Hispanic populations.* Newbury Park, CA: Sage.

Marriott Seniors Volunteerism Study. (1991). Commissioned by Marriott Senior Living Services and the United States Administration on Aging, Washington, DC.

Marvit, E. (1984, Summer). Recruiting and training retired adults as volunteers: An Israeli experience. *Journal of Volunteer Administration*, pp. 6-12.

McClelland, K. A. (1982). Self-conception and life satisfaction: Integrating aged subculture and activity theory. *Journal of Gerontology, 37,* 723-732.

Mellinger, J., & Holt, R. (1982). Characteristics of elderly participants in three types of leisure groups. *Psychological Reports, 50,* 447-458.

Menchik, P. L., & Weisbrod, B. A. (1987). Volunteer labor supply. *Journal of Public Economics, 32,* 159-183.

Midlarsky, E. (1984). Competence and helping: Notes toward a model. In E. Staub, D. Bar-Tel, J. Karylowski, & J. Reykowski (Eds.), *Development and maintenance of prosocial behavior* (pp. 291-308). New York: Plenum.

Midlarsky, E. (1990). Helping as coping. In M. S. Clark (Ed.), *Prosocial behavior* (pp. 238-264). Newbury Park, CA: Sage.

Miller, H. B. (1982). Altruism, volunteers and sociology. In J. D. Harmon (Ed.), *Volunteerism in the eighties: Fundamental issues in voluntary action* (pp. 45-53). Washington, DC: University Press of America.

Miller, L. E., Powell, G. N., & Seltzer, J. (1990). Determinants of turnover among volunteers. *Human Relations, 43,* 901-917.

Minkler, M., & Stone, R. (1985). The feminization of poverty and older women. *The Gerontologist, 25,* 351-357.

Moore, L. F. (1985). *Motivating volunteers.* Vancouver, BC: Vancouver Volunteer Center.

Morgan, J. N. (1986). Unpaid productive activity over the life course. In Committee on an Aging Society (Ed.), *Productive roles in an older society* (pp. 73-109). Washington, DC: National Academy Press.

Morrison, M. H. (1986). Work and retirement in an older society. In A. Pifer & L. Bronte (Eds.), *Our aging society: Paradox and promise* (pp. 341-365). New York: Norton.

Morrow-Howell, N., Lott, L., & Ozawa, M. (1990). The impact of race on volunteer helping relationships among the elderly. *Social Work, 35,* 395-402.

Morrow-Howell, N., & Mui, A. (1989). Elderly volunteers: Reasons for initiating and terminating service. *Journal of Gerontological Social Work, 13,* 21-33.

Moss, M. S., & Lawton, M. P. (1982). Time budgets of older people: A window on four lifestyles. *Journal of Gerontology, 37,* 115-123.

Mussen, P., Honzik, M. P., & Eichorn, D. H. (1982). Early adult antecedents of life satisfaction at age 70. *Journal of Gerontology, 37,* 316-322.

Myers, G. C., Manton, K. G., & Bacellar, H. (1986). Sociodemographic aspect of future unpaid productive roles. In Committee on an Aging Society (Ed.), *Productive roles in an older society* (pp. 110-149). Washington, DC: National Academy Press.

National Association of Social Workers. (1978, March/April). Volunteers and Social Services System. *Governor's Office of Volunteer Services Newsletter,* pp. 4-5.

Newman, S., Vasudev, J., & Baum, M. (1983). *Experience of senior citizen volunteers in intergenerational programs in schools and the relationship to life satisfaction* (Final report for Generations Together). Pittsburgh: University of Pittsburgh, Center for Social and Urban Research.

O'Connell, B., & O'Connell, A. B. (1989). *Volunteers in action.* New York: Foundation Center.

Okun, M. A., & Eisenberg, N. (n. d.). *A comparison of office and adult day care center volunteers: Social, psychological, and demographic differences.* Unpublished manuscript.

Okun, M. A., Stock, W. A., Haring, M. J., & Witter, R. A. (1984). The social activity/subjective well-being relation: A quantitative synthesis. *Research on Aging, 6,* 45-65.

Olsen, M. (1970). Social and political participation of blacks. *American Sociological Review, 35,* 682-697.

Orenstein, R., & Sobel, D. (1987). *The healing brain.* New York: Simon & Schuster.

Organ, D. W. (1988). *Organizational citizenship behavior: The good soldier syndrome.* Lexington, MA: Lexington.

Ozawa, M. N., & Morrow-Howell, N. (1988). Services provided by elderly volunteers: An empirical study. *Journal of Gerontological Social Work, 13,* 1, 65-80.

Pardo, M. (1990). Mexican American women grassroots community activists: Mothers of East Los Angeles. *Frontiers, 9,* 1-7.

Payne, B. P. (1977). The older volunteer: Social role continuity and development. *The Gerontologist, 17,* 355-361.

Payne, B. P., & Bull, C. N. (1985). The older volunteer: The case for interdependence. In W. A. Peterson & J. Quadagno (Eds.), *Social bonds in later life: Aging and interdependence* (pp. 251-272). Newbury Park, CA: Sage.

Pearce, J. L. (1983). Job attitude and motivation differences between volunteers and employees from comparable organizations. *Journal of Applied Psychology, 68,* 646-652.

Pearce, J. L. (1985). Insufficient justification and motivation to volunteer. In L. Moore (Ed.), *Motivating volunteers* (pp. 201-213). Vancouver, BC: Vancouver Volunteers Center.

Perkinson, M. A. (1980). Alternate roles for the elderly: An example from a Midwestern retirement community. *Human Organization, 39,* 219-226.

Perry, W. H. (1983). The willingness of persons 60 or over to volunteer: Implications for the social services. *Journal of Gerontological Social Work, 5,* 107-118.

Petty, B. J., & Cusack, S. A. (1989). Assessing the impact of a seniors' peer counseling program. *Educational Gerontology, 15,* 49-64.

Phillips, M. (1982). Motivation and expectation in successful volunteerism. *Journal of Voluntary Action Research, 11,* 118-125.

Piliavin, J. A., & Callero, P. A. (1990). *Giving the gift of life to unnamed strangers.* Baltimore: Johns Hopkins University Press.

Piliavin, J. A., & Charng, H.-W. (1990). Altruism: A review of recent theory and research. *Annual Review of Sociology, 16,* 27-65.

Pitterman, L. (1973). *The older volunteer: Motivation to work.* Washington, DC: ACTION.

Pizzini, M. (1986). Volunteers: 1986. An answer for information and referral in the 80s. *Information and Referral, 8,* 58-80.

Pynoos, J., Hade-Kaplan, B., & Fliesher, D. (1984). Intergenerational neighborhood networks. *The Gerontologist, 24,* 233-237.

Rakocy, G. (1981). Senior volunteers: Finding and keeping them. *Generations, 5,* 36-37, 45.

Reddy, R. D. (1980). Individual philanthropy and giving behavior. In D. H. Smith, J. MacCaulay, & Associates (Eds.), *Participation in social and political activities* (pp. 370-399). San Francisco: Jossey-Bass.

Riley, M. W., & Riley, J. W. (1989, May). The lives of older people and changing social roles. *Annals of the American Academy of Political and Social Science,* pp. 14-28.

Romaniuk, J. G., & Romaniuk, M. (1982). Participation motives of older adults in higher education: The elder hostel experience. *The Gerontologist, 22,* 364.

Romero, C. J. (1986). The economics of volunteerism: A review. In Committee on an Aging Society (Ed.), *Productive roles in an older society* (pp. 23-51). Washington, DC: National Academy Press.

Rosenblatt, A. (1966). Interest of older persons in volunteer activities. *Social Work, 11,* 87-94.

Rosenwaike, I., & Dolinsky, A. (1987). The changing demographic determinants of the growth of the extreme aged. *The Gerontologist, 27,* 275-287.

Rosman, A., & Rubel, P. G. (1971). *Feasting with mine enemy: Rank and exchange among Northwest Coast societies.* New York: Columbia University Press.

Rushton, J. P. (1984). The altruistic personality: Evidence from laboratory, naturalistic and self-report perspectives. In E. Staub, D. Bar-tel, J. Karylowski, & J. Rykowski (Eds.), *Development and maintenance of prosocial behavior* (pp. 271-289). New York: Plenum.

Sachs, M. (1983, March/April). Housing CSI—A successful senior housing cooperative. *Aging,* pp. 14-18.

Salovey, P., Mayer, J. D., & Rosenhan, D. L. (1991). Mood and helping: Mood as a motivator of helping and helping as a regulator of mood. In M. S. Clark (Ed.), *Prosocial behavior* (pp. 215-237). Newbury Park, CA: Sage.

Schaffer, K. B. (1992, March). *Reaching out: The portrait of minority senior volunteering in Minnesota.* Paper presented at the American Society on Aging Annual Meeting, San Diego, CA.

Schiman, C., & Lordeman, A. (1989). *A study of the use of volunteers by long term care ombudsman programs: The effectiveness of recruitment, supervision and retention.* Washington, DC: National Center for State Long-Term Care Ombudsman Resources.

Schram, V. (1985). Motivating volunteers to participate. In L. F. Moore (Ed.), *Motivating volunteers* (pp. 13-29). Vancouver, BC: Vancouver Volunteer Center.

Seguin, M. M., O'Brien, B., Berton, V., Hummell, E., & McConney, P. (1976). *Releasing the potential of the older volunteer.* Los Angeles: Ethel Percy Andrus Gerontology Center.

Seville, J. (1985). The Good Samaritan Program: Patients as volunteers. *Activities, Adaptation and Aging, 6,* 73-78.

Sheppard, H. L., & Rix, S. E. (1977). *The graying of working America: The coming crisis in retirement age policy.* New York: Free Press.

Simmons, R. G. (1991). Presidential address on altruism and sociology. *Sociological Quarterly, 32,* 1-22.

Smith, C. (1985). *Relationships between selected meanings of leisure, volunteering, and work of senior center program participants.* Unpublished doctoral dissertation, Texas Woman's University, Denton, TX.

Smith, D. H. (1975). Voluntary action and voluntary groups. *Annual Review of Sociology, 1,* 247-270.

Smith, D. H. (1982). Altruism, volunteers, and volunteerism. In J. D. Harmon (Ed.), *Volunteerism in the eighties: Fundamental issues in voluntary action* (pp. 23-44). Washington, DC: University Press of America.

Smith, D. H. (1984). Churches are generally ignored in contemporary voluntary action research: Causes and consequences. *Journal of Voluntary Action Research, 13,* 11-18.

Smith, D. H. (1986). Outstanding local voluntary organizations in the 1960s: Their distinguishing characteristics. *Journal of Voluntary Action Research, 15,* 26-35.

Smith, E. P., & Gutheil, R. H. (1988). Successful foster parent recruiting: A voluntary agency effort. *Child Welfare League of America, 97,* 137-146.

Solomon, G. F., Temoshok, L., O'Leary, A., & Zick, J. (1987). An intensive psychoimmunologic study of long-surviving persons with AIDS. *Annals of the New York Academy of Sciences, 496,* 647-655.

Statistical Abstract of the United States. 1991. Washington, DC: U.S. Department of Commerce, Bureau of the Census.

Stevens, E. S. (1989-1990). Utilizing a "rich" resource: Older volunteers. *Journal of Volunteer Administration, 8,* 35-38.

Stevens, E. S. (1991). Toward satisfaction and retention of senior volunteers. *Journal of Gerontological Social Work, 16,* 33-41.

Sundeen, R. A. (1988). Explaining participation in coproduction: A study of volunteers. *Social Science Quarterly, 69,* 547-568.

Svanborg, A. (1985). Biomedical and environmental influences in aging. In R. Butler & H. P. Gleason (Eds.), *Productive aging: Enhancing vitality in later life* (pp. 15-28). New York: Springer.

Tierce, J. W., & Seelbach, W. C. (1987). Elders as school volunteers: An untapped resource. *Educational Gerontology, 13,* 33-41.

Tobis, J. S., Crinella, F. M., Ashurst, J. T., Rook, K. S., Sandman, C. A., Wilson, A. F., Mosko, S. S., Swanson, J. M., & Reisch, S. (1991). *The effects of intervention on psychobiological decline in aging* (Final report of Program Project #PO1AG03975). Washington, DC: National Institute on Aging.

Tomeh, A. (1981). The value of voluntarism among minority groups. *Phylon, 42,* 86-96.

Torres-Gil, F. (1982). *The politics of aging among elder Hispanics.* Washington, DC: University Press of America.

Townsend, E. J. (1973). An examination of participants in organizational, political, informational, and interpersonal activities. *Journal of Voluntary Action Research, 2,* 200-211.

U.S. Bureau of the Census. (1974). *Americans volunteer.* Washington, DC: ACTION.

U.S. Department of Labor. (1965). *Americans volunteer.* Washington, DC: Manpower Administration.

Vaillancourt, F., & Payette, M. (1986). The supply of volunteer work: The case of Canada. *Journal of Voluntary Action Research, 15,* 45-56.

van Iwagen, M. N. (1986). Volunteers and the ethics of advocacy. *Journal of Volunteer Administration, 6,* 1-8.

Van Til, J. (1987). The three sectors: Voluntarism in a changing political economy. *Journal of Voluntary Action Research, 16,* 50-63.

Van Til, J. (1988). *Mapping the third sector: Voluntarism in a changing social economy.* New York: Foundation Center.

Vosburg, W. W. (1982). Client rights, advocacy and volunteerism. In J. D. Harmon (Ed.), *Volunteerism in the eighties: Fundamental issues in voluntary action* (pp. 75-93). Washington, DC: University Press of America.

Wandersman, A., Florin, P., Friedmann, R., & Meier, R. (1987). Who participates, who does not, and why? An analysis of voluntary neighborhood organizations in the United States and Israel. *Sociological Forum, 2,* 534-555.

Watts, A. D., & Edwards, P. (1983). Recruiting and retaining human service volunteers: An empirical analysis. *Journal of Voluntary Action Research, 12,* 9-22.

Weitzner, B. (1979). Notes on the Hidatsa Indians based on data recorded by the late Gilbert L. Wilson. *Anthropological Papers of the American Museum of Natural History, 56,* 278-292.

Wheeler, C. M. (1986-1987). Facing realities: The need to develop a political agenda for volunteerism. *Journal of Volunteer Administration, 5,* 1-12.

White, O. F. (1982). Professionalization of volunteer organizations as a "problem" in the theory of human action. In J. D. Harmon (Ed.), *Volunteerism in the eighties: Fundamental issues in voluntary action* (pp. 125-127). Washington, DC: University Press of America.

Williams, J., Babchuck, N., & Johnson, D. (1973). Voluntary associations and minority status: A comparative analysis of Anglo, black and Mexican Americans. *American Sociological Review, 38,* 637-646.

Worthy, E. H., & Ventura-Merkel, C. (1982). *Older volunteers: A national survey.* Washington, DC: National Council on Aging.

Wuthnow, R. (1990). Religion and the voluntary spirit in the United States: Mapping the terrain. In R. Wuthnow & V. Hodgkinson (Eds.), *Faith and philanthropy in America* (pp. 3-21). San Francisco: Jossey-Bass.

Wuthnow, R. (1991). *Acts of compassion: Caring for others and helping ourselves.* Princeton, NJ: Princeton University Press.

Wyant, S. (1991, Fall). Give a little—Get a lot: A citywide volunteer recruitment campaign. *Volunteer Leader,* pp. 8-9, 15.

Zsembik, B., & Singer, A. (1990). The problem of defining retirement among minorities: The Mexican-Americans. *The Gerontologist, 30,* 749-757.

Index

About the Authors

Lucy Rose Fischer, PhD, directed the Older Volunteers Project for the Wilder Research Center, at the Amherst H. Wilder Foundation. Currently she is Research Scientist at Group Health Foundation, Minneapolis, Minnesota. She is the author of *Linked Lives: Adult Daughters and Their Mothers* (1986) and the first author of *Older Minnesotans: What Do They Need? How Do They Contribute?* (1989). She has written professional articles and research reports on topics in aging, family relations, and health care. She is a Fellow of the Gerontological Society of America and has been on the faculties of the University of Minnesota and St. Olaf College.

Kay Banister Schaffer, MA, was Research Associate for the Older Volunteers Project. She is a Doctoral Candidate in Sociology at the University of Minnesota. Her dissertation examines issues of race/ethnicity in senior volunteering. She has done research on stereotypes of elderly, exceptional elders, and prosocial behavior among community elite.